AF477682

The Language of War Monuments

ADVANCES IN SEMIOTICS

Semiotics has complemented linguistics by expanding its scope beyond the phoneme and the sentence to include texts and discourse, and their rhetorical, performative and ideological functions. It has brought into focus the multimodality of human communication. *Advances in Semiotics* publishes original works in the field demonstrating robust scholarship, intellectual creativity and clarity of exposition. These works apply semiotic approaches to linguistics and non-verbal productions, social institutions and discourses, embodied cognition and communication and the new virtual realities that have been ushered in by the internet. It also is inclusive of publications in relevant domains such as socio-semiotics, evolutionary semiotics, game theory, cultural and literary studies, human–computer interactions and the challenging new dimensions of human networking afforded by social websites.

Series Editor: Paul Bouissac is Professor Emeritus at the University of Toronto (Victoria College), Canada. He is a world renowned figure in semiotics and a pioneer of circus studies. He runs the SemiotiX Bulletin [www.semioticon.com/semiotix] which has a global readership.

Titles in the series include:

Buddhist Theory of Semiotics, Fabio Rambelli
Introduction to Peircean Visual Semiotics, Tony Jappy
Semiotics of Drink and Drinking, Paul Manning
Semiotics of Religion, Robert Yelle
The Visual Language of Comics, Neil Cohn

BLOOMSBURY ADVANCES IN SEMIOTICS

The Language of War Monuments

GILL ABOUSNNOUGA AND DAVID MACHIN

BLOOMSBURY

LONDON · NEW DELHI · NEW YORK · SYDNEY

Bloomsbury Academic

An imprint of Bloomsbury Publishing Plc

50 Bedford Square	1385 Broadway
London	New York
WC1B 3DP	NY 10018
UK	USA

www.bloomsbury.com

Bloomsbury is a registered trade mark of Bloomsbury Publishing Plc

First published 2013

© Gill Abousnnouga and David Machin, 2013

All rights reserved. No part of this publication may be reproduced or
transmitted in any form or by any means, electronic or mechanical,
including photocopying, recording, or any information storage or
retrieval system, without prior permission in writing from the publishers.

Gill Abousnnouga and David Machin have asserted their right under the Copyright,
Designs and Patents Act, 1988, to be identified as Author of this work.

No responsibility for loss caused to any individual or organization acting
on or refraining from action as a result of the material in this
publication can be accepted by Bloomsbury Academic or the author.

British Library Cataloguing-in-Publication Data
A catalogue record for this book is available from the British Library.

ISBN: HB: 978-1-6235-6333-2
ePub: 978-1-6235-6896-2
ePDF: 978-1-6235-6821-4

Library of Congress Cataloging-in-Publication Data
Machin, David, 1966–
The language of war monuments / David Machin and Gill Abousnnouga.
pages cm. – (Bloomsbury Advances in Semiotics)
Includes bibliographical references and index.
ISBN 978-1-62356-333-2 (hardcover) – ISBN 978-1-62356-821-4 (ebook (pdf)) –
ISBN 978-1-62356-896-2 (ebook (epub))   1. Semiotics–History.
2. Semiotics–Social aspects.   3. Semiotics–Political aspects.   4. War and society.
5. War memorials.   6. Representation (Philosophy)   7. Memorialization–Social
aspects.   8. Memorialization–Political aspects.   9. Collective memory–Political
aspects.   10. Collective memory–Social aspects.   I. Abousnnouga, Gill.   II. Title.
P99.M23 2013
725'.94–dc23
2013018694

Typeset by Newgen Knowledge Works (P) Ltd., Chennai, India
Printed and bound in Great Britain

CONTENTS

LIST OF FIGURES

Introduction: Monuments and Multimodal Critical Discourse Analysis

In cities, towns and villages around the world we find monuments erected to those our societies wish us to mark as somehow outstanding. These are erected through official processes, sometimes drawing the public into their design, in order to celebrate the kinds of ideas, values and identities we are to consider most embody who we are at best, what we should ourselves strive towards, those to whom we most owe and fundamentally to remind us who we are by signposting points and personalities from our shared national or local histories. One particular category of monuments comprises those that commemorate people who died in wars on behalf of their nations. These too are described by historians as celebrating and heralding specific sets of human characteristics and actions. We may pass by them every day in central squares, parks and outside civic buildings, not necessarily consciously noticing them. Perhaps once each year we become more aware of them when our news media offer coverage of national ceremonies where such monuments provide the focal point while official figures, former and contemporary soldiers, often including school children and other services such as the fire-brigade, form processions accompanied by national flags and national music, celebrating those who gave their lives in service of the nation. And we may become vaguely aware that new monuments are unveiled in our locality to commemorate those who gave their lives in a more recent conflict that may have been the focus of news media attention – a conflict about which we may have understood quite little in terms of political reasons for our involvement, what it is specifically that the enemy want and even who exactly they are. Nevertheless, our heroes who died serving their country should be honoured.

In this book we take a very different view of these war monuments. Discourses that legitimize and help to maintain war as a reasonable and justifiable social practice are disseminated not only by political speeches and news items but also by entertainment media such as movies and computer games. Such discourses are communicated in school books and other history-related learning material that can be read, played with and collected. These same discourses are disseminated by routine public events such as royal parades and through annual commemorations. They are also communicated by war monuments. It is in this way, through different media and different modes of communication, that warfare and the discourses that shape our understanding of it become a mundane and accepted part of our everyday lives.

The war monument, we show in this book, has been one important way by which discourses of war that reflect the interests of the powerful in society have been communicated in British society. These are discourses that normalize and legitimize wars, obscuring and silencing the reasons that they take place and the actual effects of war on bodies, civilians and society. Through these discourses war becomes a solution that is broadly acceptable. War becomes something that we are encouraged to think about in terms of the public service of the soldier and not in terms of maiming, starvation, terror, pain, fragmented families and misused power. And it is certainly not something that is presented in ways which foreground the strategic interests of those in power who instigate and maintain wars in places like Afghanistan and Iraq. Monuments play their role in this process by placing these discourses in public, everyday places where they claim to house our collective values and ideals.

As broader discourses of war have changed over time, as the official reasons and justifications for war have changed, so have the nature of war monuments. In earlier wars the ruling elite could more openly throw away the lives of tens of thousands of men in a day in the name of facing up bravely to an evil yet more or less equal enemy. They could more easily allow millions of these men to live in squalid trenches where a third of them would die from diseases. In more recent wars, in contrast, the public have become less tolerant of the deaths of 'our own boys'. And the nature of warfare has itself changed. There are no longer any front lines or an identifiable enemy (Smith, 2001). Wars can no longer be carried out so plainly in the name of the power of the nation. Nor is a clear aim for these conflicts given apart from unfocused ideas of humanitarianism. These changes require different discourses to justify war, even if fundamentally the reasons: access to resources and wealth, are the same they were thousands of years ago. The monuments, built to commemorate those who die in these wars, just as do the speeches of the politicians who tell us the need to carry them out, must reflect these changing discourses. War monuments are one way that we are reminded about the consensual view of war, the cohesiveness of the public view of war.

War monuments, like other monuments that we find in our towns and cities sanction and signpost what our societies collectively value, what kinds of personalities and actions are to be celebrated. We tend to find statues of famous capitalists, not those who worked for collective equality. We tend to find statues of those who fought in wars, not against them. The celebration of humanitarian acts is reserved for those who acted as such in ways that provide no threat to the overall set of values dominated by nation, industry and capitalism. The war monument, we want to argue in this book, is one such case where, looking a little deeper, we find the core of values of the capitalist nation-state and its need to justify and maintain the practice of war through which, in part, it maintains itself. And in each monument the identities of those who fought, the ideas, values and attitudes, associated with their actions must be communicated by appropriate design choices that support the legitimacy of the nation-state.

One such example of such a war monument is the Cardiff monument (Figure I.1) unveiled in 1927. The monument is comprised of a circular version of a Greek temple where members of the different armed forces, resembling beautiful Greek statues, stand on its steps looking upwards, impassively, holding wreaths above their heads. Within the temple there are fountains and above a range of Christian imagery such as a large dolphin.

An example of a more contemporary monument is found at Wootton Bassett (Figure I.2) unveiled in 2004 where we find a globe held aloft by hands standing in a busy high street. Both of these monuments carry inscriptions telling us about acts of selflessness in conflicts done in the name of nation. Both use visual elements and form to communicate ideas,

FIGURE I.1 *The Cardiff WWI monument.*

FIGURE I.2 *Wootton Bassett.*

values and identities associated with those who are remembered. Both were bought into being by official, institutional processes.

Given the predominance of the monuments placed in towns and cities around Britain passers-by, and those who participate in the fund raising and commemorations based around these monuments, tend not to question the kinds of representations that they carry. But to what extent is it that each of these monuments represents the realities of warfare? Of course, one answer might be that they are not intended to show the realty of war per se, but to *symbolize* what these soldiers did so that we can pay our respects and remember them. But symbolic choices in design are themselves deeply political and ideological. What exactly *is* being symbolized is one set of ideas, sequence of events, values and identities as opposed to another set. And in the case of war monuments such as those found in Cardiff and Wootton Bassett the kinds of imagery and material forms used serve a very specific purpose in recontextualizing the reality of war to deliberately shift attention away from its nature, is causes, results and what war is used to accomplish. Just as in political speeches speakers must choose words carefully to communicate those ideas and values that justify and legitimize their actions so must the monument commissioning committees and designers choose material semiotic resources that will do the same.

Designers of these monuments since World War I (WWI), as we will discuss later, have been instructed to avoid references to violence, maiming or even to fear and in many cases they were specifically instructed to use these designs to foster nationalism in an environment of fear of workers' movements. And it is here where our specific interest in this book lies. *How do monuments communicate such ideas, values and identities?* In this book our aim is to develop a tool kit, in the tradition of Multimodal Critical Discourse Analysis (MCDA) that allows us to answer this question. And it aims to place the analysis that this permits into the actual ongoing social and political context of monument building.

If we were to create a faithful representation of war to remember what took place, what the soldiers went through, what would we need to include: how it took place, its participants and its consequences, devastated cities, lost homes, shattered families, hunger, disease, maimed children, mutilation, dismembered body-parts? These are the kinds of things that form the accounts of novels written by front-line soldiers (Remarque, 1987; Sajer, 2001). Yet these monuments feature none of the components, participants and processes that constitute actual elements of war. Instead, we find a range of elements and symbols, forms and materials that relate to: religion; mysticism; references to ancient civilizations; Classical characters and narratives and other quite specific, yet non-war-related, ideas and attitudes such as sport, ancient aboriginal peoples and art forms. In this book our aim is to show how these choices can be studied systematically in a way that allows us to reveal the kinds of discourses they communicate, to show what kinds of ideas, values and identities they represent in order to recontextualize what war actually comprises.

In Britain, war monument building as a systematic state-led enterprise began during WWI through a well-documented programme designed to foster nationalism from a ruling elite running scared of communism and of a public disillusioned with the wastage of what had appeared to be a pointless war where millions of young working-class men had died, many of disease or drowning in fields of mud. The cartoon 'Crucified', 1927 (Figure I.3), by Arthur Stadler reflected this feeling where the working classes of Europe had been used by a greedy and cruel ruling elite. We would like to imagine how it would have been had such representations of a used soldier surrounded by bloated, callous ruling elites been realized in stone and placed in the square, parks and shopping streets of our town and cities? How would this have influenced our background sense of the meaning of warfare? We could equally say that such an image would have helped us to remember and respect what these soldiers experienced. The novels of front-line soldier usually portray a sense of helplessness and resentment to those who force them to be there, to kill and maim young men very much like themselves. How would such soldiers wish their pointless suffering and death to be recalled: through them represented as Greek Gods or where the avarice and cruelty of the elite were revealed so that people would have a better understanding of war? The novels of front-line soldiers often express bitterness and irony at the knowledge of the

FIGURE 1.3 *Crucified by Arthur Stadler, 1927.*

great chasm that lies between how people back home are being encouraged to celebrate their actions as opposed to how they experience them.

Crucified by Arthur Stadler (1927)

After the largest wave of monument building, about which we will have much more to say later, construction continued throughout the twentieth century. Sometimes as the names of those fallen in later conflicts were added to older monuments, sometimes as monuments were erected to those not formerly remembered and celebrated and sometimes to honour those fallen in new wars as the case of Wootton Bassett above. And in each case slightly different objects, figures and material form used as discourses of war were changing. Each, we argue, playing its role in helping to recontextualize war at particular times, each time in the context of the needs of the ruling elite to justify its economic aims. And as new names are added and new monuments erected to honour 'those who served' in different wars, their purposes, aims and consequences, fuse in the minds of the public, each simply an example of where 'our boys' did their part for us.

What we argue in this book is that these monuments play their part in the recontextualization of the social practice of war. They form part of the banal (Billig, 1995) placement of discourses that are largely celebratory and which distract from the actual meaning, causes and nature of warfare in our societies in everyday places: the Cardiff memorial sits in a city centre park where many local government workers and students sit and eat lunch; the Wootten Bassett memorial sits in a bustling shopping street. Rick Iedema (2001:24) discusses the resemiotization of discourse as meanings are translated from one domain to another with increasingly more durable and therefore less negotiable meanings. Discourses of war can be heard in the speeches of our leaders who speak of the need to save civilians from obscure enemies whose aims are never made clear. We also find the same discourses in the news media. But they are also realized in solid stone and bronze and placed in common places, in streets where we pass on our way to work, or in parks where we stroll and relax. During the last Remembrance day one of the authors saw young cadets being photographed in front of a memorial depicting an impassive, powerful looking, handsome soldier. They stood side-by-side with their chests stuck out in pride. The author became mindful of the images from the 1924 book by Ernst Friedrich 'War Against War' which juxtaposed images of young, fiercely patriotic cadets, alongside those of appallingly disfigured survivors of the trench warfare of WWI. And he also became mindful of the accounts of Guy Sajer of his experiences on the Eastern Front in WWII – of the brutalized lives of civilians and his own constant hunger, fear, diseased body and the sheer pointlessness of what he was experiencing as nationalism waned into a realization of the squalor, waste and horror that is war. War monuments are one way by which such nationalism is naturalized and maintained.

Critical Discourse Analysis and the language of war

The questions as to *how* social practices such as war are recontextualized through language have lain at the heart of the tradition of Critical Discourse Analysis (CDA) of which this book is a part. Such studies (Wodak and van Leeuwen, 1999) have focused on the ways in which language and grammar have been used to recontextualize social practices by substituting elements, the actual participants, micro-processes, locations, times, etc., from the actual social practice with others, by deleting substitutions and additions; a process which reshapes representations to serve the interests of a particular group. Norman Fairclough (2003) has pointed to the importance of paying particular attention to the abstraction of actual participants, processes and relations in texts in order to gain clues as to the nature of the ideological interests they serve. He recommends we look carefully at what kinds of identities, processes and settings are foregrounded, backgrounded or silenced completely. We can then ask why this is the case and in whose interests this might serve.

Specifically as regards the recontexulization of war in language a number of key themes have emerged though CDA. For the most part this has shown that in political speeches explaining the decision to go to war and in media coverage there has been a backgrounding or silencing of actual social and political histories that underpin conflicts with a foregrounding of creating clear and exaggerated differences between the shared common interest of the Western powers and an evil other. Johnson's (2002) study showed how American President George W. Bush and UK Prime Minister Tony Blair justified a military response to the attacks on the Twin Towers in New York in 2001 (9/11) by creating binary oppositions between how 'the good' way of life characteristic of the United States juxtaposed with 'the evil' of the terrorists who wish to destroy the freedom it provides. Armed aggression therefore is explained not in terms of clear political objectives, nor placed in longer histories of international relations and political and military interventions, but in terms of a broadly protective way of life.

The theme of the 'evil other' also appears in a study by Graham et al. (2004) who show similarities in speeches given by key Western political leaders in speeches spanning around a thousand years: 1095 (Pope Urban II), 1588 (Queen Elizabeth I), 1938 (Adolf Hitler) and 2001 (George W. Bush). They point out that the war discourses of each leader across time draw on common themes: superiority due to beliefs and practices, a greater good such as being in the name of God, truth or democracy and the need to stand up to a threat presented by an evil other. Such themes substitute actual political aims such as the seizing of territory, resources or the fostering of political alignments for economic gain.

Lazar and Lazar (2004) show how binary oppositions are used in the speeches of the presidents of the post-Cold War period. They found a consistent 'Orientalization' of 'the enemy' who are the very mirror image of the civilized democratic West, being backward and against progress, hot-blooded, inferior and dangerous. These themes are also identified in their 2007 study which analysed Bush's war discourse. Their analyses revealed that notions of Western superiority are reinforced through claims that the act of war is defensive, 'civilizing' and serves as a route to peace.

Van Dijk (2003) focused on the manipulative aspect of the UK Prime Minister Tony Blair's speech to Parliament in which he defended his government's decision to invade Iraq in 2003. Again, rather than actual clear evidence about a real threat presented by an enemy or clear political aims, Blair drew on ideological polarization strategies including moral superiority, national democratic spirit, discrediting the opponents and emotionalizing the argument.

Hodges (2007) analysed the language of Vice President Dick Cheney to show how the argument for the 2003 invasion of Iraq was delivered via the linking of Iraq's then leader, Saddam Hussein, with the terrorist organization Al Qaeda that claimed responsibility for the September 2001 attacks on the Twin Towers in New York. Hodges notes that the Bush/Cheney linking of Iraq with al Qaeda was accepted as 'the truth' by the US public, despite the findings of the official 9/11 Commission that concluded they could find no link between Iraq and al Qaeda. However, Iraq and al Qaeda became part of the broadly accepted discourses of the War on Terror.

Drawing on the same critical linguistic perspective, other authors (Hodge and Kress, 1988; Van Leeuwen, 2005; Kress, 2010; Machin and Mayr, 2012) have pointed to the important role played by visual communication in this process of the recontextualization of social practice. There have been a limited number of studies that have explored the visual realization of discourses of war. For example Chouliaraki's (2005) semiotic-based, multimodal study of BBC World's coverage of the Allied bombardment of Baghdad revealed that the pictures that accompanied the reports showed fire-power and destruction only of non-human targets such as buildings, presenting therefore, a view of war as a material process void of any human suffering. What she describes as a '. . . spectacle of rare audio-visual power and intensity' (2005:148) not only compels the audience to become voyeurs of violence, it also allows them to view violence without having to confront the consequences of the bombing:

> By cancelling the presence of the persecutor and the sufferer, the footage presents the bombardment of Baghdad, not a scene of suffering, but a site of intense military action without agency. (Chouliaraki, 2005:153)

Chouliaraki's work reveals how violence and consequential suffering can be 'aestheticized' to remove both the horror and responsibility for these acts and helps to show how by eliminating agency, the authors of the text avoid opposing or criticizing the perpetrators of the bombardment of Baghdad. Moreover, the text does not encourage the viewer to question or criticize the act of war; resulting in, at least momentary, hegemonic control over the viewer.

Concentrating on the visual aspect of war discourse, Machin's (2007a) discussion of photographs of the invasion and occupation of Iraq in 2003 reveals differences in comparison with images of earlier wars; specifically the American invasion and occupation of Vietnam and the First Gulf War.

Machin argues that, predominantly, these images construct a story of peacekeeping rather than large-scale involvement of armed forces, killing and brutality, where civilians are represented as helpless and aimless or with clichés of innocent children. Turning to the images of torture of Iraqi civilians by British and American soldiers, Machin argues that these images are presented as isolated events in contrast with the 'real' identity of the allied soldiers. So, Machin argues, while the images seemingly reveal undesirable practices, they actually conceal the brutality of war. But the nature and aims of the conflict are absent.

While Chouliariki's study shows us that sometimes we can watch war without having to consider its victims and Machin's study reveals the way in which visual war discourses serve to repackage the brutal social practice of war into a caring practice in the form of peacekeeping, Konstantinidou's (2008) study of visual representations of the second Iraq war in a Greek newspaper shows us how those who opposed the Allied invasion were represented not as in any way representative of a broader public interest but simply random insurgent groups or rebel fighters whose aims were never articulated. In such news coverage even images of civilians horrifically maimed in the Allied bombing are absorbed into a discourse that supports a humanitarian discourse and therefore legitimation.

Machin and Van Leeuwen (2005) and Machin and Sulleiman (2006) also looked at the realization of discourses of war in computer games that allowed gamers to play as US soldiers in Somalia and Lebanon. These authors point to the importance of looking at the way that discourses of war are communicated not only by political speeches and newspapers but also through entertainments media. The computer games they analysed showed special-forces soldiers who were able to skilfully accomplish missions that required guile and sophisticated technology. Importantly these battles are represented as 'realistic'. The weapons reflect the physics of real weapons as does the kind of planning and communication. But the political reasons for the battles and their effects on the civilian population are absent. Wars and the broader chaos and terrible suffering that they cause are replaced by the intricate actions of a few highly skilled soldiers who, it has been argued (Newsinger, 1997) played a very minor role in such conflicts.

Machin and Van Leeuwen (2009) showed how discourses of war could be also disseminated by children's toys. Examining a range of children's war toys such as soldiers' uniforms, machine-guns and toy soldiers they show how war is represented as adventure. While toys in the 1970s represented a war of bravery and national armies where soldiers were relatively identity-less, more recent toys represent peace-keeping and highly trained technologized special-forces where enemies are absent. Here soldiers are given much clearer individual identities and skills. But the reasons for war are absent and the effects of war limited to cartoon depictions of explosions on packaging. Ethnographic evidence where children speak about their play with these toys revealed that they saw themselves fighting as part of a small but superior force against a poorly organized larger force in order to protect civilians.

Roderick, I., (in press) has looked at the visual representations of weapons in US 'militainment' televisions shows. Weapons, such as machine-guns and tanks are aestheticized and discussed in terms of their power, range and accuracy which are displayed on trading cards as if in a children's game. But what is always absent in these programmes is who the weapons are used against and for what purposes. Some of such programmes might show the weapons being tested against dummies to the sounds of heavy metal music. But they suppress their effects on society, bodies and the families they are pointed at. For Roderick such programmes align people alongside the idea of arms as a legitimate and unproblematic form of power. We could imagine a similar programme about weapons that depicted the different kinds of people who become the goals of such weapons, where we see terrified families, children and refugees and those disfigured and orphaned from carpet bombing.

Machin and Richardson (2012) explored the way that nationalist music, in terms of both lyrics and the actual sounds, rhythms and melodies, can also be used to communicate very specific discourses that legitimize war. Analysing two songs from WWII from Germany and Britain show how they present war not in terms of chaos, pain and suffering, but through unity of purpose, forward motion and also through a spiritual connection between body and landscape.

Put together, the body of work in CDA helps us to start to understand some of the strategies used by those in power to disseminate different discourses of war that make it seem like a reasonable, legitimate and natural social practice – that silence the actual nature aims and effects of war and foreground the need to oust evil enemies and role of the serving soldier in protecting our values and the innocent civilians under threat. These discourses are realized in different media and can be participated in vicariously through computer games, toys and songs. In this book we are interested in one other form where these discourses are realized, where the process of the recontexualization of war takes place: the war monument. Following this critical tradition we seek to draw out the less than obvious discourses and ideologies buried within war monuments, developing a methodological tool kit that will allow us to do so.

In this book we provide an account of a model of MCDA appropriate for the analysis of three-dimensional communication, drawing on the principles of social semiotics while also remaining faithful to the aims of CDA. We analyse the semiotic choices found on monuments since WWI. The book places these into the processes that create the monuments looking at historical and design documents as well as showing how the use of such monuments to foster nationalism was very much part of the consolidation of the nation itself as a political force of which militarism was one central feature.

We look at the emergence of the monument in one of the largest public construction project ever leading from WWI and as subsequent monuments have been erected for different wars. But we also show more recently a profitable war-related tourist industry exists worldwide; thousands of people flock to memorials, war museums and battle sites to view places, objects and artefacts that facilitate, or commemorate, death in war. The tourism of the sites of previous wars has 'commodified' war death; it is exploited by politicians, business people and educationalists (Lennon and Foley, 2000). In this way we show that war has become merged with different discourses of learning, cultural exchange and consumerism.

We also place our analysis within the literature that considers the central role of the nation-state in war commemoration, the way that this is bound up with the legitimation of war. The war sociologist Shaw (2003) makes the point that war and genocide, while not exclusively carried out by established states, are predominantly forms of violence that are organized by nation-states: 'States are the practitioners of slaughter *par excellence*' (Shaw, 2003:58). He argues that state power is constituted and maintained primarily through violence where new states only reach recognition once they have exercised such power. Shaw speculates on the future of war concluding that as long as state and state-like organizations are considered to be legitimate, 'legitimate war' will be an ever-present option as a resolution of conflict.

Posen (1993), also connecting the nature of warfare to the state, argues that that commitment to military participation is achieved by the promotion of nationalism via literacy and ideology and is delivered to citizens through schools, entertainment and media, as well as within military establishments. In this book, we show monuments as one part of the way by which the state carries out this process of legitimation.

The chapters in this book

In Chapter One we lay out the theoretical basis of the approach we take in this book. Here we follow in the traditions of social semiotics and CDA following what Machin and Mayr (2012) call MCDA. We consider the basis of the theoretical approach that allows us to understand the way that monuments like the Cardiff memorial, and that at Wootton Bassett, communicate. We begin by looking at what is meant by a social semiotic view of communication, which in short is to do with the way that all communication is based around a system of semiotic resources that all have potential to mean when used in contexts. In acts of communication we choose from these for the purposes of the moment and what we think will best accomplish what we want to get done. This may involve different forms of semiotic tools. A political speech may use certain kinds of words and grammar along with choices in clothing and setting. An advertiser may use a particular kind of photograph, colours or fonts. A person on a bicycle who wished someone to get out of the way will use sound – although the wrong kind may get them in trouble. For honouring those who served in war, likewise appropriate modes of communication and semiotic choices must be made. A more careful look at what these are reveals something of the intriguing nature of communication through material designs. We then go on to show how we wish to place these observations with the tradition of CDA which looks at the details in language and grammar to reveal the underlying discourses and ideologies. So too can we look at the details of all forms of communication, of the semiotic choices available and drawn upon in combinations to communicate broader discourses. We also here look at the contribution that can be made by the work on iconography and iconology by Barthes (1973) and by Panofsky (1972) respectively where we are encouraged to think about the origins and meaning of symbolic elements. What we argue is that we can best draw out buried ideologies by looking at the way that semiotic choices are used to recontextualize social practices. In this case we are looking at the way that material choices in monument design seek to recontextualize war in a way that serves the interests of the powerful but replacing and transforming, identities, causes, sequences of activity, settings, etc. Finally in this chapter, following Fairclough (1995) we look at the need to place textual analysis into social and political context which comprises an important part of the analysis in this book.

In Chapter Two we lay out some of the available semiotic resources for meaning making in three-dimensional designs. In terms of the monuments in Cardiff and Wootton Bassett considered above, what kinds of resources for meaning making have the designers drawn upon? We begin by looking at a number of meaning potentials that are available to designers to create social relations between monuments and viewers. Here we look at the semiotic meaning of size, height, elevation and boundaries. All of these choices influence the way that viewers are positioned in relation to the monument. They can create a sense of relative power and accessibility. They also communicate at a metaphorical level in terms of objects that area idealized which we look up at and those placed on the same level. We then go on to look at meaning potentials of the material form itself. Here we look at a range of semiotic tools such as angularity versus roundedness, softness versus hardness, solidity versus hollowness. We also look at the meaning potentials of some of the materials that are chosen for monuments. We then move on to a number of tools that are drawn from Halliday (1985) and Kress and van Leeuwen (1996) where concepts are drawn from linguistics. The first of these is 'modality' or 'visual truth'. Through this concept we can draw our attention to the ways that figures and elements on monuments are represented naturalistically or not. If they are not we can ask in what ways and as regards which specific features. Are some aspects realistic, whereas other aspects are not? Such detailed observations, as in the study of linguistic details in CDA, allow us more concrete information on which to make conclusions about the discourses that are being communicated – as regards how the social practice of war is being recontextualized. The second of these tools is transitivity analysis. Here drawing on Halliday (1985) we look at a number of categories of verbs that we can use in order to ask what figures on monuments are represented as doing and to whom. In CDA this has proved useful in order to think about levels of agency and also about what kinds of actions have been deleted or changed.

In Chapter Three we look at the existing literature on monument analysis from across a number of disciplines. We do this for two reasons. In the first place, of course, much can be learned about what is productive or not as regards analysis. And one criticism of much work that has been done as part of the emerging body of multimodal analysis is that it does not pay sufficient attention to work outside of linguistics that deals, already often extensively, with the particular area of analysis. In the second place, consequently, this process allows us to show just how MCDA can take us one small, but important, step forwards. In this chapter we look at a selection of work within the disciplines of and from social semiotics which looks at the politics of institutional aspects of commemoration. We look at work in cultural studies which approaches monuments more in terms of textual meanings. Following Ashplant et al. (2000, 2004) and Niven (2008), we conclude that indeed there is need for an approach that is able to provide more systematic analysis of the way that monuments communicate and where matters of design and institutional control are also considered. We conclude this chapter by showing how the approach and tools we have laid out in Chapters One and Two provide a solution to the limitations in the field across disciplines.

In Chapter Four the analysis of the war monuments begins. In this chapter we provide contextual socio-historical and sociopolitical information that saw the first wave of monument building in Britain in the period following the WWI, discussing arguments made by a range of historians that describe the political mood of the politicians, trades unions and soldiers at the time. We find the ruling class at this time in a position of incredible fear as regards the politicization of the working classes and resentment as to the losses of loved ones incurred in the war which appeared pointless from their point of view, bitterness felt by returning soldiers, the massive social inequalities still experienced by many of these people and at the same time the awareness of the success of workers movements in other parts of the world at the time. Monument building and the promotion of nationalism were seen as one way to steer attention away from these things and foster a national sentiment and loyalty. The chapter goes on to discuss previous studies of British WWI commemorative monuments by historians who have looked specifically at sociopolitical context.

In Chapter Five we begin our analysis of the way the monuments themselves communicate allowing us to show how the designers realized the kinds of communicative purposes established in the previous chapter. In this chapter we begin by looking at some of the iconography and iconology found on monuments. We look at the kinds of Classical and Christian references used on the monuments to communicate high ideals and the destiny of the nation. In the same way we look at the figures that we find represented on the monuments which also tend to draw on Classical designs and forms as well as personification of the nation and war through the use of Classical deities. We then move onto the meaning potential of pose, looking at the way the way that soldiers are represented not through fear or aggression but through impassivity suggesting total emersion in the cause, artless poses of the gentle or energetic and lively, or more solid protective poses. We then begin to think about social relations on the monuments by looking at the use of elevation by designers.

In Chapter Six we move onto the materiality of the monuments. We begin by looking at the materials chosen for the designs. For the most part these are those that communicate eternity solidity and ancientness, the organic and hand production, even if these may not necessarily be the most practical or durable. We look at the meaning potentials of stone and bronze. We then move onto other of the semiotic tools discussed in Chapter Two. We look at the uses of solidity and hollowness to communicate certainty and wholeness important when combining with figures of Classical beauty standing in impassive postures. Nation here is represented as eternal and durable infused with high ideals and destiny. We look at the use of gaze as a semiotic resource on the monuments as why soldiers simply must not be represented as looking at the viewer, as they must remain other-worldly and remote from the everyday. We then move on to look at transitivity on the monuments. In the previous chapter we looked at who was represented and who was absent. In this section we are concerned with what these participants are represented as doing, what is done to them and with whom they interact. This analysis is clearly useful as social practices involve actions and sequences of activity. It is important in analysis to ask whether the microprocesses are present or if they have been deleted, abstracted or substituted. We end the chapter by thinking about one monument that could be thought of as critical of one aspect of war. But applying the analytical tools developed in the last two chapters suggests something different.

In Chapter Seven we look at the representation of women on war monuments. This chapter is important as it allows us to develop our sense of the way that social practices are recontextualized through material semiotic choices. It also allows us to begin to understand this process historically as discourses have changed. Women have served an important role in war commemoration in Britain. War has been represented through discourses of protecting the Home Front, often represented through the images of women and children, since Britain has not experienced war under occupation in the fashion of much of mainland Europe. On the one hand this can be seen as problematic and serves to maintain a sense of war as something that takes place is more distant places and therefore prevents a sense of what the experience of war is like as a lived experience of the humiliations, fears and terror of occupation or of living in combat zones. The popular memory of war on the Home Front in Britain involves the hardship of food rationing and unity in the face of enemy bombing. In the war torn areas of Europe there was simply no rations with millions of people becoming refugees. On the other hand women did play major roles in the total wars of WWI and WWII yet this is largely absent from commemoration. In this chapter we look at the actual role of women in the wars and show which elements of this has been represented, in what ways and look at what has been suppressed. We continue to draw upon and develop the tools introduced in this chapter and the previous two chapters, continuing to show how they can be used to increase the sensitivity of our observations. We also look at the use of women on monuments who often appeared in the form of personifications such as the Goddess Victory and Britannia. We consider why these were so useful in the promotion of national unity and in recontextualizing war. We also look at more recent monuments that have begun to include women as active in the war, but show how these have remained very different to those commemorating men.

In Chapter Eight we look at more contemporary war monuments. In the first section we take a sample of newer war monuments erected to commemorate previous and contemporary wars to show how the discourses communicated are both different and also continue to carry some of the same elements, continuing to recontextualize war but in the context of the changed role of the nation and nationalism and as war itself has changed. In the case of each monument we look at the processes of commissioning and design as well as then carrying out a systematic analysis of the material semiotic choices used by the designers. We show how these new monuments are products of highly institutionalized and regulated commissioning and design processes. The analysis in this chapter shows the way that some monuments still draw on Classical features and Christian symbolism. But we also find a shift to abstraction and other kinds of symbolism to do with reified ethnic identities, heritage and even sport in order to communicate national identities. We find how war and war monuments have increasingly become part of culture and heritage trails and also that in the context of government policy must implicate viewers and provide learning experiences. We show how this still takes the form of discourses that are celebratory of war and that foster nationalism. But these also fuse with tourism and consumerism. We consider the implications of this for the representation of war. The chapter ends with a section where we analyse the inscriptions on war monuments. We show the changing discourses over time, and also consider how these work alongside the material semiotic choices.

In the Conclusion chapter we think more broadly about the nature of the findings from what we have done in this book. We also look reflectively on the MCDA that we have used in the book. We consider its use as part of a multi-disciplined approach. We also consider the further developments that may be possible in the study of three-dimensional communication from an MCDA perspective.

CHAPTER ONE

What is Multimodal Critical Discourse Analysis?

In this chapter we describe the theoretical model and analytical principles leading to the set of tools that we introduce and use in later chapters for the analysis of monuments. In the introduction to this book we looked at the figure of a soldier holding a wreath, standing on a step against a column structure, where there were other figures along with animals. We began to ask a number of questions about the design and purpose of these structures pointing to some of the questions that remain unanswered and placed this within the broader research on representations of warfare and soldiery. As we will see in Chapter Three of this book, there have been many studies of such objects. But scholars have pointed out that there has been no study that has provided a systematic model for their analysis that can allow the way that these objects communicate to be fully understood. This chapter explains the basis and details of an approach that allows us to carry out such a detailed analysis.

We begin by explaining what we mean by a Social Semiotic view of communication that we take in this book, which emphasizes that we should see all communication whether through language, images, sounds or objects as accomplished through a set of semiotic resources, options and choices. This kind of analysis means that we carefully consider the precise decisions made by a text maker/designer in order to produce any kind of text or communicative act. And since such choices are made from an existing set of available semiotic resources we should seek to create an inventory of those choices where appropriate and identify what kinds of uses these might be put to. Important in this view is that semiotic resources do not have fixed meanings as such. They do not 'stand for' something but have a semiotic potential to be used in contexts. They do not have specific meanings but rather 'meaning potentials' which may or may not be explicitly recognized. So as analysts our task is to show what *could be* communicated with a particular semiotic resource as well as what *is* communicated.

We then place this analysis within the tradition of CDA. This is a broad field of linguistic analysis that looks at the details of the language and grammatical choices used by authors and speakers in order to draw out the ideas and values that they are communicating that may be less than obvious to the casual reader or listener. Analysis in CDA typically shows what kinds of identities, actions and circumstances are concealed, abstracted or foregrounded in a text, pointing to the ideological and political consequences of these. We will be extending the principles and assumptions of this approach to look at the consequences of linguistic, visual and material choices in monument design to consider the kinds of ideologies that these communicate. As we will see, CDA has a number of concepts that will be useful in describing this process, namely 'discourse', 'ideology' and 'the recontextualization of social practice'.

In the last part of this chapter we show how scholars working in linguistic Social Semiotics turned their attention to non-linguistic forms of communication. In the analysis we carry out we include the monuments along with the inscriptions and linguistic information that they carry. But for the most part our analysis is of visual and material features. It is the details of these, the tool kit for analysing these, to which we turn our attention to in the next chapter.

Communication through a system of choices

Why is it so useful and important to think about communication as being through a system of choices? And why is this so useful in the case of monuments? To begin with we answer the first (broader) question. The reason: it is this position that best prepares us to see communication as being subject to social, cultural and economic situations. It is a position that best allows us to understand the position of the producer of communication in any instance, the sign-maker/designer, as being on one level able to see how to use available communicative resources for their own specific motivated purposes. Yet at the same time this allows us to understand that communication is subject to what is considered relevant or possible at any time by any individual or group due to constraints that are economic, political and social. What choices you can or will make will depend on your context, power to do so and access to the means for communicating them. In order to show why this is important we look first at a view of communication where choice is not significant.

Linguistic determinism and structuralism

One of the best-known positions on language use is based on the Sapir-Whorf theory, named after the American linguists Edward Sapir and Benjamin Lee Whorf. In this theory humans inhabit a world that is shaped and given meaning by language. Language is not just a way by which humans describe the world but is something that comes to comprise what we think of as 'the real world'. In this view different languages will shape the world differently. So the worlds different language speakers inhabit are not simply ones with different labels but are therefore distinct worlds (Sapir 1958 [1929]:69). Leach (1964) argued that the world does not contain any intrinsically separate things as such. Rather, as children we are taught to categorize this world as different things with different labels that appear naturally evident.

This view of language determining our world is called *linguistic determinism*. In fact, few linguists accept this view entirely but many accept that how we see the world might be *influenced* by the kind of language we use. And they would also argue that this is a two-way process so that the kind of language we use is influenced by the way we see the world. This notion has been important for the approach to language which we introduce in order to then show why the idea of choice is such an important development in linguistics and for our purposes in three-dimensional (3D) communication.

Throughout the twentieth century and still popular today have been structuralist views of language deriving from the work of Saussure (1959). In this model we can study the features of language, the lexical and grammatical choices as building blocks. As in the Sapir-Whorf model communication in language is based on the idea that everyone agrees to use the same words to mean the same thing. These words have no natural relationship to the world out there – the word 'tree' has no natural relationship to the thing in the world – but are arbitrary. Saussure argued that language could be studied in terms of its use, which he called *parole* and which would allow us to establish the underlying system, which he called *langue* which is the system of agreed-upon arbitrary signs. This view of language was adapted by scholars such as Barthes (1973) in his earlier work to look at the way that visual signs could communicate. So, as in language, where a culture will have an arbitrarily agreed-upon system of linguistic signs so visually it will have a system of agreed-upon arbitrary visual signs. A kind of food, such as red wine, might mean luxury and 'cultured'. A natural object such as a flower can mean 'romance'. We will be drawing on Barthes' ideas in this book. But for the most part we draw on the following theory of communication that is more concerned with looking for the underlying repertoire of signs available for use.

A Social Semiotic theory of communication

In the 1970s and 1980s Michael Halliday developed his Social Semiotic approach to language. This approach to language is slightly different to that of Saussure as it is interested particularly in the way it is used in social context and the way we use language to *create* society. Key to this theory is the shift away from looking at language as a *system* to one where we think about language as a set of *resources*. Here we are less interested in attempting to describe a system of grammatical rules of communication, but rather are more interested in the way the communicator uses the semiotic resources available to them, either in language or in visual communication to realize their interests. A Social Semiotic approach to communication is interested in describing the available choices of signs, but in the first place so that we can understand what it is that people are doing with them.

Key in this Social Semiotic view of language is that individuals are aware of the way words, visual elements, shapes, sounds and gestures have particular affordances or potentials to mean. They will be aware that certain words can carry particular potentials to mean which they can use in a motivated fashion for the purposes of the context. What is important here is that speakers can to some extent see through and around the words and concepts that they have in language at least in the sense of what can be done with them. This is why we are able to explain what we mean to people if they do not initially understand what we say and can argue over definitions. The term *meaning potential* is of importance for the analysis that we carry out in this book as we are interested in the way that monument designers are aware of the potentials to mean as regards a range of possibilities that are able to carry the intended ideas, values and attitudes about war to the public.

Through this process of use in context the meaning of semiotic resources is always slightly changing and new ones will emerge due to the necessity of meeting new circumstances. Social Semiotic analysis is therefore interested in what a sign has been used for, how it is now being used and also in how it could be used. Halliday (1978) thought that rather than determining people's worlds, language creates dispositions in them and can go on to influence the way that they build our societies. But since they can see around language there is also the possibility of more open interpretations of the world. Halliday's approach involved documenting different parts of language in terms of the resources that were available for speakers and writers such as for communicating levels of certainty or kinds of action and agency.

Critical Discourse Analysis

In the 1970s and 1980s linguists like Fowler et al. (1979) began a tradition of Critical Linguistics which, drawing on Halliday, sought to begin to explore the way that language can be used not just to represent the world but to constitute the world, and the social and political consequences of this. This was also influenced by Chomskyan linguistics and work in French semiotics (Barthes, 1973). Since language shapes and maintains a society's ideas, and values, it can also serve to create, maintain and legitimize certain kinds of social practices. Analysis, following the principles of Social Semiotic analysis, looked for the choices among options used by individuals and institutions in texts to look at the way that this resulted in representations of the world that favoured certain interests. These analysts would look for absences in texts, taken-for-granted assumptions and concepts and for kinds of classifications. They would look for what kinds of events and persons are foregrounded and which are backgrounded or excluded altogether. Kress (1989) for example was able to show how in school geography books certain agents and actions would be suppressed through language and grammatical choices. Here is one example in a sentence from a text which concealed capitalism motives in a study of Africa:

The large size of the farms is needed because of the land's poor carrying capacity.

Here the text says that 'The large size of the farms is needed.' But it doesn't say who does the 'needing'. This is missing from the text as a whole. In the text the land is described in terms of what it is bad for as seen in the extract above but never what it is good for in its own terms such as biodiversity, wildlife, being perfect for sustaining small-scale communities. This text as a whole is about economic exploitation on a large and unsustainable scale. What Kress argued was that language is a form of social practice. It is intertwined with how we act and how we maintain and regulate our societies. In the case of the school book language is used to promote a particular view of the world making it appear natural and commonsensical. Certain kinds of practices, ideas, values and identities are promoted and naturalized. The school becomes a place where through 'learning' children are presented with capitalist exploitation, the need to make profit, to see all as a business resource as natural and inevitable.

One of the main criticisms of Critical Linguistics was its lack of development of the nature of the link between language, power and ideology (Fairclough, 1992). This is important for the view of Social Semiotics that we take in this book. CDA sought to develop methods and theory that could better capture this interrelationship and to draw out and describe the practices and conventions in and behind texts that reveal political ideological investment (Fairclough and Wodak, 1997).

CDA has been associated mainly with the ideas of Norman Fairclough, Ruth Wodak and Teun van Dijk who offer their own versions of this kind of analysis and in fact many different approaches are classified as CDA. What all these authors have in common is a view of language as a means of social construction: that language both shapes and is shaped by society. CDA is not so much concerned with language itself but with the linguistic character of social and cultural processes and structures. In this book we are not so much concerned with the actual semiotic resources themselves but with the processes and structures of which they form a part. Other strands of multimodal analysis have, arguably, travelled more in the direction of considering the nature if the resources themselves are available for non-linguistic forms of communication (Baldry and Thibault, 2006; O'Halloran, 2011; Bateman, 2008), but this is not primarily our aim in this book although in the last section of this chapter we do begin to lay out some of the semiotic resources available for communication in 3D designs. In CDA it is common for authors to provide accounts of what kinds of linguistic resources tend to allow certain kinds of manoeuvres in talk and text such as metaphor for abstractions and 'modal verbs' for levels of commitment to truth.

CDA assumes that power relations are discursive. In other words power is transmitted and practiced through discourse. The term 'discourse' is central to CDA and will be important in the analysis of monuments in this book. In CDA the broader ideas communicated by a text are referred to as 'discourses' (Van Dijk, 1991; Fairclough, 2000; Wodak and Meyer, 2001). These discourses can be thought of as models of the world in the sense described by Foucault (1979). The process of doing CDA involves looking at choices of words and grammar in texts in order to discover the underlying discourse. For example, currently in society we find that war is often represented in the news media through a humanitarian discourse. Here 'our' boys are shipped out to troublesome regions of the world to help to stabilize them, to help to protect civilians or to keep warring factions under control. Often in fact in such news representations it is never made clear why the conflict is going on at all, nor what the broader aims are (Takacs, 2009). This discourse can be contrasted to earlier wars where soldiers were represented in the form of large and powerful nationalist armies fighting an enemy nationalist army over territory or resources. In fact in both cases what takes place, who suffers, the outcome and reasons for the conflict may be fundamentally the same. But the notion of discourse is important as it allows us to think about the broader model of events that is being disseminated.

Semiotic resources and recontextualizing social practice

At the heart of what we do in this book is seeking to understand both *what kinds* of discourses of war are disseminated, legitimized and naturalized in society and also *how* they are disseminated. In the introduction to this book we began to consider some of the existing literature in CDA on just this matter. What kinds of discourses are used to represent the actual horrors, squalor and abuses of war by politicians, news media, computer games, toys and movies? In this book we are specifically interested in the role of commemoration in this process. Another way of putting the process of transforming social practices through the use of discourse is 'recontextualization'. This is the process where elements of the social practice are changed as in the case of the school book seen earlier. The actual agents of exploitation are deleted and a set of evaluations are added. This serves to recontextualize the cynical exploitation and destruction of land for profit as something natural and a-political. In the CDA literature on war considered in the introduction we saw the way that the actual participants, victims, processes and motivations that constitute the social practice of war are recontextualized through the addition of simplified evil enemies, the deletion of the violence against civilians, through the invention of a common calling to a greater good such as God or truth (Graham et al., 2004). In this book we are interested in how this is done mainly through visual and material semiotic resources. But the emphasis remains the same – on pointing to how these serve to recontextualize social practices. In broad terms, how do they help to gloss over and shape representations of war and how warfare is legitimized.

One important set of tools for drawing our attention to how social practices are represented ideologically is provided by Van Leeuwen and Wodak (1999). We feel that these tools should also be seen as a key part of what doing MCDA is. Van Leeuwen and Wodak (1999) suggest that discourses represent not only models of the world and why these are legitimate but also reasonable ways of acting in the world. They use the term 'scripts' (p. 99) to describe the vision of what sequence of behaviour is associated with a particular discourse. These discourses represent a kind of knowledge about what goes on in a particular social practice, ideas about why it is the way it is and what is to be done.

Van Leeuwen and Wodak suggest that we should think about discourses as including, or being comprised of kinds of participants, behaviours, goals, values, locations, times and sequences of activity. So in the case of a news report on a particular war, we can ask how the participants are being represented. Are the enemy an unnamed 'militia' whose goals and values are never specified, whereas 'our boys' are named and humanized as we see images of them playing football with local children or keeping careful and respectful watch over civilians?

What Van Leeuwen and Wodak (1999) suggest is important here in the way that actual concrete participants, processes, causality and settings are 'recontextualized'. This is where they are not represented through actually giving a clear account of events, nor by logical argument, nor by a reasonable assessment of information, but through a process of abstraction, addition, substitution and deletion. Fairclough (1995) summarizes this process clearly when he compares an advert for a cigar which hints at production processes to how it was actually produced. Here first is the advert:

> Finest grade cigar tobaccos from around the world are selected for Hamlet. Choice leaves, harvested by hand, are dried, fermented and carefully conditioned. Then the artistry of our blenders creates this unique mild, cool, smooth smoking cigar.

Fairclough argues that wherever there is evidence that social practices have been abstracted, in other words where actual microprocesses are concealed, or where certain forms of activity are given prominence, or social relations are excluded, it is an evidence that there is ideological work at play. So to begin with we can ask if any of the participants are excluded. In this advertisement 'blenders' are the only actors. Other people who would be involved in the harvest: harvesters, dryers, transporters, carriers, landowners are all excluded. This is done on the one hand through passive verb constructs. We find this in the sentence 'tobaccos from around the world are selected'. This excludes who actually does the selecting. We also find tobacco is 'harvested by hand'. Here 'hand' stands for the whole person and brings a sense of care and human touch. But who exactly does this? Is it done by peasants without the help of machinery? Fairclough also points out that circumstance in the advertisement is not specific. What does 'around the world' mean? Is this the first world? Does blending take place inside a factory/plant?

Fairclough attempts a fictional account of what the microprocesses might well have been in the following:

> As noon approached, as the sun had gone beyond unbearable, Pedro gritted his teeth with the pain of the blisters and began vigorously cutting leaves of the southern end of the field which he knew the overseer would inspect first. The increased costs of the rents meant that he could no longer afford to be docked any money.

Here all the micro details are present. Here participants (Pedro, overseer), activity (cutting), objects (leaves) and circumstance are all clear. We can see that in the Hamlet case only aspects of the production process are mentioned that point to the quality of material and the care taken into selection and processing (fine, unique, carefully, choice, by hand, selected, the artistry of our blenders) are all given prominence by being placed in the initial position in the clauses.

Van Leeuwen and Wodak (1999) offer a number of specific categories for identifying how social practices are recontextualized in texts. We can look at how these can be used to help us to draw out the recontextualization in the Hamlet example.

- *Deletion*: A representation cannot represent all the aspects of a social practice. But what is important is to ask what has been deleted: which participants, actions, settings, etc. In the case of the Hamlet advert, for example, we find deletion of harvesting and processing, of the participants who do these.

- *Addition*: Recontextualization also involves adding elements. Three important forms of addition that play an important role in representation are legitimation, purpose and reactions. In the Hamlet example there is addition to bring a sense of the quality of materials and care of selection.

- *Substitution*: This is where the details and complexities of activities can be substituted by generalizations or abstractions. For example, social actors can be represented by types, either through functionalization, described by their role, or identification, by what they look like. So in the Hamlet example the details of processes and circumstances are substituted by passive clauses.

- *Evaluation*: In texts recontextualization always also involves evaluation of the social practice that is written about. Events and people in each recontextualization are represented according to the goals, values and priorities of the participants. In the Hamlet case the evaluation is provided by the artistry of the blenders and the human touch of the 'hand' picked.

What we will be showing in later chapters, and what we believe is an important part of doing MCDA, is how non-linguistic semiotic resources can equally be used in the process of recontextualization of social practice, that they too can be used in the processes of deletion, addition, substitution and evaluation. Specifically we are interested in what visual and material semiotic resources are used systematically, in the recontextualization of the social practice of war in the process of commemoration.

Ideology and power

Along with the idea of discourse, a key term in CDA is 'ideology' (Fairclough, 1995). This is a term that is derived from the work of Karl Marx and Antonio Gramsci (1971) that, like discourse, is used to capture the way that we share broader ideas about the way the world works. But ideology here is used to describe the way that the ideas and values that comprise these views reflect particular interests. For example, in our societies it is common to find discourses that promote being tougher on crime. But here crime is identified as the relatively minor actions of the least powerful members of society, rather than those of banks and corporations that seek to reorganize society in their own interest for reasons of profit (Jewkes, 2011; Minkes and Minkes, 2008). In this case we can ask in whose interests these discourses serve.

The aim of CDA is to draw out ideologies, showing where they might be buried in texts. Drawing on Gramsci (1971), Fairclough argued that, while many institutions and forms of social organization clearly reflect ideological interests, one place where we can observe exactly how these interests operate is in language. This is simply because language is a common social behaviour where we share our views of how the world works, what is natural and common sense. It is through language that we share the idea of things such as crime and war and what they are like. People and institutions then draw on this language as it appears to be neutral and 'common sense'. Of course ideologies and power can be found communicated through other semiotic modes and not only through language, but also though other kinds of semiotic choices. We can ask what kinds of interests are served by the stream of visual images we find in the news media that most often represent war not as the destruction and awful maiming of bodies, the shattering of families and communities, but as the humane intervention of a small number of well-trained and disciplined professional soldiers defending civilians from un-named generic militia whose aims are never identified. We can also look at the way that the interests of the powerful operate through the shaping of material objects in public places such as monuments and other forms of architecture.

Ideology characterizes the way that certain discourses become accepted in this way and therefore obscure the way they help to sustain power relations. Ideology obscures the nature of our unequal society and prevents us from seeing alternatives. It limits what can be seen and what we think we can do. In present common sense we take for granted that 'business' should be at the heart of everything, that it is the lifeblood of our societies and of human existence. Such is the power of this view that alternatives are viewed with ridicule. These discourses find their realization not only in language but also in social practices, in the way we organize our society, the institutions we create and the buildings that we construct (Kress, 2010). This realization in everyday life plays an important part of naturalizing these discourses, of making them appear neutral. In British society we see soldiers at the Queen's parade marching through London where those who fought in different wars carry medals and march to national music. 'Our heroes' are introduced to spectators at national football matches. We can go to air shows where we watch military aircraft on manoeuvres. Children can buy war toys such as soldiers or guns or collect actual war memorabilia from classic battles, or they can join cadets. In motorway cafes we can relax playing video games where we can shoot enemies. Schools may participate in competitions to design new monuments which will stand in the local shopping area, funded by local business people. School children will learn about key historical battles mostly in terms of strategies rather than what happened to the civilians in the areas where they took place, what happened to the orphaned and crippled children or the financing of the conflict. The first thing they learn is certainly not how the arms industry, one of the most profitable industrial sectors on the planet, works, nor of the hundred billion dollar a year private military contracts paid out by the United Kingdom and the United States (Wulf, 2005). In this sense discourses have a natural presence in society. Ideologies therefore can be found across whole areas of social life, in ideas, knowledge, institutional practices.

The question of power has been at the core of the CDA project as it is in this book. The aim for CDA has been to reveal what kinds of social relations of power are present in texts both explicitly and implicitly (Van Dijk, 1991:249). Since language can (re)produce social life, what kind of world is being created by texts and what kinds of inequalities, interests might this seek to perpetuate, generate or legitimate? In the context of this book, we ask what are the kinds of social relations of power that are present in war monuments, what kind of world is being created by them and what kind of interests might this seek to perpetuate, generate and legitimate? We show how specific semiotic resources have been used to represent warfare through Classical higher ideals, through other-worldliness, through the stoic and impassive concern with homeland and later through humanitarianism, among other things. But importantly these are at all times celebratory, if melancholic. As such these monuments have played their part in recontextualizing warfare and conflict as a natural and inevitable practice of contemporary societies, concealing actual processes, causes and consequences. They therefore act in the interests of those who seek to gain from the continuance of warfare as it is used to access resources, territory, align alongside other powerful economic interests and to make vast profits from the sales of arms (Graham and Luke, 2003). In this view, therefore, semiotic resources are not simply vehicles of communication, or even of persuasion, but are a means of social construction. The discourses they signify and realize do not merely reflect social processes and structures but themselves to contribute to the production and reproduction of these processes and structures.

Halliday (1978) believed that language can create dispositions within us. Writers like Fairclough, following from Foucault, believe that one way to put this is that language constitutes us as subjects (Fairclough, 1995). This is because the person who comes to think through the discourses of business is thinking of themselves, their identity, their possibilities, through this discourse. So too in this book we show that all semiotic resources can be used to help constitute us as subjects. Korpela (1989) points to the power of objects and locations to become part of the spaces through which we define who we are and know ourselves. The discourses they realize become embedded deeply into our mundane sense of self-awareness in ways that those realized in written discourse might not. War monuments infuse not just our public physical spaces, but also our internal mental spaces with discourses that legitimize war, soldiery and militarism, helping to shape our moral order. Critical theorists have stated that the structure of public spaces or any other constructed or natural physical environment should be thought about in terms of the way they have psychological and cultural effects since they come to house human thoughts and feelings (Sack, 1992).

Social Semiotics and multimodality

While there have been many decades of research into communication through non-linguistic means, through paintings, photographs, gestures and objects in fields like Media Studies, Film Studies, Psychology and Anthropology let alone a century of analysis in Semiotics, linguists began to turn their attention more to the visual and kind of communication in the 1980s and 1990s, particularly after the appearance of the pioneering and highly influential work of Kress and Van Leeuwen (1996, 2001). While these two authors were both heavily influenced by Halliday's Social Semiotics they were also familiar with existing work on visual communication, particularly in semiotics and psychology. And both were already writing about language in the context of Critical Linguistics and the emerging CDA.

Kress and Van Leeuwen (1996) were interested in developing a set of tools that could bring some of the rigour of analysis characteristic of Halliday's work that had been able to show what kinds of resources were available to communicators in language, to provide a more systematic approach to visual design. This would allow the analyst to show how in visual communication too we can think not just about the way that people use individual signs to communicate, such as the colour red to mean danger, for example, but to describe the underlying system of meaning potentials. For example, the colour red can be either very saturated and rich or very dilute and weak. In each of these cases what it can communicate is different – for example, a flag would be unlikely to use a dilute pale red as a bolder, richer colour is required to communicate the vibrancy and passion of the nation. And the meaning can also be changed through the other visual elements it is combined with.

What is of importance for the approach we take in this book is that in the work of Kress and Van Leeuwen there was still a strong critical element seen especially in the later work of Van Leeuwen (2005) in his

Introduction to Social Semiotics. But this critical stance has tended to be absent from other multimodal work.

Linguists working in multimodality have since sought to refine and develop our understanding of the way that non-linguistic modes of communication work drawing on the kinds of principles developed by Halliday in terms of the kinds of systems of options and functions of language. Some of these have looked, for example, at art (O'Toole, 1994) at space and exhibitions (Stenglin, 2009) at advertisements (Baldry, 2004), at mathematics (O'Halloran, 2004) and at social interaction (Norris, 2004). For the most part, despite the critical tradition from which multimodality emerged in the work of Kress and van Leeuwen (1996) work in this field has sought in the first place to understand the nature of different modes more fully rather than engaging with how they are used from a critical perspective. In the tradition of linguistics, from where many of these authors come, their aim was to understand the nature of language and its use and this pattern was reproduced in their studies of visual and other modes of communication.

While some work in multimodality appears to clearly help our understanding of the details of how modes communicate, for example, Kress and Van Leeuwen's (1996) own work on photographs and composition, much of this work has been criticized for producing over-complex jargonized accounts that yield little other than obvious conclusions (Forceville, 2010) and others have expressed the view that multimodality has simply not been able to deliver on its early aims (Cobley and Randviir, 2009). Others yet have pointed out that without also engaging with other theories of the visual it is very likely that multimodality will end up simply reinventing the wheel and falling into the very same dead ends as experienced by those theories (Machin, 2009). But it is also clear that much of this work has indeed started to introduce some new insights into the ways that different kinds of semiotic resources work – what can we communicate with an image that we cannot communicate with language, for example? The cliché 'a picture is worth a thousand words' is not necessarily true if you want to communicate something very specific that requires the precise denotation of language. And, as we show in this book, the dissemination of discourses that legitimize war and foster nationalism may be better accomplished through the placement of particular kinds of objects, made of specific kinds of materials, in towns and cities across the country. These will be able to communicate in ways that could not be accomplished through language.

In multimodality the task still remains to show how different modes can be used in the Social Semiotic sense. Rather than seeking to apply Hallidayan concepts to other modes, one more fruitful way forward may be to look at what is done through different kinds of semiotic tools. How are discourses realized in different modes of communication, what can be done for example, through material semiotic choices that cannot be done through language or through photographs? In this book, however, while on the one hand we seek to understand more about the meaning potentials available for communication in 3D objects, as is the difference between CDA and broader linguists, not so much with modes of communication themselves but with the Social Semiotic character of social and cultural processes and structures of which they form a part.

Semiotic modes and meaning making

The earlier work of Kress and Van Leeuwen (1996, 2001) pointed to the need for linguists to pay attention to the way that meaning was produced also by other non-linguistic modes in many of the texts that they analysed. So while a linguist might produce a careful analysis of how language communicates 'fun' and 'assertiveness' in an advert through the use of imperatives, lots of adjectives and personal pronouns they will miss much of the way that the advert actually works by paying no attention to the image on which the text is placed (Machin, 2007b). Multimodality, therefore, was driven by the idea that modes other than the linguistic mode should be studied if we are to understand meaning making. So if we want to understand speech, as well as the grammar and language used we should deal also with tone of voice, posture, gesture and setting. As noted above some linguists have sought to clarify the nature of these different modes.

On the one hand revealing the nature of different modes has been problematic as it is not clear what the boundaries of modes are. Bateman (2008) has shown that many of the assumptions of what are modes in multimodality are incorrect. What Bateman starts to do is to show how what is a mode may be less easy to pin down than had earlier been assumed. In fact in 2001 Kress and Van Leeuwen had already begun to question the ease that this could be done and in 2005 Van Leeuwen leaves the issue alone and deals more with discourse and communication.

On the other hand the need to identify the rules and boundaries of different distinctive modes may be more a task that tells us more about what linguists do than of the nature of communication itself. Perhaps this is a question born out of a desire to apply linguistics models, principles and tools to other kinds of non-linguistic communication. One of the core purposes of linguistics has been to document and explain how language works as a kind of system, to discover its rules. This drive has been transferred to other 'modes'. In this book we are not so much concerned with what modes are in themselves but with how different kinds of semiotic resources can play a part in realizing discourses and to recontextualize social practices. Forceville (2013) too suggests that the concern to differentiate modes may result in little more than arbitrary findings and may itself not be necessary to make progress in our understanding of non-linguistic communication.

As Kress (2010) points out different kinds of resources have different affordances. As we see in our analysis of this book some of the meanings communicated by material choices in stone could simply not be appropriately expressed through language. If we see a news item about a particular issue in a Muslim community and we find an image of a woman in a full Burhka to represent 'Muslimness', it would not be possible to write 'all Muslims look like this', or 'this is representative of all Muslims'. Yet the image works. As many theorists on the visual have observed, images do not have such specific denotative meaning as language and therefore it is a less easy matter to pin down what meanings they convey precisely. What is important in our analysis is the way that each of these different semiotic resources allows the sign-maker to do different kinds of work in terms of recontextualization.

This can be illustrated further with Kress' example of plant cell being described using two different modes and the kinds of evaluations that this involves (pp. 16–17). He imagines a teaching asking two different questions:

Who can tell me something about a plant cell?
Who can draw a plant cell?

The verbal answer could be: 'The cell has a cell wall and a nucleus.' But the drawing would have to do something more and make a commitment about shape and about where to put a dot for the nucleus – in the centre, for example. The dot has to be placed somewhere. But language would have to make a commitment to naming as in 'cell wall' and 'nucleus' whereas the drawing can just be of a circle with a dot in it. In language there would also have to be a commitment to the relation of the names such as 'the cell *has* a nucleus'. In drawing no such commitment is necessary. What Kress suggests is that these different ways of describing a plant cell involve different kinds of *epistemological commitment*. In language it is naming and relations. In the drawing it is spatial and size relations. But each can be used precisely since such commitments may be avoided. And it is this kind of epistemological commitment of semiotic resources that is of primary interest to us in this book. As we show in later chapters ability of semiotic resources to allow certain qualities to be glossed over and others communicated more specifically that provides a useful tool for designers and for the multimodal process of communicating about the meaning of war. So too can this be a useful tool for the analyst when thinking about the way that monuments can represent war its participants and process while avoiding certain aspects of these. Critically it is important to identify the work that different kinds of semiotic resources can do in the recontextualization of social practice. So how do choices in material, such as marble, bronze, tin or wood for a sculpture create different kinds of meaning from the inscriptions that can avoid certain kinds of epistemological commitments and make others that are useful in the process of deletions additions and substitutions?

Semiotic resources and meaning potential

Above we looked at the way that Kress (2012) and Van Leeuwen (2005) speak of the way that semiotic resources come to have meaning potential. We have also thought about the importance of being mindful of the way that different kinds of semiotic resources have different kinds of affordances that bring different kinds of epistemological commitments and how these, therefore, can be used in the contextualization of social practice. In this section we discuss ways that these resources come to be infused with meaning. We distinguish two kinds of meaning origins: provenance and associational. In each case we look at a number of scholars whose work we later draw upon.

Provenance

This is simply when a semiotic resource comes to have a particular meaning through cultural accumulation of associations. Barthes (1973), looking at the way that visual signs could communicate gave examples of the way that a kind of food, such as red wine, might mean luxury and 'cultured'. A natural object such as a flower can mean 'romance'. Every culture will have an agreed-upon set of signs, although these will be always slightly in flux and new ones will emerge, that work at this level. Barthes (1973, 1977) was influenced by Saussure's view that communication in language is based on the idea that everyone agrees to use the same words to mean the same thing. These words have no natural relationship to the world out there – the word 'tree' has no natural relationship to the thing in the world – but are arbitrary. In this sense words like tree could be said to gain their meaning through provenance, in other words through use in particular cultures. It would then be possible to trace the origins of these meanings in time. This is one way that we can draw out their constructedness which was one important part of Barthes' work.

In our analysis of monuments we will be drawing on Barthes' two-step analysis. At the first level of analysis we must describe carefully what we see in any representation independent of our interpretation of it. Only then can we take the second step and think about what ideas and values, the people, the places and objects in images stand for – what their arbitrary meaning might be. In fact it is the first level that people often find the most difficult. We are more familiar with saying what an image means to us than we are with describing its details. The first level of analysis asks what is denoted, or simply, what do we see. So in the case of a monument we need to document all the elements and forms that we see. Of course we never really see any image in this kind of innocent way as simply depicting something. For example, whether we photograph a person alone or as part of a group can influence whether they are shown as an individual or as a type, whether we are encouraged to identify with an individual or just see them as an anonymous part of a crowd. Denoting people in particular places or in groups, from different angles, in distance or close up, will have an effect on how we will see them. But all these too can be carefully described and classified.

At the second level of analysis we look for the connotations of those elements and forms. Once we have identified what is depicted we can ask what it means, what are the cultural associations of elements, features in, or qualities of, the image?

Barthes listed a number of key carriers of connotation that we will be considering in our analysis including architectural styles, materials, objects and poses. According to Barthes there exists a dictionary of poses in our heads. For example, a soldier, at attention, stands straight, rigid and tense. The pose is regular and precise. The rigidity and discipline over the body can have the association of discipline, subjection to the confines and restraint of authority. We might find a teenager in the street deliberately and consciously striking a sloppy and loose pose in order to connote the very opposite of this subjection to authority. This may be no less deliberate than the rigid pose, but can connote the opposite of control and rigidity. These will be important in the analysis of the figures we find on the monuments. We can ask whether poses connote rigidity, stability, fear, caution, etc.

The work of art iconographer Panofsky (1970, 1972) is also important in the way we approach meaning that comes from provenance. Panofsky offered three levels of iconological interpretation for understanding the visual elements in paintings. At the first level, the viewer *identifies* elements in a painting by means of familiarity, being able to identify and name objects they see – akin to Barthes' denotation. The second level involves *iconography*, the *linking* of objects with themes, concepts and conventions, knowledge of literary sources and the manner in which themes or concepts were expressed by objects and events. As we analyse the monuments it is important to carry out this process of linking to historical traditions in art symbolism and style in sculpture. One simple example is where Panofsky explains the meaning of the way a man might feign doffing an invisible hat when seeing someone in the street. The meaning of this has its origins in medieval knights who would remove helmets in this way to indicate they offered no threat.

The third level is the *iconological* level of *interpretation*, going into the domain of 'symbolical' values; it is at this level that much deeper levels of meaning are realized. For Panofsky it is at this level that we can show how our analysis is able to reveal how iconographical choice, including symbolism, perspective and materials can reveal the 'basic attitudes of a nation' (1972:7). In the case of the monuments we show the way that choices in style, designs, poses, gestures and perspectives, etc., can allow us to make broader conclusions about the attitudes that are being fostered and legitimized at different points in history as we look at changing monument design over a century since WWI. The extension of Panofsky's work is important to the interpretation of the commemorative war monuments under analysis as it helps to unlock the meanings in the symbols found in the sculptures.

Experiential meaning potential

The meaning of semiotic resources may also derive from associations of things in the real world. Arnheim (1997:117) argued that communication is steeped in 'experiential associations'. He explains that 'human beings are naturally aware of the structural resemblance uniting physical and non physical objects' (p. 118). So we might clap our hands together to suggest a conflict of interest between two people. There is no actual clapping or physical collision going on in the interaction but communication works by drawing on an experiential association of these to understand something of the way that people may not agree. In the same way the sound associated with crashing objects could be thought to suggest conflict as opposed to a gentle drifting sound that might mean some kind of mutual attraction.

Much of the best work of Kress and Van Leeuwen (1996, 2006) and Van Leeuwen (1999, 2005) arguably draws on semiotic resources based on experiential or associational meaning potential. For example, Van Leeuwen (2005) has shown how typefaces that are wider tend to suggest stability and weight as opposed to slimmer, taller typefaces that can suggest less stability but therefore perhaps something more elegant. While what we see on the page is of course not stable as it is comprised of ink, these forms bring associations of wider and more stable things in the world such as a tree. Curved typefaces can suggest something softer, gentler, more organic, than those with harsh angles. A product for something soft and nurturing will tend to avoid harsh angularity. Again there is an association with things in the world that are soft and nurturing being curved as opposed to harshly angular. This kind of meaning potential is important in monuments which rely on things like form, angularity, elevation and height that all create meaning through reference to our experience of things in the world.

Historical context

To fully understand the monuments critically it is essential that the analysis goes beyond a reading of the texts and extends to an exploration of the context of their production. The significance of contextual factors to the interpretation of texts is acknowledged within the CDA itself. Fairclough and Wodak (1997) discuss the value of the inclusion of historical contextual information in the analysis of discourse, citing earlier work such as Van Dijk's analysis of racist discourse during the 1980s and Wodak et al.'s work on racist discourse in Austria in the early 1990s. Fairclough and Wodak (1997) go on to demonstrate the significance of a 'discourse historical' approach in their example of an analysis of a speech by the ex-British Prime Minister Margaret Thatcher, concluding that the speech relates to a number of earlier events: speeches and proclamations; laws; media reports and other actions. They conclude their discussion by pointing out:

> The discourse history of each unit of discourse had to be uncovered. This naturally again implies interdisciplinary analysis; historians have to be included in such an undertaking. (1997:277)

Kress (2010) also explains the relevance of contextual information to a Social Semiotic analysis of a text by listing the first question a social semiotician asks of a text: '*Whose interest* and agency is at work here in the making of meaning?' and pointing out that the third perspective that multimodal Social Semiotics takes in the theorizing of the meaning of *mode* is a description of '. . . its histories of social shaping and the cultural origins/provenance of elements of that mode', emphasizing that both culture and meaning are required in a full theory of meaning (Kress, 2010:61).

When we look at the production of war monuments we find that they are co-produced; the end product was not solely shaped by the designer, the sculptor, but by a chain of agents. These agents in all cases were directed by those who occupy powerful positions in society. Earlier in the chapter we considered Fairclough's point that not everyone in society is in the same position to communicate their viewpoints. Just as only certain persons have the power to explain wars on national television news only some have the power to place their versions of events in the form of stone monuments in public squares.

The majority of British monuments were erected following the WWI and marked a radical change in the way Britain commemorated war through public sculpture. The monuments occupy a unique position in British political history, so the analysis in this book begins in Chapter Four with a discussion of the post-WWI political climate that sparked the nation-wide programme of war commemoration by public art. It then goes on to provide contextual information on commemorative war monument design considerations, giving details of guiding trends that directed designers of the monuments. It then goes on to analyse more contemporary monuments again providing details about the process of commissioning and design.

The inclusion of this contextual information will demonstrate that multimodal analysis does not provide the analyst with a fixed, universal method of unlocking meaning that permanently resides within semiotic resources, but it recognizes that *sign-making* is a process that stems from both the interests and needs of society at a given time (Van Leeuwen, 2005).

Kress (2001:67) argued for the necessity in a new way of thinking about meaning: one that delivered the promises made by Saussure (1959) and Peirce (1935, 1958); the: '. . . all-embracing theory [that] would provide an account of human semiosis in all its manifestations'. Indeed, perhaps the greatest theoretical leap from those earlier schools of thought is the stance Social Semiotics takes on different semiotic modes: it does not seek to make separate descriptive or functional accounts of these, but examines how semiotic modes are brought together in the process of sign-making to create new meanings (Van Leeuwen, 2005) and fundamentally sees signs as motivated, arising out of the interests of sign makes (Kress, 2010). Kress explains:

> *Social semiotics* and the *multimodal* dimension of the theory, tell us about *interest* and *agency*; about *meaning(-making)*; about *processes* of *sign-making* in social environments; about the *resources* for making meaning and their respective *potentials* as *signifiers* in the making of *signs-as-metaphors*; about the *meaning potentials* of cultural/*semiotic forms*. The theory can describe and analyse all signs in all *modes* as well as their interrelation in any one text. (Kress, 2010:59)

The importance of context lead Kress and Van Leeuwen (1996) to make one more point that is relevant for our own analysis. In their discussion of the emphasis on the relevance of culture in the 'grammar' of visual design they make it clear that their 'grammar' is not intended to be a universal grammar, but acknowledge that their analysis of signs within Western cultures, does not necessarily apply to visual communication generated by non-Western cultures, or that people from non-Western cultures read Western communication in the same way that Westerners do:

> A glance at the 'stylized' arts of other cultures should teach us that the myth of transparency is indeed a myth. We may experience these arts as 'decorative', 'exotic', 'mysterious' or 'beautiful', but we cannot understand them as communication, as forms of 'writing' unless we are, or become, members of these cultures. (Kress and Van Leeuwen, 2006:33–4)

This is an important point in relation to the meaning potentials we consider in the next chapter. These war monuments are all of British origin, created for a British audience and placed in British public space. If their full meaning potential is to be established it is important to use a theoretical approach that acknowledges the relevance of culture and it is also important to remain mindful of cultural relevance during the analysis.

Conclusion

In the introduction to this book we looked at two monuments. The first of these, standing in a park in Cardiff city centre depicts soldiers in the form of Classical Gods standing on the steps of a rounded mini Acropolis. In this book we seek to understand how and what such monuments communicate. On the one hand we place the analysis that we carry out within the tradition of CDA. The aim here is to draw out ideologies through analysis of the details of language and grammatical choices. This is important as it is through language that we share the idea of how the world works, what is natural and what is common sense. Ideology points to the way that what becomes natural and common sense in fact serves the interests only of specific groups, most likely at the expense of others. Ideology characterizes the way that certain discourses become accepted in this way and therefore obscure the way they help to sustain power relations. Ideology obscures the nature of our unequal society and prevents us from seeing alternatives. People and institutions then draw on this language as it appears to be neutral and 'common sense'. The 'common sense' can be analysed through the specific choices made by the authors of texts which they make from a system of options. So we can analyse the speeches of politicians, for example, to look at the way that they legitimize and naturalize certain events and actions, such as war, in terms of the subtle linguistic choices, to reveal their ideology. We can look at what it is that they gloss over through their language use, the substitutions that they use and which actions they represent only as abstractions. In this book we assume that ideologies and power can be found communicated through other semiotic modes and not only through language. And in the same way we can look at the details of these different kinds of semiotic choices and how these are used to recontextualize social practices like war. In terms of the Cardiff monument how do the semiotic choices made by the designer delete, substitute and abstract the actual microprocess of the practice of war and the death of soldiers? In the next chapter we look at some of the semiotic resources, some of the specific meaning potentials, which are available to monument designers in order to accomplish this. But before we can go on to apply these to actual monuments we will need, in Chapter Four, to look at the social and political context which lead to their creation.

CHAPTER TWO

Three-dimensional Social Semiotics

In the previous chapter we laid out the basis for MCDA based on a Social Semiotic view of communication. Here all communication, through speech, writing, colour and material objects, etc., is accomplished by text-makers on the basis of choices with specific communicative aims in mind, from a set of available resources or meaning potentials. And these choices are motivated and ideological in that they select and shape how persons, events, ideas and identities are represented, to background certain aspects and foreground others. It is through this process that text-makers recontextualize social practices to support their own interests. In this chapter we look at some of the semiotic resources, the meaning potentials, available specifically for 3D communication.

In this chapter as well as drawing on the iconography and iconology of Barthes (1973) and Panofsky (1970) we use the ideas of provenance and experiential association to draw out an inventory of meaning potentials. We indicate not only how these can be used to create meanings in the context of monuments specifically, but also point out how these can have wider use. In later chapters we then go on to use these to build up complete analyses of individual monuments.

We begin with those that can be thought in the first place in terms of creating social relations and then move onto materiality which can be thought of in the first place as communicating ideas and attitudes. We end by looking at three sets of tools drawn from Halliday's (1978) linguistics by Kress and Van Leeuwen (1996) and by Van Leeuwen (1996, 1999) adapted here for 3D communication.

We point out here that meaning in 3D is never made through individual semiotic choices but through combinations which can activate meaning potentials in slightly different ways. In this chapter we deal with each individually and in isolation for practical purposes. In later chapters these will be brought together.

Semiotic resources that communicate social relations

Elevation

The height that a statue is positioned as regards the viewer has important meaning potential. It is usual to find older WWI soldier figures raised up on a pedestal, whereas more recent statues find soldiers closer to the ground. Van Leeuwen (2005) has discussed the metaphorical associations of height with status, as in 'upper class'. We also associate height with 'loftiness' of ideals, although this can have a negative connotation where we say someone has their head in the clouds. The opposite of this is that a person can be said to be grounded and down-to-earth or the opposite of lofty ideals could be baseness. It is from these associations that Kress and van Leeuwen (1996:193) suggest we think of that which is placed at the top of visual compositions as the 'ideal', whereas that placed at the bottom is the 'real'. So in an advertisement a beautiful woman might appear in the ideal as the fantasy, and the product in the real at the bottom. From this we can think about statues raised onto pedestals as being placed into the ideal, as being higher than the real and the everyday. Of course the extent to which they are raised must not be too extensive. Figures of WWI soldiers are typically raised up several metres so that the viewer is literally at his feet. We can imagine the difference in meaning if we put a statue of a soldier who sacrificed his life for God and country on a pedestal of 10 m. Such height is normally reserved for national figures who have gained some kind of mythic status such as in the case of the Duke of Wellington statue in London where there is extensive idealization. We will be showing that more recent monuments have placed soldiers closer to ground level in the 'real'. Of course it is clear that such soldiers should not be placed too low down. We can imagine the difference in meaning when they are placed in a shallow, or even deep, hole in the ground. This could mean inferior. But it can also mean part of the land/organic which has also become important for more recent monuments where representing nation and nationalism has become much more abstract than in former times.

Angle of interaction

Elevation and size also position the angle with which the viewer interacts with the depicted soldier. Jewitt and Oyama (2001) have discussed the meaning potential as regards the way that photographs can depict participants looking up at them, looking down or at the same level. As regards the monuments where we look up at the soldier, we may look up and find ourselves looking up to them in terms of status, power and respect. We can imagine the same feeling if we look down at them where we may see them with less power or status – although not necessarily both. Of course this could have the effect of making us, as viewers, feel weak when looking up or powerful when looking down. These would be useful meaning potentials to harness depending on the discourse. What we find in our analysis is that earlier monuments tended to place the soldiers much higher using pedestals or a series of steps that meant that viewers had to look upwards at the figures. Later figures are positioned at ground level and on occasion in postures that require the viewer to look down, suggesting equality or placing the viewer in a position of power or the soldier in a position of vulnerability. In this case we will relate this to the process of discourses that represent soldiers themselves as human, as citizens not unlike civilians, who themselves suffer and experience trauma as the struggle in demanding conflicts abroad. Humanitarian discourses of war, in contrast to nationalist discourses require more consistent representations of humanized and individualized soldiers.

Size

Size of the figure on monument itself carries meaning potential. We can imagine the meaning potential if a soldier was represented in the size of a giant or conversely as the size of a doll. If we look around the world at very big statues we find these generally represent dictators or states where there is a high degree of control over the population. An example is the figure of Saddam Hussein attached to the Ishtar Gate in Baghdad in the 1980s. Another massive statue is the 87-m high 'Motherland Calling' statue in Volgorad which commemorates the fight to expel the German army from Stalingrad. Kruk (2008) has discussed the outsized statues of Stalin in the Soviet Union that were meant to symbolize not so much the man himself but the collective communist spirit. Michalski (1998) describes the use of such massive monuments as part of a 'ruler's cult' (p. 197). As a rule for the monuments we will be analysing in this book, earlier figures on those erected around the WWI were larger than a human figure by about half a meter, so they were not greatly larger than a real person but still suggested something larger than life. On later statues we find soldiers represented in a much more human scale. At this point in time it is unlikely to find them commemorated through doll-like figures. In their analysis of toy soldiers Machin and Van Leeuwen (2009) looked at the way that figures had tended to become larger and more individualized than earlier toys. Here too size conveys a shift away from the small anonymous expendable soldier who fought in large national armies to the more humanized soldier who is highly trained.

Gaze/interaction

The gaze of the soldiers on these monuments is also very important. Kress and van Leeuwen (1996) suggested that it is useful to think about the way that images can be thought of as fulfilling the speech acts as described for language by Halliday (1985). Adapting this model to visual communication, Kress and van Leeuwen show that there are two kinds of image act: 'offer' and 'demand'. These are useful for thinking about the way that the soldiers depicted in monuments interact with the viewer. In demand images the subject looks at the viewer, who is therefore addressed. In such images the viewer's presence is acknowledged. And as when we are addressed in social interaction we are required to respond. Of course the image will not know whether we respond appropriately or not, the viewer will feel what is required. The kind of demand that is made will depend on other factors such as facial expression and posture. So the subject, through looking sad, may demand that we feel pity. In offer images, the subject does not look at the viewer and the viewer remains unacknowledged. Kress and van Leeuwen suggest that we are encouraged to look at the scene or individual solely as an onlooker or as a voyeur. In such a case the viewer is offered the scene as information available for scrutiny. These authors argue that there is important ideological significance in which kinds of objects we are encouraged to interact with through offer image acts. For example, toys for young children, such as trains, clocks and telephones tend to have eyes. Other objects such as toy carpentry tools and medical equipment do not have eyes. In this sense children learn to create personal bonds with transport, time and communication.

Gaze can also have metaphorical meaning. Since 'up', in Western culture can have associations with positive moods or with aspiration and 'down' with negative moods and inward looking, these meanings can be transferred to visual communication. Often in photographs in lifestyle magazines we will find a woman looking off frame and upwards for an article on 'how to get on at work'. A politician represented favourably might be depicted looking upwards or towards the horizon while one represented on the cusp of defeat may look slightly downwards introspectively.

Distance/proximity

Material objects can be created so that they can be approached, touched or can be kept at a distance from viewers or framed off by some kind of boundary. For example, a neighbour might erect huge thick walls around his garden to signify the privacy of his property whereas another might plant a row of flowers. A third neighbour might, hypothetically, place a low single row of barbed wire around theirs. Each lays claim to privacy of a space, but semiotically each communicates different ideas and attitudes. The wire symbolizes an aggressive kind of privacy where doing harm to those who transgress is not felt to be a problem. However, this is a kind of privacy which suggests physical isolation but where onlookers can see into the private domain. The huge wall, in contrast suggests a protection even from their view – isolation in all manners from the outside world. The materials used for such a high boundary would also influence what was communicated. Solid stone might be different than were it a wooden fence. A neighbour with a high wooden fence may eventually invite you in for coffee. The neighbour with the thick stone wall may not. The boundary comprised of flowers suggests a willingness to be involved in passing conversations and community participation. In this sense we will also be thinking about the way that monuments can be interacted with to what extent they are boundaried off from viewers.

Some monuments can only be looked at frontally. Others we can walk around and others walk into. The latter of these has been part of an important shift in the way that discourses of war have changed across the media. Drawing on Arnheim's (1982) theory of the positioning of 3D sculptures, Kress and van Leeuwen (1996) make an important observation on the relevance of context to the physical positions available to the viewer from which to view the sculpture; for example, where barriers prevent close access which impacts on the social distance of the interactive relationship. Such barriers can be in the form of simple chains, or elevation where figures are out of reach, or other physical barriers that frame the monument away from the viewer.

More recent changes which have seen a shift away from barriers towards closer interaction even encouraging touching can also be linked to more recent changes in British Government policy as regards these kinds of public art and displays. Karp and Lavine (1991) describe a drive where public displays, such as in museums have to be lively and people-friendly places which 'implicate' audiences. As part of this process war monuments become not only sites of mourning but of learning and may even tend towards the quasi artistic and curious, with instructions on how to understand complex symbolism. Newer monuments often point out that they are arranged so that they catch the sun's rays on a certain day, or that they align with certain stars, or face a city far away. All this, say Karp and Levine, is about the veracity of the experiential. Many of these monuments are designed to 'implicate' as opposed to being made to look at and walk around.

Social Semiotics of materiality

We now move on to the material semiotic choices. Here meanings are for the most part based on experiential association.

Curvature and angularity

Van Leeuwen (2005) in his discussion of typefaces describes the meaning potential of angularity versus curvature. The significance of these may be based on experiential and cultural associations with round or angular objects. Roundness can mean 'smooth', 'soft', 'gentle', 'emotional'. It can also mean 'fluidity', 'ease' and 'organic'. In contrast, angularity tends to be associated with 'harsh', 'technical', 'masculine', 'objectivity'. These may be positively or negatively evaluated. We see these meaning potentials on the fonts in advertisements. While an advert for a female face-cream will use lighter curved fonts, the related men's produce will use more angular fonts. A movie poster for a male superhero will be unlikely to use the same light curvy fonts as we might find for an animation about princesses. In the case of 3D communication forms can emphasize gentle sweeping curves or harsh angles. Often they can combine the two so that gentle curves can be combined with straight edges and corners to combine organic and softer meanings alongside rationality and truth. One of the authors has a daughter of just over one year who has toys that are representations of everyday objects yet much more curved and rounded. This is not so much about safety per se but about communicating 'gentle' and 'emotional' to parents. As regards the monuments we analyse in this book, in many older monuments, we find stress on roundness often drawing on Classical architectural forms. Later monuments use angularity to suggest conflict and aggression, although these meanings are usually diluted through levels of abstraction.

Regular–irregular

The organic and non-rational versus technical and rational can also come from the meaning potential of regularity versus irregularity. Whereas the Classical statues emphasize symmetry and order some later statues emphasize irregularity. Regularity in form suggests formality, certainty, conformity, unity and seriousness. Other monuments might have irregularly positioned stones, objects and figures. Irregularity can have the meaning potential of not following rules and therefore informal and organic. It can also mean playful or even chaotic. These meaning potentials are important tools in communicating that war or nation are either something regulated, controlled and official, or something more of ordinary people in a more personalized idea of nation.

Solidity/hollowness

Solidity versus hollowness can have important meaning potential for monument designers. The monument depicting the figure of Oscar Wilde to the front of Charing Cross station in London is hollow and it is possible to look straight through it. The meaning potential here is openness, transparency or even vulnerability and complexity or encouraging us to look beneath the surface as would be appropriate for Wilde. For the most part, statues of soldiers are represented as solid. They are not vulnerable, and we are not encouraged to look beneath the surface. But this is precisely because they are used to depict solidity of character, a single uncomplicated view of a figure to be revered rather than analysed. We can imagine the difference had these boys who were killed were represented as hollow. We will, however see some variations on this solidity in more contemporary monuments where soldiers have become more humanized as discourses of war have changed. Soldiers are no longer supposed to give their lives for the high ideals of a powerful nation-state but are ordinary people involved in peacekeeping missions that often put much strain on them and where they need the support of the public.

Materials

Material itself can be a crucial carrier of meaning. Whatever the object that has been designed we can think about the material chosen and its affordances. On the one hand clearly there will always be a practical aspect to materials. We may not wish to make a boat out of paper, or a furnace out of plastic and in the case of monuments there will be issues of weather resistance, vandalism and a material's suitability for sculpting. But on the other hand there will always at the same time be a semiotic aspect to such choices although this will be to different degrees in different contexts. This can be illustrated through a 'SALE' sign we find in a shop window as compared to a plaque found on the wall by a solicitors' office door. The first will be made of paper or cheap card in order to communicate something of its spontaneity and immediacy. We can imagine it would be inappropriate were it made of solid shiny brass. Likewise it would be inappropriate for the sign by the solicitors' door to be made from a scrap of paper. Such signs must communicate permanence, solidity and expense. In the same way a cheap-looking plastic would not suffice. Recently one of the authors visited his bank relating to a mortgage. The desk of the manager was of solid heavy wood with a leather inlay which had a gold-coloured inlay pattern around the edge. Such desks suggest a former era of administration and writing done with a pen and inkwell. This was different from the shiny clear glass table he sat at during a recent interview with managers at a new online business-news company. The latter would have been inappropriate at the bank which sought to communicate the trust of tradition and also of durability. And in the same respect the online company looked for the sleekness of glass to show modernity. Business schools in universities where they have purpose-built new buildings will often use shiny glass and bare metals. The glass in itself brings associations of openness, vision and light, as opposed to closedness, tradition and gloominess of the older businesses such as the bank.

In the case of monuments, materials must communicate durability, after all these monuments must appear to be long lasting or eternal. A monument to an important leader made of paper or even wood would not be appropriate. But some materials that are durable would also be inappropriate. Plastic could be extremely durable but this has connotations both of cheapness and of modernity. Materials like marble, granite and bronze suggest something ancient and timeless. Rocks suggest mountains and eternity and bronze can suggest ancient times or the values and attitudes of the ancient warrior. Those who are commemorated in this book are represented as part of timeless national spirits projected backwards and forwards into eternity. This would be crucial since of course ordinary people would be less willing to throw their lives away in war for the rather contemporary nature of nations that sociologists and historians describe.

Plastic and aluminium may also not be suitable as they connote something manufactured as opposed to something carved or forged by hand as in the case of marble or bronze. But designers indeed use stainless steel, aluminium or titanium if the aim is to communicate modernity, science or technology and also where a smaller monument is involved. Here the scarcer use of a more valuable material appears inappropriate favouring materials that side-step this. And materials that communicate modernity may be appropriate where the intention is not to place the commemoration into and eternal timescale but to place it in the present and into contemporary thinking.

Soft/hard

This meaning potential sounds obvious but a designer has the choice of whether to make something hard or soft. Softness could be communicated though a material-type texture or fur that could communicate comfort and invite physical contact. A teddy bear is soft and invites squeezing and physical contact. It must communicate this. One that is hard would not do so. So an animal that is very dangerous is represented in a way that invites tactile interaction. We could imagine figurative monuments that featured soldiers who were soft and invited squeezing. While the toy bear communicates comfort thorough the softness, the monuments do not. Softness could also be communicated through lack of rigidity. So if we pressed the surface it could give in to different degrees. The dashboard of our car may do this if we press our finger against it. Here this too communicates a sense of comfort, ease and accommodation rather than resistance. But if a figure of a soldier gave in when we pressed it, perhaps in the fashion of a piece of foam or polystyrene, this kind of accommodation would suggest a sense of pliability or weakness. A figure of a soldier that left the imprint of our finger if we poked it could suggest a more sensitive soldier who was easily affected by events.

In fact more contemporary monuments are designed for interaction and engagement in a way that older ones were not, but this is certainly not in terms of tactility, comfort nor accommodation. Commemoration does not involve physical contact but contemplation. Machin and Van Leeuwen (2009) showed that children's war toys could usefully be analysed in these terms. For example, a boys' Special Forces uniform while carrying camouflage and Special Forces emblems was made of soft cotton material like that used for pyjamas. Warfare for the 6-year-old can feel comforting and cozy rather than harsh and durable. Children's construction toys can be made of softer material such as plastics as opposed to steel for older children. Another example of the use of softness working in design is the case of adult sex-play handcuffs that come covered with soft pink fur. The lightweight material of the cuffs themselves would not necessarily cause harm to the skin so the fur is not so much for protection but to diffuse the meanings of the harshness that might be associated with this kind of sexual activity involving restraint.

Of course there are degrees of softness and this is utilized in the design of monuments. Different kinds of stones can communicate different degrees of hardness and softness. In our analysis we will show that some monuments use softer-looking, lighter-coloured stone that communicate differently than heavy darker bronze. An artillery man might stand over us eternally in dark heavy immovable bronze whereas a woman nurse is represented as sitting gently in light stone which has been softly and roundly shaped.

Static/mobile

Objects can be designed so that they can move or not. Of course, the point of some objects is to be mobile; such as a car or vacuum cleaner, or a toy clockwork mouse. These can be propelled in different ways – battery motor, by hand, clockwork. Clearly monuments are not designed to be moved around. But asking why this would be inappropriate can reveal some of the meanings of monuments. Imagine a monument is unveiled in a public square to commemorate the deaths of soldiers in a recent conflict and it is on wheels. After the ceremony people can therefore wheel it around the square, even ride on it. We can also imagine that it would be inappropriate for a figure of a soldier to move in the manner of a wind-up or battery-operated toy so that limbs moved in a marching or attacking motion. The meaning potential of stasis is important in the sense of the measure of eternal time. We can see this in the meaning of slow-motion versus speeded-up. Pop videos will show a band walking in slow motion across a landscape. This makes it epic and momentous as they move like slow epic time where every movement appears deliberate. Were they speeded up so that they moved in rapid jerking movements this would appear as slightly silly and trivializing where movements are inaccurate and unmeasured. At funerals in Britain those who carry the coffin walk at a slow deliberate pace as a sign of solemnity.

Heaviness versus lightness can also relate to mobility. In more recent decades lightness has come to mean something positive with mobile technologies. So weight can also be related to mobility/immobility. Monuments must appear heavy and immobile. Were they made of plastic and moved slightly in the wind this would not be appropriate. But in some cases heavier can have meaning potential of worth. Lightness can mean lack of generosity with materials. Weight can also suggest quality through quantity of materials. A manufactured product such as a coffee machine that otherwise has quite light parts will be weighted to give the impression of quality. Objects designed to communicate the ancient history and eternity of nation should not be lightweight.

Fixed/articulated

Some figures such as dolls are designed so that limbs and head can move. These can have the communicative purposes of learning or play so that children can manipulate them. What is interesting is that different kinds of toy figures are articulated in different ways which is ideological. Machin and Van Leeuwen (2005) explain how toy soldiers were formerly rigid moving towards later more articulation and individuality in appearance. This reflects an ideology of a shift towards the humanization of soldiers as part of humanitarian discourses, where formerly they were anonymous and served as part of large armies. Newer toy soldiers will be designed to be posed in different ways, although their joints will be oriented to the limitations of engaging with the weapons that are designed for them and not say for gently hugging distressed civilians.

In the case of monuments, while they are now often about learning, it is inappropriate that they should be manipulated. Other objects are designed so that they can be taken apart so that children can learn about the parts they are made up of. Monuments could be designed so that helmets, rifles and other equipment could be taken off and examined. Again even in the case of monuments that seek to engage and communicate learning these are designed for the purposes of learning about spiritual feelings or about cultural heritage symbolism rather than factual learning. This observation in itself tells us that these monuments even when they are designed with learning in mind have a specific kind.

Granular surface/polished surface

This is the meaning potential that can be associated with the organic, natural and more functional as opposed to the manufactured, designed and carefully maintained. This can be the difference between opaque and glossy. The packaging for an organic product may use a more granular effect in its surface as opposed to a smooth glossy one that we might find for a travel brochure or for upmarket hotels. O'Toole (1994:101) points out that smoothness can be associated with status where the higher you rise in a company the smoother your floors will be polished 'just as the rough edges of your native dialect and behaviour have been smoothed away by your training for high office'. Designer shops and corporate spaces will use glossy, shiny surfaces to suggest luxury and also the clean minimalism of modernity. Polished objects also literally shine and can be brilliant and reflect as mirrors; Gage (1993) has discussed the use of polished surfaces in design in terms of the way they can increase levels of light and vibrancy in colours to add to optimism. The value of gloss can be seen in the history of things like the development of patent leather as a luxury item.

Shine and brightness have also need associated with positive feelings as opposed to muted, darker shades, as is reflected in the metaphors 'I am feeling bright today.' Polished can mean cared-for, or it can mean overused and worn as when garments and other objects become worn and shiny, in this sense the difference being between something that is deliberately man-made and that which happens through natural processes of use, time and weathering. Grittiness, can, however also mean worn and dirty.

Some monuments, as we shall see use more shiny surfaces both to point to luxury and high, almost invisible, production values. This can be seen on Classical designs, especially marble brickwork and pillars on WWI monuments. Here there is a sense of simple, clean lines, impeccable order and luxury to the surfaces which support and house soldiers represented as Greek Gods. Other monuments use rougher edges and suggest something more organic and timeless as the mountains from which they came. Such monuments can also appear more humble. Other monuments yet use shine and gloss to suggest something slightly worn and ancient in the case of those forged from bronze.

Visual grammar

There are two other sets of meaning potentials that we look at in this final section that draw on Hodge and Kress (1979), Kress and Van Leeuwen (1996) and Halliday (1978). These derive from concepts in linguistics. While the visual and material are clearly very different to language these concepts can help to draw out attention to the details of representations. The first of these is visual modality which we use here to think about the extent to which figures and objects depicted on monuments are represented naturalistically or not. In this case we can ask which elements and features are realistic and which are not. The second of these is transitivity. Here we draw on a number of categories from Halliday (1978) to think about what the figures on the monuments are represented as doing.

Modality

Surface realization on monuments also has much meaning potential. We can ask what kinds of features have their details increased, and which have them decreased. Kress and van Leeuwen (1996) refer to this as 'visual modality', although we can also think about this through metaphorical association which we come onto shortly. These authors consider visual modality as being akin to the way truth is communicated in language. In language we have a system called 'modals' for indicating levels of truth or commitment to a state of affairs. We can say 'we should' as opposed to 'we will'. The second is more committed to truth. In visual communication too we can look for the way that modality is reduced through reduction in articulation of details, in objects or surface realization. We can ask how much of what we see is articulated in the manner we would expect in everyday life. We can ask how much the details of the soldiers have been reduced in articulation of detail. We can imagine the difference were the soldiers represented as in real life in full detail. Such a semiotic choice would create more of a sense of documenting rather than symbolizing. A real person depicted on a Classical monument base might be incongruous and not serve the design purposes of recontextualization. A soldier represented in even lower modality resembling more a cartoon would represent, again, something different. We explore the way that soldiers have been represented through different levels of modality, that some are represented in almost increased detail while others are slightly simplified with lower modalities which present simplified and idealized soldiers.

Other statutes such as some commemorating those who died and suffered at the Ravensbruck concentration camp use even lower modality as the surfaces are roughened, even blurred as in the case of the Will Lambert project. Clearly something other than certainty and truth is being communicated in this case and here we may be shifting rather into a metaphorical association of lack of clarity and obscuring of vision where the sheer comprehensibility of the events represented is impossible. Although other examples, such as in the Ravensbrook Memorial to women in Amsterdam, use bright polished stainless steel and abstract forms which suggest science and modernity; perhaps here placing the memory in the present as opposed to the eternal and ancient as with bronze and stone. But each in its own way attempts to represent that which is in some ways not representable or truly comprehensible.

Were the soldiers on the WWI statues represented through considerable blurring of details, this would have had a similar kind of symbolic effect. On any monument we will be asking which features are represented in naturalistic detail, which in heightened detail and which in reduced detail. Machin and Van Leeuwen (2009) showed how these kinds of questions were useful in order to analyse children's war toys to think about which elements were suppressed and which foregrounded to place war in the realm of play. On guns it was the technology such as optic sights and sound suppressors that were rendered in greater detail although were not functional in order to symbolize sophistication and precision in warfare whereas locking mechanisms are rudimentary. The actions of firing and loading are backgrounded while the technology is foregrounded.

Kress and Van Leeuwen (1996) also include the articulation of the details of setting in their modality criteria. This is also important in our analysis of monuments. There are a range of options for the monument designer ranging from setting to no setting. Painters will often depict persons in settings such as a woman on a river bank among flowers. A wood carving might depict a person in woodland. Alternatively, no setting can be shown. It is usual to see sketches of figures with no setting often as studies of form and style as opposed to representation of a person, place or mood. We find such differences too in photographs. While documentary photographs will show people in actual places those found in advertisements and in lifestyle magazines may show people in settings that are out of focus or simply blank spaces. Such images tend to symbolize moods and concepts as opposed to documenting times and settings. The people depicted are not specific persons but types of persons.

Memorials tend not to provide actual settings. Soldiers tend to be positioned against an obelisk or within or in front of a series of columns. The ground on which they are depicted as standing may be rough like a battle field. But for the most part they are not depicted against actual scenes of war with other dying people around them, nor the enemy present. We can ask why this might be. By decontextualizing the participants in war, as with the advertising images, they are allowed to do more symbolic work. It also allows the other iconography to do more work. We can imagine how the idealized figures we often find in monuments would appear if depicted as standing on battlefields strewn with body-parts and terrified bewildered young men in agony as is often depicted in novels written by former front-line soldiers.

Colour also has relevance to modality. A figure of a soldier could be represented with the full naturalistic colour palette in the way they would have been seen had we been present at the time. But colour is not often used on monuments and when it is we find monochrome. As opposed to full-rich colour monochrome suggests moderation and restraint. Monuments generally tend to reply on the colour of the stone itself. In part this comes from the convention of the perception of the use of colour on Classical sculpture which historians now question. Nevertheless this provincial association is now well established. Likewise the dark, burned and shining hues of bronze serve to connote the ancient and eternal associations of this metal.

Transitivity

In CDA one useful level of analysis is carried out at the level of transitivity. This is simply a study of what participants are represented as doing in texts. The analyst can look for what choices have been made in language and grammar as regards how participants are given active or passive roles, although these can be of different orders. In other words this is a study of the kinds of verbs that are found in a text. Are certain people represented as being active while others always as passive? This will have consequences as to the kinds of identities of the persons who are represented. For example, it has been observed that women in women's lifestyle magazines are often represented as very passive as either carrying out very trivial tasks or as recipients of the actions of others.

We can be more precise with these observations by drawing on Halliday's (1985) classification of verb processes. These are useful for our purposes as while they may not necessarily translate from language to visual and material communication so easily and as images don't have clearly listed verbs for us to classify but nevertheless they draw our attention to the details of what is being depicted. Machin (2007a) applied these concepts to news photographs of the war in Iraq showing that civilians were always represented as idle and aimless while soldiers kept watch and guarded. There was neither attacking nor violence. Machin and Mayr (2012) also show how there is much analytical worth in analysing texts for transitivity at both the linguistic and visual levels since these may not be the same in both cases. So in news coverage of war soldiers may be represented as attacking and shooting linguistically whereas visually they are seen being thoughtful and watching. These are the categories used by Machin and Mayr:

1 Material processes which describe processes of *doing*. Usually, these are concrete actions that have a material result or consequence, such as 'The police arrested the burglar', although they may also represent abstract processes such as 'Prices have fallen.'

2 Behavioural processes, like *watch, taste, stare, dream, breathe, cough, smile* and *laugh* denote psychological or physical behaviour. They are semantically a cross between Material and Mental processes. For example, 'look at' and 'listen to' are classed as behavioural, whereas 'see' and 'hear' would be mental processes.

3 Mental processes which involve thinking or sensing when the agent engages in a mental task such as 'wondering' or enacts one of the five senses such as 'seeing'. It is often the case that participants who are made the subjects of mental processes are constructed as the 'focalizers' or 'reflectors' of action. These actors are allowed an internal view of themselves.

4 Verbal process – that is saying something, when the agent is verbalizing, such as 'ordering' people to move away; the relational process – when something is being used for comparison, that is when representations show a similarity or difference between two or more people or groups.

5 Existential process represents that something exists or happens, as in 'There has been an increase in enemy activity.' Existential processes typically use the verb 'to be' or synonyms such as 'exist', 'arise' or 'occur' and they only have one participant, as in 'There was *an attack*.'

It is important to emphasize again that analysing a text means that we can see easily whether a participant is represented as 'shooting' or 'thinking'. In the case of images and monuments there is a level of interpretation. But as Machin (2007b) and Machin and Mayr (2012) showed, this can still allow us to engage more systematically with what we see. Machin and Mayr analysed websites for hospitals during a time of sweeping privatization, spending cuts, job freezes, low-staff morale and the reliance on agency staff. In their analysis they found language that relied on abstraction and signifiers of action, 'innovative excellence' and 'vision', with an emphasis on 'partnership' and 'co-operation'. Linguistically the websites foregrounded acts of working together and communication with a lack of material processes with outcomes. Such language served to give the impression of there being dynamic action, where in fact there was none.

Visually they found that the websites depicted telephone operators, people speaking and a doctor smiling. Visually no actual treatment taking place; neither was illness/suffering depicted. What was foregrounded therefore was acts of communication, listening and internal moods. So in terms of the verb processes represented there was a predominance of behavioural processes as three of the participants smile at the viewer representing also mental process of 'caring' and 'welcoming'. Machin and Mayr suggest that there could have been images of actual workers carrying out the material processes characteristic of health care such as a nurse bandaging an arm, a surgeon examining someone's head, a health support worker demonstrating how a piece of equipment worked. Those who are visually represented as engaged in work are a woman working at a computer and another, smiling, operating a telephone switchboard. So the material work processes represented are related to communication and administration and not to actual health care processes. The practices of the health service are therefore backgounded, while communication and dealing with clients is foregrounded. Overall the actual quality of treatment and facilities is therefore substituted with the attitudes of the worker who work as a team and their responsiveness to patients.

In the previous chapter we showed how we could reveal the ideology of texts by looking for the way social practices have been recontextualized through deletion, addition, substitution and abstraction. Here we can see that the practice of care for patients in a hospital has been recontextualized through deletion of material processes of caring and for suffering or illness. We find addition of mental processes and reactions of the participants. The material processes involved in care and treatment are substituted for those related to communication. The same process is now taking place in British universities as academic staff are required to continually show students (customers) that they are responsive to their needs and preferences by gathering and responding to constant feedback. Less emphasis is on the intellectual quality of what is taught but 'student experiences'. Both in the university and the hospital this is part of a shift to a customer/management lead model. And both these shifts take place in an environment of reduced state financial support and preparation for full privatization of each system.

What this case study by Machin and Mayr (2012) helps us to see is that attention to transitivity to what participants are represented as doing is useful in helping us to understand how a social practice is being recontexualized. What is so important about the practice of CDA is that its tools allow us to show *how* texts communicate meanings as well as to understand *what* they communicate. A casual listener to a political speech may have a sense that they are being offered little in concrete and that there is an element of manipulation of events taking place. But CDA can show us exactly how this takes place through language and grammar. So too MCDA must be able to help us show not just what meanings are communicated but how these are done. When we turn our attention to monument analysis in later chapters asking exactly what kinds of transitivity process we find represented on the monuments is a useful tool to think about the recontextualization of the actual actions and verb processes that comprise war.

Conclusion

In the previous chapter we explained how our approach to monuments was social semiotics in that it saw communication as being done through choices made from an existing repertoire of semiotic resources. These would be used for specific ideological purposes by designers who would have a sense of how to combine different meaning potentials to communicate specific meanings in contexts. We discussed how these semiotic choices, in the tradition of CDA, could be analysed in order to reveal the ways that social practices represented have been recontextualized, through things like deletion of agents, actions and settings, their substitution for others or their complete abstraction. By doing this we would be able to reveal the less apparent discourses and ideologies. In this chapter we have begun to think about some of the semiotic resources that are available to monument designers. As we apply these to a range of different kinds of examples in later chapters we will be able to say more about their consequences and more about the way by which they realize different meaning potentials as they combine with other semiotic choices.

CHAPTER THREE

How monuments have been studied

In the last two chapters we have laid out our theoretical and methodological positions. We have explained the broader concepts that form the basis of our approach to monument analysis, looking at the principles of Social Semiotics and CDA. We have also introduced some of the specific semiotic resources available for 3D communication. In this chapter we place our own approach and analysis in the context of existing work on monuments and commemoration. One criticism of multimodality, more broadly, has been its sometimes lack of engagement with earlier and existing scholarly traditions that have already trodden the same ground in the areas chosen for analysis such as in the analysis of advertisements, visual design and film analysis (Machin, 2009). This can lead to reinventing of wheels and wasted efforts travelling down the same dead ends. And it has become clear that scholars working in innovate areas of multimodality (see Bateman, 2011) are now addressing this shortcoming. On the one hand it is important for any research and form of analysis, if they are to clearly demonstrate what they contribute, to show what has already been explained and understood and how precisely they have something useful to add that takes knowledge and analysis a step further. On the other hand, simply there is much in this literature that can of course guide our own analysis and upon which we can ourselves draw.

What we show in this chapter is that while there has been much excellent research done on monuments our own work is able to make a very specific and unique contribution. We show, in fact, that our approach does fulfil some calls from a range of authors from within monument and commemoration studies to provide a new approach which is more sensitive both to how monuments communicate meanings (Danzer, 1987) and which also understands the importance of context and the processes and institutions that manage and bring monuments into being (Niven, 2008). In this chapter we begin by examining the analytical approaches taken by prominent historians and art historians, which form the largest body of theoretical work on how society commemorates war. We then go on to look at analytical approaches taken by some cultural critics. In each case we explain the process, data and methodological approaches and motivations of the different studies as this best allows us to build up a sense of where lie the different kinds of answers and paths of investigation to which we might contribute.

Commemoration as political ideology

Ashplant et al. (2000, 2004) have summarized and critiqued much of the scholarly work done on war commemoration. They identify two main paradigms. One comprises those studies that view war commemoration as fundamentally political, where it is viewed primarily as an institutional tool used by governments and social institutions which utilize ritual forms of activities in order to promote their own particular ideologies of war. The second comprises those studies that take a more psychological approach to focus on the views and reactions of those who visit monuments and participants in acts of commemoration. We begin with the first of these.

Rausch (2007) is one author who has been interested in the way that different ideologies that favour the powerful have been communicated through war commemoration such as the legitimization of the colonial wars. She argues that through the analysis of public rhetoric and commentary on public monuments in different countries it is possible to isolate the interpretive patterns of national self-understanding and achieve a more critical and deconstructive analysis of the interpretive patterns. Rausch begins the British section of her comparative study with a detailed discussion of the historical context in which the constructions of nineteenth-century war monuments were erected. Referring to two prominent examples, Nelson's Column and the Duke of Wellington in London, Rausch outlines the general attitude of the government to war at the time and also refers to the attitude of the wider population. Throughout the discussion her analysis weaves between historical detail and press accounts of Britain's wars and reaction to them. Her conclusion is that the central function of the commissioning of war monuments was the promotion and legitimation of the nation-state arguing that monuments, their ceremonial unveiling and their promotion through the print medium that were:

> . . . part of an extremely complex didactic used to pass on a national message. . . (Rausch, 2007:75)

Rausch argues that circumstances in the different European states meant that despite an attempt to manipulate collective memory, the public's response to attempts to legitimize the nation through the construction of statues did not result in an automatic acceptance of national war myths, although it must be said that her evidence for this claim is based on press comments, not on records of interviews with individuals from wider society. She urges that monuments should be studied on an individual state basis taking into account historical contextual factors that lead to '. . . different programmatic connections between war and nation' (2007:75). Indeed later in our own analysis we show the different discourses in operation in monuments commissioned at different times.

In the nineteenth century, according to Rausch, not only did different states vary in their approach to war commemoration, there was also variety in the approaches each state adopted to its different wars. For example, in comparison with Prussian and French monuments the representations of British imperialism, through the construction of numerous monuments in the late nineteenth century, distinctly emphasized the aggressive and missionary aspects of colonial campaigns. During the latter period of the century, the emergence of monuments celebrating various successful campaigns in Africa and India gave the message that Britain depended on war and colonial expansion to enhance the power of the nation. This coincides with the physical locations of the battles Britain was fighting at the time that were now no longer within European boundaries, but further afield.

Rausch argues that these colonial exploits were presented to the public, through the monuments, in terms of religious ideology; a type of Christian militarism, Rausch notes that there was little opposition to this message from liberal critics. Again, Rausch uses newspaper comment as evidence for this assertion, citing the London newspaper, *The Standard*. Rausch quotes a passage that clearly shows that reactions to the nineteenth-century empire-building wars and their commemoration revealed a nationalist ideology that based itself on the belief that the British race was superior to those native occupants of its territorial conquests. Writing of the unveiling of a monument to the first High Commissioner of South Africa Sir Bartle Frere, it says:

> Accustomed from youth to deal with inferior and subject races, he [i.e. Frere, H.R.] could not conceive of any tribe, or race, or people confronting British power with any chance of success. His one duty in life was to . . . bring to their knees, those who did not at once recognise [England's] authority . . . it was the destiny of the British Empire not to shrink but to expand. (*The Standard*, quoted by Rausch, 2007:87)

To emphasize her point on the variation of representations in war commemoration, that differed depending on the particular war that was being commemorated, Rausch quotes the *Telegraph*'s piece on the unveiling of the statue of Major General Sir Charles Gordon who was defeated and killed by 'the enemy' in Khartoum, Sudan. Rausch notes how the newspaper presents Gordon as a 'humble and earnest Christian' (*Daily Telegraph*, 17 October 1888, quoted by Rausch, 2007:87), a description that perhaps seeks to excuse his defeat.

Rausch's exploration of reports of unveilings of monuments suggests that at the end of the nineteenth century religion was a powerful and acceptable justification for war and conquest. Rausch argues that wrapping war in this religious ideological perspective profoundly differs from the perspective taken in the commemoration of WWI when commemoration of war sought to legitimize the events by linking them with the cause of the nation. On this point, Rausch comments that memorialization of this conflict publicly exposed the war myth for the first time:

> This only became possible after the Great War of 1914–1918, when the disillusionment caused by the experience of mass death allowed the development of new symbolic languages and modified through still one-dimensional versions of legitimising the nation through war across Western Europe. (Rausch, 2007:91)

Having generally discussed samples of nineteenth-century war monuments through the press reports of their unveilings, Rausch concludes that these nineteenth-century monuments to the heroes of WWI shaped conceptions of war in general by their representations of these heroic public figures. Although Rausch's paper does not include a study of WWI monuments themselves, she asserts that only after this war, in an attempt to maintain public support for the war, do we see complex symbolism which sacralized violent death.

Rausch's work, from our own point of view is useful as its basis is to identify, what we would view as, the discourses of war that were dominant at particular times. What we do not find in her work was detailed discussion of the actual representations found in the monuments themselves. For this kind of approach we turn to two historians, first Calder (2004), a historian, poet and essayist and Wingate (2005), an art historian who analysed visual representation of the American WWI soldier known as the Doughboy.

Calder (2004) explores the topic of war in a collection of essays in which he examines representations of war in various genres: poetry, art, films, theatre, memoirs and commemorative sculpture. He does not claim to offer a single theory on the way war is represented, saying that different methods are employed in each genre. However, he says that they all succeed in transforming 'fact' into myth by incorporating 'real' manifestation into '. . . pre-existent discourses and narrative structures' (2004:x). He discusses

WWI monuments in terms of their commemoration of imperialistic activity and asks an important question about the role of future war commemoration:

> We may wonder how fresh imaginations born into the twenty-first century will respond to, and perhaps make use of, the values projected in the Great War memorials. (2004:27)

Calder's approach to the analysis of the war monument begins by providing the background to the practice of commemorating war deaths by the erection of public monuments, noting that they were not common in medieval or early modern Europe but only much later. In his discussion he exemplifies his points by drawing on Scottish examples of war monuments; focusing primarily on the Scottish National War Memorial at Edinburgh Castle. He begins by providing details of the process of its erection; such as who designed it, how many people were involved in creating it and its physical location in castle. He then goes on to describe the elements that make up the monument, contrasting its heroic representations of the Scottish soldier with historical fact relating to the death toll in WWI; the war that it commemorates. For example, of the large hall of honour that features decorated bays dedicated to the 12 Scottish regiments Calder comments:

> . . . statistics dissolve the Valhalla of the kilted soldier in flames and ruin. (2004:20)

In contrast to many writers on the topic, it is clear from Calder's description of the Scottish National War Memorial, as with his other examples, that he has spent many hours studying its form and noting its every detail.

Calder's discussion of the projected 'values' and the role commemorative war monuments will play in the twenty-first century raise some important questions about the entwined existence of nation and war. For example, he suggests that the role played by the nation's military in the twentieth century is very different from the imperial role it played in WWI; citing the case of NATO intervention in the former Yugoslavia during the 1990s, he comments that military intervention is now widely viewed as one of a peacekeeper's, rather than an imperialist's role (Calder, 2004). Yet it is frequently the case that the names of the 'fallen' in new wars, in Iraq and Afghanistan, are simply added to these old imperialistic monuments fusing these acts together. This is something that we ourselves look at in greater detail in later chapters.

Although Calder's discussion provides more details of the elements of the monuments his analysis remains at a broader interpretative and impressionistic level rather than considering the communicative potential of each element in the way a Social Semiotic-based theory provides. However, we can see more of this kind of attention to detail in the work of Wingate (2005).

Wingate (2005) analysed the American WWI commemorative monuments that feature the Doughboy, which is the popular name given to WWI American soldier. Wingate begins her discussion of the monuments by setting out the views of various members of 'elite' groups that existed in 1919 that reveal their attitude towards public representation of the Doughboy through art; she does this by quoting the views of: the chairman of the National Commission of Fine Arts, an art critic and a painter who all offered their particular view on the function, purpose and symbolic power that a public representation of a Doughboy should carry. She then goes on to discuss nine prominent American WWI commemorative monuments, interspersing her discussion with references to the proliferation of images of the Doughboy at the time.

Taking examples from contemporary film posters, magazine covers and other popular publications, Wingate illustrates how these images '. . . helped to shape the way the public remembered the soldier's experience' (2005:32). She points to two stark anomalies in the representations of the Doughboy: first, the contrast between the widespread poor health among the WWI soldiers and the 'glowing health' of the soldiers portrayed in the monuments through their strong facial features and their sturdy poses; secondly, the lack of representation of African American soldiers citing only one example of a monument to mark the contribution made by African Americans in Chicago: *The World War Black Soldiers' Memorial*. In both instances Wingate's comments on the examples are set in the context of historical evidence; such as the writer who wrote of his approval of the 'development battalions' that were created to improve the fitness of recruits and a contemporary article by a writer called Du Bois that recognized the significance of and promoted the contribution of African Americans. Through the use of comparative illustrations of the Doughboy in contemporary publications, evidence of government strategies in articles that promoted them in popular publications and her own commentary on the general style of the representations of a Doughboy in her examples of commemorative war monuments, Wingate makes a compelling case that the function of the WWI American war monument ultimately served to connote loyalty to the nation and mythologized constructions of American masculinity.

Wingate also refers to a fear of communist influence in the United States at the time and comments on the power of the war memorials to combat any 'Left-leaning' political persuasions by offering images that would encourage patriotism and, consequently, commitment to a capitalist dominant ideology. Wingate comments that sculptor after sculptor designed and produced a soldier statue that fulfilled ideological aims of nationalism by connoting patriotism and idealistic masculinity (Wingate, 2005).

According to Wingate, two of the most notable sculptors able to achieve these communicative aims were John Paulding (1853–1935) and Ernest Moore Viquesney (1876–1946). While commenting on the similarities in the designs of their work that produced representations of soldiers in battle, Wingate describes how the work of Viquesney was considered to be a 'perfect' representation of the American soldier by the American Legion in their weekly magazine and local newspapers. They used the sculptures to promote the dominant ideological stance in direct reply to war protests by a radical labour union. Wingate further illustrates how the use of the image of the charging Doughboy was frequently used in the wider culture, such as advertisements for cigarettes, articles on sport and song sheets to connote the health and virility of the American male and, by association, the health of the American nation. The Doughboy was therefore part of tutoring viewers in the American way and being a good American.

Wingate does not offer a systematic analysis of monuments in the fashion we intend in this book. But she does show the importance of placing the monuments firmly within their wider sociopolitical context where representations of the fighting soldier must be considered in the context of the widespread anxieties the American public was voicing over the health and well-being of the returning soldiers. She also connects this to concrete observations about intrinsic features of the designs, noting that later in the 1920s and into the 1930s Doughboy statues featured soldiers in various poses of grief, such as bowed heads over graves; seen by Wingate as romanticizing the soldier. Linking the Doughboy statues and the various uses of the image to the American nationalist cause, it is clear that the outline of events that she provides shows clearly how the military, artists and the media come to the aid of the nation in America at that time.

A psychological approach to war commemoration

Some authors have approached the meaning of war monuments by asking what a typical war monument should achieve for the viewer; asking what its purpose or role is within society. One such author is Rowlands (2001) who discusses the commemoration by using two prominent war monuments: the Vietnam Veterans Memorial in the United States and the Sydney War Memorial to the Anzacs in Australia. But again such analysis can point to the way that such visual and material designs connect to prevailing discourses about war and soldiery.

Rowlands begins his analysis of the Sydney monument by turning to the history of its commissioning process. Citing the work of Kapferer (1988), he explains that early design proposals for the monument caused a certain amount of controversy that resulted in its rejection. The design, that featured a naked female in a crucifixion pose surrounded at her feet by the dead bodies of soldiers, was rejected in favour of a naked soldier lying next to a sword on a shield supported by three clothed women who were said to represent: a mother, a sister and a wife. Of this decision Rowlands comments:

> Sacrifice of the nation embodies a classical theme of the warrior as a heroic, young and sexually potent male whose death is justified by the preservation of the regenerative powers of women. (2001:134)

A significant stage of Rowlands's analysis is to ask what purpose war monuments have in the twentieth century. He argues that a successful design is one that offers the viewer a resolution of mourning, concluding that monuments become memorials when they satisfy three functions for the living. These can be summarized as follows:

1 To acknowledge the importance of death and destruction that constituted the sacrificial act while acknowledging the loss incurred by relatives, communities and nations and indicating an acceptance that the violence and suffering took place and that the sacrifice will not be forgotten.

2 To show an acceptance that violence takes place in a context where it is claimed that something has been gained instead, providing a transformation of a sense of collective loss into an object of devotion and passion.

3 To ensure that the dead are deified as part of that devotional logic in the sense that they become embodied in the idea of the collective while giving the message that that the role of the living is to recognize the debt and express a willingness to reciprocate.

In his conclusion, he argues:

> The relief from trauma lies in the detail. Recognising the nature of sacrifice as an act of surrendering the self is in this sense part of a wider understanding of what constitutes humanity, which is the ideal object of devotion imaged in the war memorial. (2001:144)

In this kind of analysis we do get a sense of the details of design choices coming under analysis which are also placed in the context of commissioning.

But from our perspective, and in the context of the work by historians that we have considered in the previous section, what is missing is a critical sense of the monuments and of the motivations of the designers. In the following chapter we place the commissioning of such WWI monuments in Britain as part of a huge fear of the working classes and worker movements. Rowlands's analysis, and the recommendations he makes, gloss over such motivations and context and rather foster myths of willing sacrifice and worthy cause.

We find further approaches to the analysis of commemorative war monuments that tend to fall within the psychological paradigm as described by Ashplant et al. (2000, 2004) in a much larger body of work, residing within the discipline of critical studies. Much of this deals specifically on the analysis of the Vietnam Veterans Memorial (the VVM) erected in Washington, DC, USA, in 1982. Although discussions of this monument tend to be mainly structured around its psychological significance for the viewer, mainly through the observation of the behaviour of those who visit the monument, some authors have also centred their attention on the monument's intrinsic features. Designed by Maya Lin, the monument features more abstract elements not previously seen in commemorative war monuments and it represents a radical departure from traditional commemorative war monument design.

The VVM is a black V-shaped wall upon which are comprised panels inscribed with the names of the American war dead. These names are set out in a representation of a time line throughout the war. The panels also carry two inscriptions specifying the purpose of the memorial; one after the date of the first American death and the other after the date of the last. As a result of widespread criticism of the original design, the monument does not stand alone as intended. After much debate, a 'compromise' was agreed upon by allowing a second and third memorial to be erected near Maya Lin's memorial. This second memorial sees a return to commemoration by representing human figures; three male soldiers: one black and two white, dressed in combat gear appear to be coming out of a wooded area; gazing towards the names of the dead on Lin's memorial, there is also an addition of a flagpole with an inscription.[1]

When analysing the monument, authors make reference to two starting points: the claim by Lin that her design has no intended meaning, and that at the instigation of the design competition the commissioners of the monument requested a design that was both therapeutic and conciliatory (Griswold 1986; Haines 1986; Carlson and Hocking 1988; Blair et al., 1991; Abramson 1996). Both the claims by the artist and the requirements of the commissioning body act as a focal point for the discussions and analyses of the monument, albeit with a slightly different focus in each analysis.

Abramson (1996), who specializes in architecture and urban design, seeks to explain the meaning of the design choices made for the VVM in terms of the requirements of the design committee, the proclaimed aims of the designer Maya Lin and ideological impact of the use of the time line, a prominent feature of the VVM. In his discussion of the commissioning of this monument and two other designs by Lin: one commemorating female presence at Yale University and the other commemorating the American Civil Rights Movement, Abramson (1996) points out that the design was guided by the requirements set out in the competition to select the successful designer. He argues that the designer Lin responded to directions of the VVM given by the fund and architectural adviser stipulating that a list of names of the dead soldiers (around 58,000) should be included and the tone of the monument should be '. . . "harmonious", "conciliatory" and "contemplative and reflective"' according to the design programme (Abramson, 1996:685). The commissioning body also took the surrounding landscape into consideration when specifying the shape of the monument: it should emphasize horizontal rather than vertical elements and it was to be set in a large garden area. Abramson argues that these guidelines resulted in Lin's winning design, and while Griswold (1986) points out that the winning design was not at first widely appreciated or admired due to its distinct departure from traditional forms of commemorative war sculpture, although Abramson (1996) claims that the design was not as radical departure from tradition as people think.[2]

Abramson supports this statement by drawing attention to the timelines that appear on the monument. He comments that in basing the VVM on chronological time lines when listing the names of the dead, Lin brings personal memory and political memory together '. . . in the name of social reconciliation and historical continuity' (1996:708). Abramson argues that Lin, in claiming that she set out to create a monument that aims to simply record events and make no ideological point, has actually managed to propose a 'remarkable ideological conceit' (1996:702). How can she presume that people will read the monument in the way she intends? Yet, he argues that the use of time lines to portray historical events is: '. . . the ideological tool par excellence of American educational culture' (1996:698), making the point that American viewers of the monument will be used to seeing representations of their nation's history in their classroom wall charts and textbooks. Abramson concludes that the VVM is closer to an: '. . . annal in its "list like objectivity . . ."' (1996:700).

As with the work we have discussed so far, Abramson utilizes public records, comments by the designer and newspaper articles to support various points made during the analysis. His approach involves examining the features of the VVM in the form of the time line on the original monument and coming to the conclusion that instead of challenging authority, Lin's VVM supports official narratives of the Vietnam War.

Griswold's (1986) work carries out a more psychological analysis of the VVM. He comments that the addition of the flagpole and statue enables a more palpable and traditional representation of '. . . the heroism of the veterans and the nobility of their cause' (p. 718). Throughout his discussion of the VVM, its physical location in relation to other famous landmarks and memorials, the reactions of its visitors and the dedication ceremony, Griswold (1986) emphasizes the meanings of the memorial as therapeutic, encouraging the viewer to question the purpose and consequences of war not only for the individual but also, in his view, encouraging a reaction that espouses a positive sort of patriotism; one that is in itself therapeutic. He asserts:

> The VVM embodies ability of Americans to confront the sorrow of so many lost lives in a war of ambiguous virtue without succumbing to the false muses of intoxicating propaganda and nihilism. (1986:713)

Yet, revealing a seemingly contradictory position, Griswold goes on to describe how the design of the monument, set into the soil and reading as a chapter in a book, leads the viewer to think of the war in terms of the preserving of the American nation:

> . . . it admonishes us to write the next chapter thoughtfully and with reflection on the country's values, symbols of which are pointed to by the Memorial itself. (1986:708)

An approach that focuses solely on the psychological effect that the monument has on the viewer can be found in the work of Carlson and Hocking (1988) who offer a more critical reading of the monument. In their analysis of the significance of the messages left by visitors to the VVM, they comment that it is not a memorial to the war, but to the individuals who took part and died fighting in it. They view the original design, Lin's VVM, as the focal point of commemoration, describing the memorial as '. . . deceptively simple' (1988:205). They offer no other analysis of the actual monument, instead choosing to concentrate on the reactions and messages left by its visitors. They conclude that the meaning of the VVM is only realized by its visitors and that the visitors define its meaning by their reactions to the sacrifices made by the people who are named. As we demonstrate in later chapters such an approach neglects the communicative potential of visual semiotic resources. As we began to discuss in the previous chapter, even a large glassy surfaced marble wall can realize very specific discourses of war and soldiery.

Some authors opt for reading the original monument as a separate entity from the additions of the figurative work and the flagpole, such as Griswold who views Lin's monument as a separate entity from Harts' statue.

For Haines it is the ambiguity of the design that makes the VVM '. . . vulnerable to political manipulation' (1986:17). However, as with Carlson and Hocking, Haines does not base his comments on an analysis of the monument itself; instead Haines' work focuses on the actions of the visiting veterans, noting that some veterans are so deeply traumatized by war that they commit suicide at the memorial site. Haines describes how many others go there to 'speak' to their dead friends after locating their names on the wall, while others leave their messages at the wall in written form. In this short paper Haines discusses the attempts of political elites to utilize the VVM for their own ideological aims and links the VVM to power. His reading stands apart from the other readings discussed here in that he makes the crucial claim that the VVM rather than being a monument that resists a particular reading has the potential to become an argument in favour of future wars and future sacrifices on behalf of the nation. This view of the commemorative war monument's potential for future legitimation of warfare is not the position taken by Blair et al. (1991) and Blair (1994). They argue for a collective reading, moreover, one that 'deauthorizes the authors' (1991:273). They assert that the addition of Hart's monument and the flag alter any readings the original design would have offered if it had been placed alone. With its multiple authors and postmodern, rather than modernist, categorization they argue that the monument site '. . . tells multiple stories' (Blair et al., 1991:279), asking questions (as Griswold also argues), yet offering contradictory interpretations. They assert:

> The Memorial stands as a commemoration of veterans of the war, and as a monument to political struggle. (Blair et al., 1991:281)

Blair et al. (1991; Blair, 1994) discuss the intrinsic features of the VVM and consider the monument within the context of postmodernist thinking, asserting that it can be categorized as falling into a postmodernist, rather than modernist, category due to its departure from generic norms of commemorative monuments and its non-functionalist element. Moreover, Blair et al. suggest that the VVM may be considered as a 'prototype of postmodern memorializing' (1991:264). Postmodernism and its relationship to architecture, the field within which monuments can be placed, is discussed by Jencks (1987, cited by Blair et al., 1991; Blair, 1994) who claims architecture is a verb. Blair et al. assert that this is demonstrated by the rhetoric of the VVM that: '. . . acknowledges Vietnam veterans both as a group and as individuals', '. . . allows for legitimate commemoration . . .', '. . . invites active engagement by the visitor', '. . . invites doubt and critical differentiation of the issues' and that it invites its visitors to '. . . weigh the cause against the cost' (Blair 1994:278).

Clearly, Blair et al. are emphasizing their pluralistic reading of the monument, stressing that:

> The goal is not to locate *the* message but the multiple, frequently conflicting, messages. To attempt a unified, centered reading, thus, is to miss the point. (1991:269)

And although they stress its resistance to a singular reading, they reject the idea that the VVM is an apolitical piece of work as claimed by the designer Maya Lin; concluding that the monument makes a political statement by virtue of its departure from the norms of commemorative memorials. This departure, Blair comments, allows the monument to tell '. . . multiple stories' (1994:369), and in doing so realizes a conflict in opinions on the war, resisting one single account. Blair et al. argue that the fact that for many Americans the war on Vietnam was 'unpopular', even 'immoral' (1991:276) meant that there was no consensus for the 'valorization' of the war dead. It is this lack of public support, or consensus, for the war, Blair et al. claim, that 'allowed' the memorial to take a multiple stance. Blair et al. (1991) comment further that in the light of the differing opinions on the war there could be no typical response in its commemoration; it required one that would '. . . honor the veterans . . .' without '. . .valorization of the war dead', something apart from awarding political merit to the war itself (Blair et al. 1991:366).

In their analysis, Blair et al. argue for a reading of the two elements of the VVM: the original wall and the statues added later by Hart, as one monument. Therefore, in their analysis they consider the elements of the whole monument collectively; the flag, statues and original wall are all discussed. They focus on their possible individual meanings and their meanings when considered in relation to each other, adding that the addition of the flag and the statue intensifies the political character of the original design; commenting that they '. . . "question" one another's legitimacy indefinitely' (1991:367). Blair et al.'s approach does involve an examination of the features of the monument, they discuss: the angle of the wall; the way the names inscribed on it are chronologically sequenced; the motifs and its height. They also consider its surroundings, or physical location, and discuss all these features in relation to how they can guide a viewer into multiple, sometimes conflicting readings of the monument. For Blair et al., the postmodern design of the VVM is a political piece because it results in 'interrogative features': '. . . constitute the political message; questioning *is* the point, and that point is a thoroughly political one' (1991:275). Their positioning of the analysis within this postmodern context leads them to Foucault's point that discourse is always open to multiple interpretation due to its nature as a constant reference to other texts, or as they describe: '. . . not an entity given in reality. Its character is a premise of critical argument' (1991:282). At first, Blair et al.'s approach seems completely at odds with the approach we propose in this work, yet, as with all of the work we discuss in this chapter, we share some aspects of each approach. However, as you will see in subsequent chapters, we propose a more systematic approach to the analysis of the commemorative war monument.

Danzer (1987) also argues for a more systematic approach to the analysis of commemorative war monuments. He says that monuments in public places have an important function for the individual and their identity:

they tell us who we are and how we should behave. He claims that in representing an event from the past, they guide contemporary viewers and lead the way for future generations. Danzer argues that an analyst should examine key elements of any memorial under investigation, these being: its history; design; materials; site; inscription (or lack of); connections to other people, places and times and their subsequent life (e.g. whether the monument has undergone a change in its use). In Danzer's work we find not only a defence of the analysis of memorials as a valid academic enquiry, but also a proposal of a systematic approach to their analysis.

Danzer goes on to apply his approach to a discussion of the Washington Monument (Washington, USA) and makes a brief reference to the VVM that sits on the same site. He provides much detail of the historical circumstances surrounding various elements of the monuments, yet, despite calling for analysis of a number of 'key elements' such as design, Danzer's approach does not offer a reading of the monuments that make more precise observations and analysis of things like form, materials, surface and size. For example, Danzer makes a claim about the VVM monument's possible effect on its viewers stating that when leaving the VVM, visitors can see the Washington Monument that '. . . rises directly in front, a symbol of hope' (Danzer 1987:14), yet, precisely *how* this monument gives people hope is not clear as the theoretical approach Danzer applies does not provide a systematic framework for the analysis of the elements that make up the monument. After reading Danzer's discussion of the Washington Memorial, we understand much more about how the monument came about and what led to the decisions reached on each aspect of its construction. However, our understanding of *how* these monuments may construct meanings for their contemporary visitors through their intrinsic features is not further advanced.

Approaches to the analysis of the material content of the VVM memorial vary widely. Some take the whole site into consideration, including not only the additions of the flagpole and the statues, but also the other major landmarks in the immediate area. Others only consider Lin's work without paying attention to its physical setting and context. While some do discuss the symbolism found in the intrinsic features of the monument itself and their possible meanings, they do not take each physical element of the memorial and the surrounding space into account in a systematic way and then consider their meaning potential realized as a combined channel of messages.

Much closer to the analytical model we propose in this present volume is Kruk's (2008, 2010) analysis of the history of public monumental art in the Soviet Block that looks at the ideological, political and financial constraints faced by sculptors working under the control of communist Soviet Union. Kruk (2008) begins by considering the effects of pre- and post-Stalin Soviet ideological positions on public art, showing how they moved from communicating socialist ideology to expressions of 'subjective psychology'. Kruk considers the use and origins of iconographic representations by giving much background detail of external social and political transformations. He looks into the mechanisms of funding for artists and he considers how artists supported the dominant discourse of power in their quest for financial support of their art. However, Kruk's work, while providing fascinating insights into the iconography of Soviet sculpture and the way it can be connected to ideology, falls more into line with what Van Leeuwen (2005) describes a more traditional form of semiotic analysis which provides a list of individual sign meanings rather than attempting to document the kinds of meaning potentials and semiotic resources available for monument design. However, Kruk's enquiry into the social practice of art funding within Soviet culture provides compelling evidence for the importance of this aspect of semiotic enquiry – that is, who has power to regulate the use of semiotic resources and to what political ends are these put.

Finally we outline work on monument analysis that has been especially influential on our own work. We draw on her work in later chapters to support our own observations about the commissioning process for monuments. Here we deal with the specific approach taken in her research. Catherine Moriarty, an art historian, was the coordinator of the Imperial War Museum project to provide the first comprehensive online database of British commemorative war monuments. Moriarty's approach, we suggest, defies Ashplant et al.'s categorization of commemoration work as falling within two main paradigms of monument research; as although Moriarty (1995) states that her interest lies in the response by communities to the task of commemoration, she analyses British WWI commemorative war monuments from both the political and the psychological perspectives.

Moriarty (1995) begins her discussion by setting out the historical context of death and mass burial of soldiers who were killed on the battlefields of WWI. Providing historical details of the recording procedures adopted by the British government, she lists the terms they used when informing the families of the missing or dead soldiers. She also looks at documents describing how many bodies could not be identified as they had often been blown apart and disappeared into the mud. She explains that, where possible, what remained of the soldiers' bodies was buried in mass graves near the site of the battle as the repatriation of the bodies of soldiers was not the policy of the government at the time. She explains the official measures that were taken to identify and remove soldiers' remains to the newly created war cemeteries that were established and managed by the *Imperial War Graves Commission,* a newly established government department as a response to the huge numbers of WWI deaths.

For most of the dead soldiers' families a visit to one of these overseas cemeteries was impossible, a situation that added to the grief of the bereaved. Moriarty describes how this situation, the absence of a body to bury and over which to mourn, led to the erection of the Cenotaph, a word derived from the Greek *Kenotafion* meaning 'an empty tomb', that was intended to be a focal point of grief for all bereaved families. In 1920, a remembrance ceremony at the cenotaph was combined with the burial of the body of an anonymous dead British soldier *The Unknown Warrior* whose remains were transported back to London from the battlefield and buried in Westminster Abbey. Moriarty's extensive historical detail is supported by contemporary photographs illustrating the searches made for the bodies of dead soldiers and their removal for burial in one of the overseas war cemeteries.

Moriarty attaches great significance to the erection of the Cenotaph in Whitehall, explaining that its abstract form failed to fully satisfy the '. . . need for a focus of grief' (1995:15). She explains, citing the records of the Imperial War Graves Commission, that smaller communities across the country wanted to import their own *unknown soldier* from the battlefield and it was the impossibility of meeting this request that led to the many commissions for a sculpted body of a soldier to be featured in the commemorative war monuments of so many British towns. Moriarty illustrates her discussion of monuments featuring sculpted bodies by the inclusion of 14 photographs of monuments that exemplify her particular points of discussion.

In her analysis, Moriarty considers the psychological benefits a bereaved viewer may gain when viewing a figurative sculpture on a commemorative war memorial; an example of this kind of discussion is her comment that bereaved spectators could 'engage' with both the soldier figures and, where they were included, the figures that represented mothers, wives or sisters. However, throughout her analysis Moriarty also contrasts the representations in the monuments with the reality of the WWI soldier's appearance and environmental and physical conditions, an approach that views the monuments as an institutional tool used to convey an idealistic image of war. For example, she cites the practice of awarding commissions to eminent sculptors, such as: Royal Academicians; professors in art schools; members of the Royal Society of British Sculptors and ex-soldiers, such as Charles Sargeant Jagger whose service record would appeal to the commissioning committees.

Throughout her discussion, Moriarty provides an extensive account of artistic methods and practices as an explanation of how the figures in the WWI monuments were designed and created. She describes how, in the case of a traditional bronze piece, a sculpted body was created from the sketch to the wooden frame to which clay or wax was gradually added to build up a body that would later be cast in bronze. However, in the case of the WWI monuments, Moriarty explains that the bodies were created in separate parts and then '. . . joined together to create an illusory appearance of solidity and wholeness' (1995:37). Through this analytical process that utilizes historical records, accounts of the needs of the bereaved and an analysis of art practices, Moriarty concludes that the absence of the dead soldiers' remains was responsible for the idealization of the WWI solider in the monuments, creating what she calls 'public myths' regarding their physiques and the circumstances of their deaths. We will return to Moriarty's work later in the book.

Conclusion

In this chapter we have learned something of the type of work that is carried out in the study of war commemoration through the overview it has provided of the work of some authors in the field. In their discussions of commemorative war monuments we have seen a variety of approaches that seem to share many stages of analysis. Historical documents play a major role in the analytical process for many authors; as we saw, Moriarty (1995) takes her starting point from historical documents, as does Wingate (2005) and Rausch (2007), while others tend to take a different perspective. For example, Abramson (1996) and Blair et al. (1991; Blair, 1994) concentrate on reading the monuments within a particular theoretical framework rather than using historical context within which to frame their arguments. Other authors such as Griswold (1986) and Carlson and Hocking (1988) tend to focus on the behaviour of the monument's visitors to try to understand their interpretations, and hence any possible messages that the monument carries.

We have seen authors argue the importance of nationalism as a contextual feature of the commemorative war monument, by emphasizing the ideological relevance of war commemoration. Their work suggests that death and sacrifice is a crucial feature of increasing military participation and a key feature in the nationalist message that is passed on to members of the nation-state in order to perpetuate and sustain a level of military recruitment. Commemoration of past wars is one way of disseminating this message and the work of authors reviewed here suggests that twentieth century commemorative war monuments play a significant role in this dissemination.

It must be emphasized that the work we have discussed in this chapter is a very small proportion of the body of literature that exists on the topic of commemorative war monuments. The selection has been chosen to give an overview, not only of their arguments, but of their approaches to the analysis of the monument. While we may agree with many of the points made by these authors in our own analysis, we argue here that an MCDA approach should include historical context, but that the communicative potential of the physical elements of the monuments themselves is the key to assessing the effect a monument may have on its viewer. But there is much in this literature in terms of what historians tell us especially, that we take into how we contextualize out textual analyses.

Notes

1 'THIS FLAG REPRESENTS THE SERVICE RENDERED TO OUR COUNTRY BY THE VETERANS OF THE VIETNAM WAR. THE FLAG AFFIRMS THE PRINCIPLES OF FREEDOM FOR WHICH THEY FOUGHT AND THEIR PRIDE IN HAVING SERVED UNDER DIFFICULT CIRCUMSTANCES' (Griswold, 1986:710).

2 Griswold's notes summarize a 'rancorous and heated debate' between supporters and opponents that led to the additional monument (1986:718). Whereas Blair et al. (1991:275) refer to a delegation of 27 Republican Congressmen who regard the design as making '. . . a political statement of shame and dishonor'.

CHAPTER FOUR

The political context

A number of scholars working in CDA (Fairclough, 2003; Richardson, 2007) have argued that CDA, as well as analysing language and grammatical choices in order to reveal the more buried ideologies that they contain, must also pay attention to the social goings on that lie behind texts in order to connect analysis to matters of production processes, decision-making and reception. Otherwise there is a danger that all we would be doing is carrying out disconnected textual analysis. The social goings on behind texts might be revealed, for example, through interviews with those involved in the production process of newspapers or other media. It might involve observing the process of production of texts to reveal the ways that ideologies become loaded onto them. For example, Machin and Van Leeuwen (2007) sought to understand the ideology of the texts in the global women's magazine *Cosmopolitan*, not only through textual and visual analysis, but also through interviews with editors, writers and photographers. The resulting analysis allowed them to consider the language styles, genre and narrative choices found in international versions of the magazine in the context of specific commercial strategies to create a brand which would signify specific ideas, values and identities that suffuse all contents of the magazine to align with the world of advertising and consumer culture. Interviews also allowed them to understand the way that only certain details of localization were harnesses to place a gloss over the brand in order to enter new territories.

So in this chapter we seek to place the emergence of the war monument and its designs in the context of specific political climates existing at particular points in time. In this case the contextual information is provided by the work of historians, political documents and archives which reveal information about the commissioning and design of monuments. These allow us to reveal some of the social goings on that lie behind the material objects that we analyse.

In this chapter we show how the commissioning and design process of earlier war monuments can be understood as part of a process of the promotion of nationalism in the face of perceived political threats from the left. The careful decision-making about what kinds of representations these monuments should contain and the control of the authorities over what is and is not appropriate has persisted through to later monument production. What we look at in this chapter is how and why certain elite groups made certain decisions as to what exactly the public should be called on to commemorate and what forms this should take.

The post-WWI British political climate

Keegan's (2001) account of the WWI provides an excellent overview of how seemingly inconsequential disputes between the major power holders in the world at the time led up to WWI and consequently how that war led to the demise of the Austro-Hungarian, Russian and Ottoman empires. The fall of the latter gave the victors, Britain and France, control over new territories in the Middle East; this factor is in itself having a major influence on future wars. The replacing of the autocratic Tsarist regime in Russia with the Bolshevik government caused some concern within the British government of the time. There is ample evidence to suggest that British society was undergoing a period of adjustment; changes that revealed signs of unrest at the bottom levels of society and that those elites at the top levels were concerned about the possible threats as a consequence. Arnot (1967) refers to the effect on British Parliamentary decisions following the Russian Revolution of 1917 as strikes, mutinies and opposition to the war all increased in the year following the Bolshevik Revolution.

Events in Russia were certainly in the minds of the early labour movement in Britain and influenced their early decisions in party policy (see, e.g. McKibbin, 1974; Laybourn, 1997). The fear of Bolshevism was also uppermost in the thinking of Winston Churchill at that time, who, according to Jenkins (2002:350), was intent on: '. . . strangling near to birth the Bolshevik regime in Russia'. Jenkins comments that despite having just come out of one war, Churchill was calling loudly for Britain to engage in another war; this time against the new Russian power holders.

A trade union perspective on British military involvement

Arnot (1967) describes the growth of trade unions in Britain during the first two decades of the twentieth century and how, following the war and the Russian Revolution, they became more militant. Convinced that the combined force of allied powers were determined to intervene militarily in Russia's Revolution, the unions called for a withdrawal of British troops from the force. Speakers at the conference of the Miners' Federation called for the withdrawal of troops and highlighted the role of the press in anti-Russian propaganda, although these excerpts are lengthy, it is worth seeing them in full at this point to appreciate the strength of feeling against further military participation by Britain:

> I want to submit to the conference that if we had no capitalistic money invested in Russia we should have no troops in Russia . . . It is a betrayal of the lads who have been called up to take on military service in that direction. They ought to manage their own affairs; they ought to be left alone, and it is not for us to interfere and land troops there to protect capitalist interests. (Hebert Smith of the Yorkshire Miners' Association, quoted in Arnot, 1967:148)

> This Government of ours are controlling the Press of this country, and not allowing the truth about Russia to come out; if they did, possibly three would be almost, if not quite, a revolution against the treatment that has been meted out to the men who have been fighting for liberty, and for justice, and democracy. I think it is one of the greatest scandals, and one of the greatest reflections upon what we sometimes call this free British country of ours, that our troops should be sent there in order to prevent these men and these women, who like ourselves, are endeavouring to work out their own social salvation. (James Winstone, Vice President of the South Wales Miners' Federation, quoted in Arnot, 1967:148)

We can see from these comments that trade union officials saw parity in the social circumstances experienced by British soldiers, the general public and Russian citizens. Arnot's work reinforces this perception; he describes how during this period a revolutionary spirit was spreading throughout Britain; he quotes Lloyd George from a confidential memorandum who said that the whole of Europe was:

> . . . filled with the spirit of revolution. . . . there is a deep sense not only of discontent, but of anger and revolt, amongst the workmen against the war conditions. The whole existing order in its political, social and economic aspects is questioned by the masses of the population from one end of Europe to the other. (Lloyd George, quoted in Arnot, 1967:150)

According to Arnot, this spirit of revolution existed in the British army at the time, and the mutinies of January, and the demonstration by police and prison officers in Hyde Park in June 1919 can be attributed to this revolutionary spirit. This picture of a popular revolutionary spirit is also borne out by Hobsbawm (1990) who writes that the state and ruling classes were already competing with 'rivals' for the loyalty of the British working class, or what Hobsbawm regrettably refers to as 'the lower orders' (1990:83), pertinently noting that prior to WWI recruitment could not be taken for granted:

> The political attitudes of citizens, and particularly workers, were matters of vital interest, given the rise of labour and socialist movements. (Hobsbawm, 1992:83)

Returning soldiers: Elites' and soldiers' perspectives

Once the war was underway the establishment also seemed to be concerned about the attitude of returning soldiers. Rudy, a social and political commentator of the time describes in an essay he wrote in 1918 how he is often asked his opinion by 'officers' and 'ministers of the Church' what 'Tommy' may be thinking after his war experiences. Writing while the war was drawing to a close, Rudy (1918), spoke of the contrast of the real soldiers on the front and the idealized representations of them at home, he comments on:

> . . . the almost necessary glorification of . . . men and methods out in France or wherever we are at close grips with the enemy. (Rudy, 1918:545)

The idealized versions of soldiery propagated at home never matched the bleak reality of the soldiers' lives on the front. Rudy's article warns of the 'dangers' that may face the 'homeland' (Britain) and 'its empire' when the soldiers returned from the war. When they return Rudy fears the soldiers will:

> . . . either go to the extremist camp or he will help form some powerful organisation of his own. (Rudy, 1918:551)

He talks of the enormous profits being made by businessmen involved in the manufacturing of goods for the war while living in the safety and comfort of home. The tone of his article is one of fear and demonstrates that the return of disillusioned, dissatisfied men who have now become aware of their unequal status in society through the war process was a genuine threat to the nation.

In a stark example of the social distance between members of differing economic classes, he adopts a condescending tone when speaking of the soldiers who he regarded as being: '. . . prone to mental phlegm' (Rudy

1918:546). The soldiers are, he observes, generally ignorant and largely illiterate. He urges for an education of the masses to avert any danger, but the education of the masses was not without benefits for the nation, he argues:

> . . . the State owes it to its citizens that they should be acquainted with their rights, duties and the true significance of Throne, Country and Empire. (1918:550)

Without elaborating on circumstances surrounding the events, he refers to the:

> . . . social grievances which almost culminated in 1914 in a war of classes in the United Kingdom, the citizen-soldier has added the many wrongs, or supposed wrongs, of the past four years. (1918:546)

Alerting the reader to the fact that the church no longer has power over the soldiers, he notes their lack of spiritual interest, describing them as:

> . . . essentially materialistic, highly superstitious and possessing virtues which are ethic rather than religious. (1918:551).

Above all, he mourns the loss of faith 'Tommy' has in political parties and institutions, national or: '. . . imperial . . . which stand, or ought to stand, above party strife' (1918:546). Rudy (1918:546) then gives an example of a symptom of this loss of faith: '. . . his present attitude towards the national anthem'. Rudy's comments while not supported by a great amount of detail are evidence that by 1918 soldiers were displaying their resentment of nationhood and that powerful groups had noted this resentment and feared its consequences.

The contextual information provided by the literature reviewed so far paints an uneasy picture; there were obvious tensions at government level regarding the perceived threat of the emerging Communist ideology. Signs of the level of the perceived threat can also be seen in Churchill's willingness to engage in further military activity against the new Russian power holders. The trade unions, claiming to speak for the British workers, saw a parallel with their domestic low social status and that of the Russian worker and firmly rejected notions of further British military activity. On the domestic level the perceived threat also came from within the lower ranks of the military, those who made up the mass of the British army, 'the ordinary' British citizen who was now waking up to the appalling conditions their poverty at home created for them and their families.

These are the sociopolitical factors that are significant to the conception and production of the nation-wide WWI memorial project and that the concerns we have seen expressed propelled their erection in British villages, towns and cities. It may be that *nationalism,* communicated by the wide-scale commissioning of commemorative war monuments, became the mechanism by which the elites attempted to reconcile with the average citizen.

The following section discusses the commissioning processes that preceded the erection of war monuments in British villages, towns and cities and explores the design considerations that were involved in the process of the national memorial: the Cenotaph and British commemorative war monuments in general, particularly looking at the choices made by the designers in their representation of soldiers. It begins with the spontaneous war 'shrines' that sprung up on streets throughout Britain during WWI.

Pre-conscription, spontaneous WWI commemorative shrines

Winter (1998:79) categorizes British war memorials into three distinctive 'spaces and periods': first, those scattered over the home front before 1918, these spontaneous street memorials appeared around Britain soon after WWI had started. The second category is the WWI memorials in churches and civic sites; these were constructed in the ten years following WWI. Third, those memorials erected in war cemeteries abroad.

After the onset of WWI the category defined as the first category of war memorial by Winter (1998) started to appear. Before the wave of more official public memorializing, people in small communities had already begun to erect their own small monuments, or 'shrines', to the people who had enlisted from their street, workplace or organization to which they belonged. These shrines would be a record of all the names of the volunteers from a particular community and as well as being viewed as a celebration of the act of volunteering, they were also seen as a way of promoting the war effort and contributing to war propaganda (King, 1998; Winter, 1998). Winter describes these early monuments as a method of encouragement of further enlistment and: '. . . a permanent and immediate chastisement of those who chose not to go' (Winter, 1998:80).

So, one function of the pre-conscription street shrine war monument was to encourage people to go to war by evoking a sense of shame in those who had not volunteered to go. Speaking of the proposal to erect a shrine in Islington, Alderman Saint hoped that it would:

> . . . also serve as a stimulus to the people not to be a party to an inconclusive peace which might mean a repetition of this terrible slaughter in the course of the next generation. (Saint, quoted in King, 1998:54)

It is clear that the spontaneous memorials, that numbered 267 according to Furlong et al. (2003), were viewed by some at the time as a way to encourage participation in warfare, but what role could the second category, the post-war memorials have taken?

The widespread commissioning of WWI memorials

Perceptions of the second post-war category differ from those of the spontaneously erected memorials. Winter describes these as having '. . . ecumenical and conventional patriotic elements, emphasizing at once the universality of loss and the special features of national political and aesthetic traditions' (1998:79).

It is this emphasis on 'national political and aesthetic traditions' that offers an interesting avenue of enquiry into the role played by the state in the erection of commemorative war monuments. Winter continues:

> These local war memorials arose out of the post war search for a language in which to reaffirm the values of the community for which soldiers had laid down their lives. (1998:79)

This quote suggests that Winter seems to downplay the role of the state, by aligning the 'national political and aesthetic traditions' with 'the values of the community' for which people have sacrificed their lives, Winter hints at an acceptance, a naturalization, rather than the questioning, of the concept of sacrifice of one's life for the nation-state.

In each location, war memorial committees consisting of representatives from public officials to 'lay' people and religious figures, decided on the plans for location and form of the monument to be erected.[1] The cost of commissioning and erecting a war memorial, at least in the provincial towns and villages, did not depend on central government funds. Financed largely through public donation and subscription, plans for the war memorials were considered not only for their perceived representation of both grief and gratitude, but also for their financial burden. Many plans had to be revised, for example a change of material or size of the intended monument, due to lack of funds (Winter, 1998; Quinlan, 2005). King's work highlights the financial role of the public in the commissioning process; it seems that although they were not usually actively involved in design choice, the amount of money they could donate determined the size and quality of the memorial that could be selected by the committee. King points out that spontaneous public interest alone was not sufficient to secure the commissioning of the monument; apart from disappointing levels of contributions, attendance at public meetings was sometimes low (King, 1998).

According to some historians (see, e.g. Winter, 1998; Quinlan, 2005) the primary motivating factor in the construction of so many WWI memorials was to provide the public with a place at which to mourn; according to Winter they were an expression of grief and a show of support to the bereaved (Winter, 1998). It is true that the provision of this facility was partly deemed necessary due to the absence of individual graves to mourn at; in WWI families of soldiers would be told about the deaths or the disappearance while in action of their relatives, but often nothing, or very little, else. In most cases individual bodies could not be identified or located; even if it had been possible to distinguish an individual soldier's body on the battlefield a non-repatriation policy was practised by the governments involved in WWI (Commonwealth War Graves Commission, online reference).[2] Consequently, the families had no corpse to bury. So, according to Winter the war memorials act as a 'grave' for these families to attend, providing a focal point for grief: '. . . a framework for and legitimation of individual and family grief' (Winter, 1998:93).

Viewing the war memorials solely as a facilitator of personal grief is, as has been suggested by Ashplant et al. (2000, 2004), a singular way of viewing the use of war memorials; it places their ownership and origin with the individual, rather than the collective and suggests a uniform interpretation of both the expression and the interpretation of the meaning of the war memorial. Notably, Winter's work (1998, 1999) emphasizes and discusses in some depth the memorials' function at the time they were erected as a mourning site, and locates them as an act of individuals rather than in: '. . . some state-bounded space of hegemony or domination' (Winter, 1999:60). However, looking closely at his own descriptions of the war memorials, we can see that his comments in themselves reflect multiple meanings and hegemonic influence; he describes the erection of the war memorials after 1914 as:

> . . . an act of citizenship. To remember was to affirm community, to assert its moral character, and to exclude from it those values, groups, or individuals that placed it under threat. (1998:80)

Despite this tacit acknowledgement of the hegemonic function of war memorials, Winter argues strongly for the reading of war memorials as a private, personal expression of grief rather than one of nationalism and hegemonic influence. He urges people to consider the background to their construction in order to understand their 'true' meaning and is critical of readings that focus on war memorials as political symbolism saying: 'What these people did was much smaller and much greater than that' (Winter, 1999:60). Viewing the war memorials as both a symbol of grief and a site for grieving concurs partly with the view of Gregory (1994) who, as well as acknowledging this humanistic role, also acknowledges their hegemonic function when he describes the language in their inscriptions as drawing heavily on:

> . . . pre-war rhetoric of God, Empire, King and Country, on notions of sacrifice and on presenting the war in terms of a crusade for human dignity and liberty. (1994:24)

Surely, we should conclude that whatever else they may be the memorials are undoubtedly sites of political expression? For a view of the memorials as being symbolic of a political act we can turn to King (1998) who argues that in order to reconstruct meanings of war memorials, their own creative process has to be examined; of this process, he says:

> This process was fundamentally political, because it relied for its organisation on the institutions of local politics, on the press and on other forms of association whose activities, if not overtly political, had political implications. (p. 5)

Participation of elitist groups in the commissioning of commemorative war monuments

Authors (Gregory, 1994; Gaffney, 1998; King, 1998) record the extent to which elites in each community struggled with each other for power over the decisions on the type of war memorial they would have in their areas from their conception to the unveiling ceremonies; this is clearly seen in Wales where Gaffney (1998) conducted her research on WWI memorials. In this work, Gaffney (1998) looks closely at the political debates that surrounded the construction of commemorative war memorials and monuments, the people who were involved and the political motivations and influences. While acknowledging political and hegemonic readings of the memorial process, she cautions against a singular interpretation and recognizes a plurality of approaches to the memorials seeing them as:

> . . . potent evidence of the both the catastrophe of the Great War and of the challenges faced by those seeking to commemorate the fallen. (1998:24)

The political significance of the commemorative war monument is also prominent in the construction of the monuments in the South Wales

Coalfields area where they appear in abundance. The process of their construction was managed by people who were positioned at a high level in the mining industry that dominated the area. Death was commonplace in the industry; Gaffney (1998) cites the example of the Senghennydd mining explosions, one in 1901 which killed 79, and another in 1913 that resulted in the death of 439 men and boys. Despite this major death toll, no memorial to the miners was erected at the time. However, in 1919 a war memorial committee was established and the Senghennydd war memorial was erected in the town centre: '. . . an impressive clock tower in a prominent position' (Gaffney, 1998:99).

Gaffney cites a prime example of the complex political jostling that preceded the erection of a war memorial; the events that took place during the commissioning process of the 'national' war memorial in Cathays Park in Cardiff. Attempts by the local authority in Cardiff to get contributions from surrounding councils towards the erection of the Welsh National War Memorial in its civic centre failed. Fearing that a 'national' monument in Cardiff would deny them the erection of their own memorial, councils refused to give money to fund the 'beautification of Cardiff' (Gaffney, 1998, quoted in Quinlan, 2005:59). Gaffney (1998) describes in some detail the hostile debates that surrounded the proposal to have a memorial in Cardiff that was meant to act as a memorial for the soldiers of the whole of Wales.

However, the concept of a united Welsh national identity, with Cardiff as its focus, was unattainable as Gaffney's work demonstrates:

> It is clear that the invitation from Cardiff City Council to local authorities throughout Wales was treated with a mixture of indifference, suspicion and hostility. (1998:51)

Having failed to start a national fund, the council decided that a city fund would be the only means of raising the funds (Gaffney, 1998). However, the Cardiff-based Welsh newspaper, the *Western Mail*, which had a large circulation throughout Wales, persevered with the notion of a national memorial. In an article published in 1919, they promoted the proposal for a national monument, arguing strongly that in Wales all actions are habitually taken from a national standpoint (Gaffney, 1998). Appealing to their readers to rally together as one, under a single national identity, they started a subscription fund with their own donation of a hundred pounds (*Western Mail*, 24 October 1919, in Gaffney, 1998:53).

We find echoes of the wider British political climate in Wales by looking at Gaffney's work who proposes that the *Western Mail* had its own reasons for pushing the nationalist case. She cites the emergence of socialism within many local authorities that was challenging the Liberal stronghold as the motivation for the *Western Mail's* national flag waving. According to

Gaffney, the *Western Mail* had enjoyed commercial domination in Wales and feared the emerging socialist trends within the local authorities:

> . . . the appeal for national unity provided the paper with an opportunity to assert its position in Wales. (1998:54–5)

The Welsh public responded well to the newspaper's campaign, eventually raising a large sum of money: £24,000 by the time it closed in 1920 (Gaffney, 1998). In this example we can see sacrifice, memorial and a Conservative brand of nationalism coming together to mutually support each other.

Gaffney's research helps us to see that war memorials are indeed complex cultural resources that are created with the help of many societal establishments and, in some cases, with significant input from individuals. The nature of the individual and elite input into the process leads to a conclusion that war commemoration in the form of monument commissioning can be viewed from a hegemonic perspective, as the elite establishments of government and media called for a particular response from the public who responded by giving what they could from their limited incomes, yet, despite their significant financial commitment they were not invited to participate in the design decisions or in the unveiling ceremonies.

The choice between symbolic and utilitarian memorials

The decision to put limited recourses into a war memorial, rather than much needed facilities, was a common occurrence throughout the United Kingdom. However, a war memorial was also taken as an opportunity to increase public facilities. Weekly house-to-house collections would be made in some of the most poverty-stricken areas of the country and it is the poverty in which these families existed provides a clue as to why people with so little may have given to the fund. By the selection of a utilitarian memorial, such as a hospital, library or recreational facility, rather than a symbolic memorial, Gaffney (1998) states that the memorial process enabled many communities to create facilities for themselves that otherwise would never have been provided for them by the authorities. An example Gaffney cites is that of Trehafad, in *The Rhondda Valley*, where the desire for a utilitarian memorial outweighed the desire for a symbolic monument. Local newspaper *The Rhondda Leader* wrote in 1924:

> Cinderella of the Rhondda . . . without an Institute, a recreation field, and even without a playground for children, apart from those attached to the schools. The residents, with characteristic thoroughness, are

making a splendid effort to meet these long and deeply-felt wants, and they have set their hearts upon providing a War Memorial Institute. (*The Rhondda Leader*, in Gaffney, 1998:108)

Elsewhere in historical evidence we not only see that the urge to create a symbolic monument overrode practical needs, but we also get a sense of what the commissioning committees believed they would achieve by choosing a symbolic monument. All memorial committees were faced with a similar choice when considering the construction of a war memorial: a symbolic monument, or a utilitarian memorial. Debates on this choice centred on two schools of thought: emotional urges to create a permanent memory of sacrifice for posterity in the form of a symbolic monument and a facility that provided a practical benefit for ex-servicemen. King (1998) says that, while this was a point of disagreement, they all agreed that the purpose was to honour and mourn the dead. According to Moriarty (1997) the public decided which kind of memorial (i.e. utilitarian or symbolic) they would commission through a series of public meetings. There was much disagreement over the choice of memorial, King (1998) quotes artist W. Reynolds-Stephens, designer of the memorial in Cleveland among others, who said a utilitarian monument:

> . . . evinces no real desire to keep green the memory of the great heroism of the fallen. (Reynolds-Stephens, 1918, quoted in King, 1998:66)

King asserts that social, ethical and political ideas unrelated to honour and mourning were all introduced into the debate as a means of developing a preference for a particular type of memorial. At the same time, King argues, there was no correlation between Left/Right political positions and the preference for a symbolic monument or a utilitarian memorial. He refers to two political figures: Philip Gibbs a Liberal politician, and the Conservative Councillor George King who are quoted giving different perspectives on the purpose of a memorial. Gibbs talks about the role of the memorial as an anti-war statement:

> . . . should be not only reminders of the great death that killed the flower of our race but warnings of what war means in slaughter and ruin, in broken hearts and agony. (Philip Gibbs, in King, 1998:76)

While the comments of Councillor George King reveal a different ideological position, he speaks of memorials as representing:

> . . . the great cause for which our gallant men laid down their lives – the cause of justice and freedom. (George King, in King, 1998:76)

When faced with the decision about the type of memorial to erect many communities decided on a utilitarian model, may be a hospital extension or a recreation facility, but some were able to afford both a utilitarian and a symbolic memorial. An important point to make about the symbolic monument is that, unlike a utilitarian memorial that invites certain sections of a community into it at certain times in their lives, a symbolic memorial offers the opportunity to anyone in the community to gather around it to commemorate war in future ceremonies and it is their potential for the projection of an ideological position on sacrifice for the nation-state that makes the commemorative war monuments an important cultural resource that necessitates research. Moriarty attributes the desire to create a symbolic memorial to the fear of forgetting: '. . . what the dead had died for and their example of self-sacrifice' (Moriarty, 1997:128). While King asserts:

> But it is clear that much of what was said was less concerned with the memory of the dead than with the needs of the living. (1998:82)

Although it is tempting to take a romantic view of the erection of WWI commemorative monuments as a spontaneous act taken by individuals in a community who were somehow not associated with powerful groups, evidence in the literature suggests we should view their commissioning as a deliberate act of power holders. This is evident in the story of the construction of the Cardiff monument exemplifies what King (1998:6) describes as: '. . . an exercise in official and unofficial power'. Indeed, King discusses a range of factors that influenced the decision to create a monumental war memorial rather than a utilitarian memorial and also the benefits that resulted from taking that decision; these went far beyond the realm of the simple act of remembrance of the war dead.

Discussions about the kind of memorial a town or village should have led to extensive debates on social, ethical and political ideas. Power struggles emerged to gain control of the memorial fund (King, 1998). Making it clear that, in his opinion, the erection of a war memorial was a political activity, King says that consideration of such factors is essential to the interpretation of the meaning of war memorials. It is clear that the spontaneous memorials were viewed by some at the time as a way to encourage participation in warfare. Yet, views of the role of post-WWI country-wide commissioning of central public war memorials seem to differ.

The call for more permanent war memorials in central civic spaces throughout the country was promoted by newspaper reports and political figures towards the end of WWI (King, 1998). According to Mosse (1990), the construction of the Cenotaph in London was first proposed during peace celebrations in July 1919. He also emphasizes that the proposal had a political motive: to combat a perceived threat of bolshevism in Britain. Indeed, as the earlier part of this analysis has demonstrated, the fear of Bolshevism was common throughout Europe at that time and influenced many aspects of political life in Britain.

Despite the rise of proletarian socialist movements, according to Hobsbawm it is during the WWI period and its immediate aftermath widely thought that mass nationalism triumphed against rival ideologies (Hobsbawm, 1992:123), but how would a designer go about representing nationalism in a commemorative war monument? Perhaps we can see this process in the history of the creation of the most well-known British war memorial on which the annual national commemoration of war still centres: the Cenotaph in London. As the erection of war memorials spread throughout the country, committees were faced with a vast selection of choices regarding the design of their monument. Many factors had to be considered, not only environmental factors, but also how the soldiers were to be portrayed in those monuments that featured statues that represented the soldier who had suffered severe physical and mental distress during and after the war, as King (1998) points out:

> There were also the distress and grievances caused by economic problems in the aftermath of war to contend with, especially those of ex-servicemen. (p. 156)

Perhaps these complexities were considered too vast when the choice of the design of the national monument had to be made.

Centralizing war commemoration and the issue of design

Thinking that the creation of a symbol in central London would: '. . . work up patriotic feeling' (Homberger, quoted in Mosse, 1990:95), Mosse refers to the move to construct the Cenotaph as a conscious effort to engage the public's attention and enthusiasm in the new age of: '. . . mass politics' (1990:96). It is the Cenotaph that is still the focal point of the annual Remembrance Parade each November. Originally the architect Sir Edwin Lutyens was asked to design a structure referred to as a 'catafalque'; in effect a stand on which rests a coffin. Lutyens thought that this was not harmonious with the fact that the bodies of the dead were absent, so he preferred a cenotaph. The name 'cenotaph' originates from the Greek 'kenotafion' meaning 'empty tomb' (Moriarty, 1995:13).

This style of memorial was soon adopted throughout the country, the UK National Inventory of War Memorials lists their number throughout the country as 267 (Furlong et al., 2003). The apparent lack of reference to an actual body or coffin is interesting when considering the linking of the 1920 Armistice memorial service with the burial of the body of the *Unknown Warrior* at Westminster, the body is that of a British soldier; the identity of whom is uncertain. Moriarty (1995) points out that a symbolic memorial, lacking representations of soldiers, dead or alive, is a way of appealing to each individual of the bereaved population. In the case of the *Tomb of the Unknown Warrior* at Westminster the body of the soldier buried within could be imagined by a bereaved family to be that of their relative, while at the same time the Cenotaph conveys anonymity; making it accessible to the whole of the bereaved population. Although representation of a soldier was rejected by the designer Cenotaph Lutyens, he did include a figure of a draped corpse on the top of his other cenotaph-style memorials at Manchester, Southampton and Rochdale (Moriarty, 1995:15).

It seems that although the cenotaph format was widely adopted as a commemorative monument style throughout the country, it was often modified to include figures; these were more often male soldiers, but occasionally female figures were included. Yet these figures did not reflect the physical reality of the soldiers, neither did they reflect the reality of the environment and manner in which they were killed. In comparison with Moriarty's view, King's comments on monument design process preferred by artists and committees portray innocence with regard to their expectations of the emotional needs of the public; King says:

> In memorial design, simplicity and reticence were urged by artists and critics, and it was also much appreciated by lay people – at least those whose views are recorded in memorial committee records. (1999:161)

However, Moriarty has an entirely different perspective; her description of the outcome of debates that were held over the design of commemorative war monuments alludes to the thinking behind architects' design of the images of the male soldier:

> They represented a pure race unsullied by foreign blood. The splendid physiques belied the reality of pre and post-war poverty, malnutrition and disease. (1995:20)

If King's assessment of 'lay' people's appreciation of the simplistic images of the soldiers is accurate, we are urged to speculate about why people would be more appreciative of images that idealize their dead? Moriarty explains that as with the fictitious heroic soldiers in the imaginations of people at home, representation of their actual looks and conditions in which they served on the front line was no more realistic in the memorial monuments. As Scarry (1985) commented:

> . . . the persistent content of war-injury-often slips from view by a process of omission or redescription. British war memorials played a vital role in this process. (Quoted in Moriarty, 1995:19)

During the commissioning process the designs choice made by the commissioning committees was often governed by financial constraints; the inclusion of a sculptured statue would significantly increase costs (King, 1998). But when money was available for a statue to be included, what part did reality play in the choices made in the representation of soldiers? According to King, rather than individuals on war memorial committees coming up with designs and ideas on the representation in the memorial, artists or sculptors were consulted and their opinions were usually treated with respect. Artists would advise committees on the appropriate memorial for the intended location: King (1998) cites architect Edward Warren who wrote that simple memorials, such as crosses, were appropriate for smaller communities while larger areas such as towns should opt for a figurative sculpture. King notes that although there were many disagreements regarding the selection of a memorial, artists, rather than clients, led the way in the choice of memorial.

Moriarty (1995) documents the processes that governed the choice of the bronze figure; saying that 'traditionalists', some of whom had served in the war, were awarded the majority of commissions. Awarding the work to the traditionalists had a significant impact on the resultant style of representation in the WWI commemorative monuments. The end of the nineteenth and beginning of the twentieth centuries saw a change in attitudes of modern sculptors towards the sculptural understanding of the human form. Moriarty refers to this new style as: '. . . a new acceptance of the incomplete body' (1995:20). This 'new' approach of stripping the familiar, choosing to disguise the appearance, and consequently, the meaning communicated by a representation conflicts with the choices made by the sculptors of the WWI commemorative monuments. They chose the opposite of reality; rather than thin, tired, wounded soldiers, they chose complete, healthy bodies with neoclassical forms clothed in contemporary military uniforms. Their depictions of the human form remained consistent with established tradition, redressed in WWI uniforms (Moriarty, 1995).

The selection process was largely governed through a process of institutional, elitist control, as King says, the choice was '. . . largely determined by institutional and financial power' (1999:160). Indeed, sculptors would have been trained by established design schools all advocating particular, traditional theoretical positions on representation, therefore, we would not expect to see a wide diversity in the final images of those memorials that featured human figures. Also, uniformity in approach is reflected in opinions on the choice of language.[3]

A designer who received some attention for being different was Charles Sargeant Jagger. His memorial for Hoylake and West Kirby is described by King as 'unconventional'. Sir George Frampton commented that it was one of the best, if not **the** best statue he had seen (Frampton, 1921, cited in King, 1998:114). Jagger is known for a more primitive, rugged style of art. He was a serving soldier in WWI and was injured and received military decorations. This experience may account for his style of representation; his figure of a dead soldier in his memorial in Hyde Park, London, was too realistic for some and resulted in criticism in letters to *The Times* (Compton, 2004).

Public records viewed at the Glamorgan records office during research on the Welsh National War Memorial in Cardiff show that Jagger's memorial statue for Great Western Railway in Paddington station so impressed one of the war memorial committee members in Cardiff that they invited Jagger to submit a design for the Welsh National War Memorial. However, his design did not succeed in being selected. Unfortunately, the records do not indicate what his design consisted of, or why his ideas were finally rejected (Welsh National War Memorial Order of Service at the Unveiling of the Monument, 12 June, 1928, Glamorgan Records Office, D/DX684/1). This rejection without discussion seems unusual; historians record that discussions with the artist regarding design of memorials were common, and as we have already seen decisions regarding design were usually left to the professional artist (King, 1998). A hint as to why the commissioning committee in Cardiff rejected Jagger may lie in criticisms that were made of another of his projects. According to both Compton (2004) and King (1998), he had received criticism from the committee responsible for the commissioning of the Royal Artillery Memorial in Hyde Park; they criticized his use of 'bulky clothing'. Nevertheless, this criticism had not deterred him from his design choices; Jagger's response to the criticism was:

> I am most anxious to conform to these criticisms . . . except beyond the point where to do so would seriously affect the design as a work of art. (Jagger, 1921, quoted in King, 1998:118)

An insight into what may have guided another designer of war memorials can be found in the words of one prominent architect Sir Herbert Baker, who was one of the Principal Architects of the Imperial War Graves Commission:

> My inclination for war memorials at home was the same as for the war graves cemetery, that generally they should express the sense of reverence and peace: uniting the living with the dead in manifold memories. (Baker, in Quinlan, 2005:46)

Baker's view of the function of the war memorial clearly sees spirituality as an important feature in their design. Contrast this view with that of a Colonel Earle in a speech he gave at the unveiling of the war memorial at St Alfred's school in Wantage, Oxfordshire. Colonel Earle, whose speech Quinlan (2005) quotes from, sees the war memorial as a reminder of sacrifice past an acceptance, one could say even welcoming, the possibility of sacrifice in the future:

> ... the other object of the memorial is to teach us Duty towards our King and fellow citizens – generous wholehearted duty as was given by those whose names we honour today in order that we might live and preserve all that we hold most dear. May we prove worthy of their sacrifice. (Earle, in Quinlan, 2005:70)

These two quotations illustrate the expectation that war memorials have a particular didactic function, in that they should give people a resolution to death, and also to teach respect for sacrifice of life for the nation-state. How are these ideological expectations realized in the design and construction of a war memorial?

Moriarty (1995) refers to the inclusion of a sculptured representation of a soldier as the 'instantaneous function', and argues that this is far more effective than a cenotaph, an obelisk or a cross. She cites Edmund Gosse, a proponent of the 'new' style of sculptor who believed that bronze casting 'is not a translation of the original but that original itself' (Gosse, 1894–5, cited in Moriarty, 1995:23). According to Borg (1991), Gosse coined the term 'new sculpture' that described a new realism and naturalism in British Sculpture originating in France from where many tutors came to teach at the Royal College in South Kensington, London. Moriarty (1995) says that every effort was made to create a finished image that looked whole and seamless, noting that, in some cases, efforts were made to replicate conditions that the soldiers had faced in Flanders fields; soldiers' boots sinking in mud, pitted bronze to resemble the clay models that the bronzes were cast from, claiming that the clay itself was symbolic of the mud the soldiers were living in.

Commenting on the use of bronze, Moriarty says that the figure set permanently in bronze has no fragility, the act of casting the sculpture renders the soldier immortalized, as a soldier either, sturdy in battle, ready to fight, or victorious after battle, and she claims it is this message that ensures the continuous regeneration of the acceptance and expectations of war (Moriarty, 1995). As Moriarty puts it:

> The dead's very absence facilitated the process of idealisation of whom they had been as people and the circumstances of their death. The Sculpted body shaped private personal memory as well as creating public myths. By avoiding any reference to physical and social fragmentation it engendered a literal and metaphorical remembering. (1995:37)

Although Penny wrote that the purpose of the memorials were to '... portray the typical, indeed the common, victim or participant' (Penny,

1981, quoted in King, 1998:132). King acknowledges the importance of institutional control in the war memorial process, he says that:

> . . . the expressive possibilities of war commemoration were not shaped by a system of values encoded in commemorative symbolism, but by the nature of the institutions through which commemoration took place, and by the interests of participant groups, pursuing goals determined by their own sectional values. (King, 1998:248–9)

Bourke (1996), commenting on the choices faced by committees when selecting a war memorial, cites a member of the Llandudno committee:

> . . . any memorial of a pronounced warlike or realistic character should be avoided.

Bourke notes they chose an obelisk because it:

> . . . had been used as a commemorative monument by successive civilisations for nearly 4,000 years. (Llandudno War Memorial Unveiling Ceremony and Dedication, 11 November 1922, 3, cited in Bourke, 1996:227)

Disagreeing with this view, the Colwyn Bay war memorial committee opted for a bronze figure of a soldier. However, they too were mindful of creating something that avoided association with realistic war imagery preferring that the image showed:

> . . . no suggestion of callousness or brutality associated with war

and the representation of the soldier was to be:

> . . . typical . . . Called from his uneventful civil pursuits by the stern life, whilst the knowledge of the horrors and possibilities of War enhance[d] his valour. (*Book of Remembrance*, Colwyn Bay War Memorial 1914–1918, quoted in Bourke, 1996:22)

On the subject of real and idealized war and soldiers, another intriguing design is the memorial in Burnley, Lancashire. Moriarty makes an interesting observation on the way this memorial used imagery related to childhood. This, she comments, urges the viewer to see the dead as '. . . children, rather than fighting men' (1997:139). She provides evidence for her assertion in the form of the local newspaper report that tells its readers that it was the intention of the sculptor to avoid all association with death, or 'slaughter' and to emphasize the fact that the boys had done their 'duty' (*The Burnley Express*, 11 December 1926, in Moriarty, 1997:139). The newspaper's description of the memorial tells the viewer how the memorial should be read and even offers its own view of how a grieving mother would feel when viewing the memorial:

> The cenotaph merging into the three figures of sailor, soldier and airman is intended to express the emotion felt in the human heart at the ideals of those who have fallen in the Great War. The mother, overwhelmed in this emotion, places a wreath in memory of her son at the foot of the Cenotaph, and, as she stoops, the cenotaph shapes itself in her heart into the features of her son. (*The Burnley Express*, 11 December 1926, quoted in Moriarty, 1995:19)

Moriarty also documents the processes that governed the choice of the bronze figures that are found in a large number of the monuments, noting that most of the work went to 'traditionalists', some of whom had served in the war. The end of the nineteenth and beginning of the twentieth centuries saw a change in attitudes towards the sculptural understanding of the human form. Moriarty refers to this new style as: '. . . a new acceptance of the incomplete body' (1995:20). It is important to note that this 'new' approach of stripping the familiar, choosing to disguise the appearance and consequently the meaning of a piece conflicts with the choice of artistic style of representation selected by the sculptors of the WWI memorials, they chose to follow the opposite approach; complete, healthy bodies with neoclassical forms clothed in military uniforms, portraying not new, but Classical sculpture redressed in WWI uniforms (Moriarty, 1995).

If the modernist movement was dictating a new style as art critics suggest, why did the majority of WWI war artists choose the continuation of a Classical style constituting, as it did, a resistance to new directions in art? Could it be that because of the subject matter – war – the cause of the nation-state and nationalist discourses had superseded the inherent desire of so many artists to challenge traditional methods of representation?

Moriarty also gives an account of the significant amount of religious ritual that was acted out at the unveiling of a war memorial. Religion and nationalism came together; the moment was usually covered by a Union Jack, they would then have a church service, singing hymns and saying prayers that offered the sacrificed to god. The dignitaries who spoke at the ceremonies would be influential religious, as well as political figures.

In accordance with King (1998), Gaffney (1998:120) acknowledges the cross, '. . . whether "traditional" or Celtic in design', is the most common icon featured on British war memorials. However, despite the domination of Christian ideology in Britain at that time, sects within the church existed in the form of many denominations, as did other religions, such as Judaism. The cross, which was used to symbolize sacrifice, became a popular feature in the war shrines and memorials. King (1998:129) says this image became to refer, 'in most people's minds', to the sacrifice of the soldier likened to the Christian belief that Jesus had sacrificed his life for mankind. This idea transferred easily into the:

> . . . supposedly willing and generous laying down of their lives by soldiers in defence of their country and their ideals. (King, 1998:129)

Taken from traditional funerary symbolism and markers, the torch, according to King, was used to remind people of the need to continue the struggle on behalf of soldiers who had died so far. The obelisk and inscribed wall-tablets were also commonly used in the memorials. King attributes the use of the obelisk to two motives: the use of Classicism in civic design and the tradition of aristocratic landowners incorporating an obelisk into their estates. The fact that there was an attempt to fit with current town planning design trends suggests that town planners made a significant contribution to the choice of style a centrally located war memorial would be. As he says, the obelisk is not a feature of the small village memorial, so an awareness of aesthetic appeal and contemporary trends was obviously a consideration in the debates on the commissioning of a war memorial.

Usually, it would have been the cost of a proposal, rather than the design that resulted in any drastic changes (King, 1998) and where professional designers were consulted, their knowledge was respected and acknowledged by the commissioning committees. It is also important to note that many committees, restricted by limited funds, did not approach designers for an original piece of work, instead, they chose from a catalogue of designs held by monument masons (King, 1998). Yet, when this is the case the designs in the catalogue come from the same body of designers that are approached individually; all of whom learn their trade via the same institutional process.

So far, we have been able to establish a classic approach to the design of British WWI memorials, one that aims to steer well clear of reality and present an idealized form of war and the soldier. The institutional thread that binds the programme of the commissioning process together has been traced from the political climate to the media and in the main, finds that the ultimate decision rests with the artist. The artists, of course, are products of their cultural heritage. Kress and Van Leeuwen (1996) emphasize the importance of recognizing the relevance of culture to the analysis of semiotic resources. However, it is difficult to objectively view one's own cultural norms, sometimes only by comparison with the cultural norms of others do we get a clear understanding of our own practices.

Cultural influences on commemorative war monument design

The relevance of British cultural practice and norms in commemorative war monument design is apparent when compared to the design customs in non-British territories. Representations found in mainland European memorials differ from those in Britain. Mosse's (1990) discussion of the factors taken into consideration when selecting a war memorial includes: noise, spatial awareness and whether the memorial should serve in providing some function for the living as well as acting as a memorial for the dead. Speaking of German war memorials, he notes that modernity was: '. . . absorbed by war memorials, while it was ignored by military cemeteries and the Tomb of the Unknown Soldier' (1990:101). He identifies a common European theme in the war memorials: the ideal warrior, and, in Italy and France particularly, the resurrection of the soldier. He also noted differences between the European choices of memorials; according to Mosse, England did not usually use images of soldiers in poses that were: '. . . semi nude or aggressive' (1990:105) and he highlights the role of the memorial in Germany as preserving 'the myth of the war experience' (1990:106), which, he asserts, helped the Right-wing politicians to promote nationalism, offering an alternative to the reality of post-WWI Germany.

Mosse's work on Germany's commemoration of both World Wars is interesting, as it considers the commemoration of a nation that is unable to celebrate victory in their commemorative monuments. Mosse finds that the German nation avoids tackling the topic of defeat and manages to celebrate itself by utilizing pre-industrial symbolism in their commemorative war monuments.

The German style of commemoration contrasts with that of France; evidenced by Kidd's (1997) discussion of memorials in Lorraine. He discusses the pre-1914 war memorials that commemorated earlier wars, some following neoclassical forms by their use of the obelisk. However, the diversity of the imagery used in the WWI memorials also seems vast in comparison with the British range. Kidd talks about: flags, female figures, sometimes in local costume, one wearing 'rough country shoes' (1997:144) and a wounded soldier holding a flag. He notes the

> . . . industrialisation of warfare during the First World War, and the need to commemorate millions of dead in all the belligerent countries, which 'democratized' memorial practice and production. (p. 145)

Kidd (1997:151) describes the variety of representations to be found in Lorraine memorials as: '. . . angels, crucifixes, Sacred Hearts, symbolic and 'real' female figures'. The religious emphasis in France is understandable given the Catholic tradition they predominantly follow. Mosse's comments on the German preservation of the 'war myth' are interesting, he notes that they moved towards modernist styles of representation. However, despite the alternative choice of artistic style in comparison with those chosen by British artists, Mosse's argument is that the end result is still the promotion of nationalism. This view of war memorial and commemoration as a promotion of nationalism concurs with that of Raivo (1998:6) who notes that all sites of commemoration are fundamental parts of the national iconography of modern states, saying:

> The sense of nationalism – the ideology of belonging to the nation – is an essential part of war remembrance.

Raivo's analysis agrees with Mosse's (1990) analysis of 'the cult of the fallen', focusing on German commemoration, which asserts that sites of commemoration are places where both the local community worships the nation and the nation worships itself. Mosse makes the point that the spirit of mourning was not dominant in the memory of war; pride had played a major part in coming to terms with loss. In an effort to justify the enormity of loss of life, the nation had become a worthy cause for sacrifice (Mosse, 1990). Furthermore, Mosse asserts that this newfound spirit of national pride was not spontaneous, but carefully created from a myth that was built upon and communicated through many cultural channels to glorify war and death:

> Those concerned with the image and the continuing appeal of the nation worked at constructing a myth which would draw the sting from death in war and emphasize the meaningfulness of the fighting and sacrifice. (1990:6–7)

According to Borg (1991), British WWI memorial monuments divert from previous forms, whereas earlier memorials celebrated victory through the memorializing of the leaders, the WWI memorials celebrated the ordinary soldier as the hero. However, as we have seen, the 'ordinary' soldier and the conditions they endured on the front line were not considered by commissioning committees as desirable features to include in commemorative war monument design. What were the outcomes of the cautious approach taken towards 'realistic' representation, one that avoided representing the horrors of the battlefield, by the commissioning committees?

Conclusion

In this chapter we have looked at the political context in which the WWI monuments emerged in Britain. The work of historians has shown us that monuments emerged in a climate of not just physical, but also ideological struggle. Fairclough (1995:19) commented that critical discourse analysts sometimes failed to adequately: '. . . *historicize* their data', remarking that as well as specifying the particular historical conditions within which the data was generated, analysts should pay attention to what extent the resultant form of the data owes to their particular historical conditions. By exploring the work of these historians, we hope to understand more about how these monuments were shaped and formed by the social and political conditions of the day and that this understanding enhances our analysis.

Notes

1 Quinlan gives the description of two such committees; one in Sleaford, Lincs: 'It was composed of 12 councillors, 12 clergy, 15 ratepayers, 18 ladies and 15 ex-Servicemen', and the other in Bethnal Green, London: '. . . was composed of the local council, Christian clergy, the synagogue, two benevolent funds, the friendly societies, two hospital aid funds, the Union of Boot and Shoe Operatives, the rifle club and the special constables' (2005:43).

2 Founded by Sir Fabian Ware, the Commonwealth War Graves Commission was established in 1917 and was charged with the responsibility of the burial and commemoration of war dead abroad.

3 We analyse a selection of inscriptions on commemorative war monuments in Chapter 8.

CHAPTER FIVE

Iconography and iconology

In this chapter we begin our analysis of the semiotic choices made by war monument designers. We focus for the most part on WWI monuments moving onto more contemporary ones in Chapter Eight. In the first section of the chapter we discuss the iconography and iconology of monuments looking at the way by which designers use meanings that draw on religious and Classical references placing the war into higher moral and spiritual ideals, bringing a sense of destiny to the national project. We then move on to look at the meaning of poses, then at the meaning potentials of the height of monuments and the angle of viewing which are important semiotic resources for setting up social relations between viewers and those who are commemorated.

Classicism and higher moral order

From 1914 to the mid-1920s when most of the WWI monuments were built there was a fashion in art deco and in Classicism which had been common in public buildings and monuments from the latter half of the nineteenth century. This was highly influenced by the design styles of ancient Egypt, Greece and Rome that have been much idealized in Northern Europe. These architectural styles were ideal for monuments that could connote ideas of strength and power, high ideals and thinking (Moriarty, 1997). One of the standard features on monuments drawing in this period, often used for smaller town monuments or forming the features of larger monuments, is the obelisk, itself developed by the ancient Egyptians as a symbol of their attempts to communicate with their own deity: the sun god. Egyptian obelisks were inscribed with details of battles, proclamations of victory and praise of the pharaoh (Borg, 1991). Obelisks were later adopted by the Romans who used them to symbolize victory (Borg, 1991). Later, in early Christian art they were topped with crosses; thus continuing legitimizing war by proclaiming approval of a deity for the taking of, and the self-sacrifice of life during war.

We can see this use of the obelisk on the Bridgend monument (Figure 5.1). We can also see at the base that the design feigns the appearance of large stone blocks that were characteristic of Classical Greek buildings. These would be laid on top of each other without using mortar. The base itself also resembles the kinds of pedestals used in Roman designs for their pillars on which would stand a deity or important political figure.

The UK National Inventory of War Memorials (UKNIWM) lists 730 obelisks and 441 pillars, or columns, erected to commemorate WWI along with a further 4,781 that combined with Christian iconography (Furlong et al., 2003).

FIGURE 5.1 *Bridgend monument.*

The Welsh National War Memorial at Cardiff displays many typical features of Classicism. The central figures, as seen in Figure I.1 in the introduction to this book, are surrounded by columns that resemble those at the Acropolis in Athens displaying clean, smooth lines that connote certainty and order. References of this sort connote death through both sacrifice to nation as specifically depicted in the inscriptions but visually through themes of Classical civilization with high ideals and moral balance. The monument features a winged figure, again holding a sword, and a contemporary soldier, sailor and airman; each holding wreaths. Both the winged figure and the wreath can be traced back to Nike, the Greek goddess of victory. In Greek sculpture she can be seen with her wings spread out hovering over victorious soldiers and carrying either a palm branch, a wreath or a caduceus (MacDonald, 2009). As we continue on with our analysis we introduce more elements of Classicism that were used, including uses of poses, bodily forms, and in later chapters the use of female deities, showing how these combine with Christian, and in more contemporary monuments, with more mystical symbolism and vaguely educational imagery.

Christian symbolism

Many columns were erected just after the war that developed using scaled-down versions of the kinds of columns found in Classical Rome. But these would be topped with a cross. Often these would be Celtic crosses which take the form of a cross in a circle. The circle itself has a tradition of being used to connote eternity going back to Classical times. But in this use the Celtic cross was able to connote simplicity, timelessness and something of the land. Much nationalism mythology, even in its extreme forms, such as Nazism, draws on this link between simple people and the soil and land of the nation. This would be important at a time when this commemoration, as well as pointing to glorious former civilizations, could also signify the ordinary landscape. These crosses are commonly seen in the grounds of churches as seen in the St Giles' monument in Oxford (Figure 5.2).

In this monument we find the central column is a re-interpretation of the original obelisk with the additions of steps, an inscribed base and the cross on the top. The elaborations in this monument are particularly interesting, the steps upwards, often seen at the entrances to European churches, elevates the structure towards the sky forcing the viewer to look upwards ascending towards the imagined direction of the religious notion of heaven. This upwards angle connotes power; in this case the power of sacrifice for god as an ideological goal. These ideals are given further

FIGURE 5.2 *The monument at St Giles, Oxford.*

credence in the elaborate decorative additions to both the cross and the base that provide a platform for the inscriptions.

The inscriptions appear on shield-like shapes. These themselves can connote objects used in ancient battles and are based on designs of shields used by knights in battle from the Middle Ages. Later noble families used shields carrying arms and further on institutions and organizations indicating a bond and moral allegiance and were legally protected. As they ceased to be used in warfare these shields were used on wax seals and placed in churches as families used them around their tombs. These shields came to signify inheritance, the claim to property or officialdom of office. We might ask why not use elements of weaponry or defensive technology such as the gas-mask from the war itself. Clearly the shield here serves to soldiery in this case with a long tradition of noble soldiery, tight bonds of sworn allegiance and the inheritance of the national spirit.

The inclusion of objects in the war memorial, particularly those related to religious symbolism, goes back to ancient times. To the Ancient Greeks this inclusion of objects usually represented victory or peace, a practice described by Barthes (1977:23) as '. . . accepted inducers of ideas'. The ideas associated with these objects may well have been obvious to the Ancient

Greeks, but it is interesting to consider how their meaning is understood by the minds of the twentieth-century viewer. Consider the example from Chippenham, Wiltshire, shown in Figure 5.3.

This monument, void of any represented human form, relies on a viewer's ability to attach meanings not only to objects, but also to structure, shape and form; all of which combine to give the overall message of death and sacrifice for a 'higher' cause. In this example, as in many others, the shape and form of the architectural features reflect a Classical style and symmetry that combine to give a sense of balance and elegance and, in doing so, come to represent social and moral ideals as well as connote the greatness of these civilizations and their place in history.

Several of the design features connote Classicism: the columns that are shorter versions of those found in ancient temples and the cenotaph structure, similar to the Greek burial tomb. But perhaps the most striking feature is the semi-circular stand supported by shorter columns that resembles a church altar. Church altars themselves were originally the open air focal point of early Christian worship where the sacrifice of Christ was commemorated. Before Christianity arrived in Britain altars were used to sacrifice animals to pagan gods. The inclusion of an altar in a twentieth century commemorative war monument is another example of a remaking of semiotic material carried over from ancient pagan and more modern religious practices into the commemoration of sacrifice of citizens' life for the nation during war.

FIGURE 5.3 *Chippenham WWI monument.*

In the Bridgend monument we find the combination of the obelisk, the Roman god Victory, placed in the base comprised of large stones along with a small altar in the space at the base. Here the colour is much darker signifying something more solemn as opposed to the brightness of the Classical forms. Here the Christian place of worship is placed with the domain of the Classical space, overshadowed by its great ideas and nobility of purpose.

The urn has been used to contain the ashes of human remains since ancient times, so its presence on a monument to commemorate the sacrifice of dead soldiers is unremarkable, but its iconographical history suggests something more in terms of its design use. According to Cirlot (2002), it is a symbol of containment that has a wider connection to earthly things: gold, silver or other precious materials. In ancient Greece it was used as a symbol of mourning where the body was a container of the soul. This was taken up into Christian symbolism and to symbolize a container of life itself, particularly the womb of the virgin. So we can see its profound significance in the context of a commemorative war monument. The urn serves two purposes: it connotes not only death and sacrifice, but also rebirth; thus providing the message for grieving relatives of dead soldiers and future soldiers that death, particularly death in war for the nation, leads to life in an alternative form. Above we also see that the very urn itself is raised up on its own smaller set of columns. The very bodily remains of the soldiers themselves become sacred – perhaps ironic given the way that their lives were so callously thrown away.

Many WWI monuments also include a human form, either of soldiers themselves or often featuring characters and objects that stem from Classical art. The idea of the 'hero' in war commemoration was established by the Greeks who represented them in aggressive, commanding poses often offering gifts of thanks for their victory (Borg, 1991). The modern use of similar objects is well illustrated in the example we saw earlier in Cardiff and in the monument at Exeter (Figure 5.4).

The Exeter monument features the Roman goddess Victory holding a dove upwards towards the sky in the right hand and a downwards facing sword in the left, with the downwards direction signifying the end of its use for the present time. The dove in ancient Greek mythology was the bird of Athena and symbolized the renewal of life, it was later employed in Christianity to symbolize the Holy Spirit arriving from heaven. What is interesting about its use in this monument is its appearance alongside the sword. The sword appears in ancient Greek art with Themis, the goddess of justice. It can be seen today held by statues outside courts, such as the one at the Old Bailey in London where the figure holds a sword in one hand and a pair of scales in the other. So, in the Exeter monument the message provided by the inclusion of the dove and the sword is the renewal of life, a message that is brought about by the use of a sword which, with its connotations of justice, tells us that it was a *just* war. Also important

FIGURE 5.4 *The monument at Exeter.*
http://www.flickr.com/photos/simonwaters/

on the Exeter monument is the fact that Victory is depicted standing on a dragon. Often in Classical art Victory is depicted standing on or over the defeated. The figure is often interpreted in art history as Deceit, Intrigue or Rebellion. So in this case the end of the war of attrition is represented through Classical figures, the foe as an allegorical creature.

On the Cardiff monument (see Figure I.1), we find a male nude according to the design information representing Victory in a winged version as in the Classical statue Victory of Samothrace. Although given that Victory was female it appears here that this is fused with Christian imagery appearing also as a winged angel – in Christian symbolism dominion angels often carried swords or sceptres and represented the power and authority of god. However, a look at the face of the angel points to a clear Classical influence and this could easily look down from a pedestal in a Roman city. Angels were important in war monuments, often shown blowing trumpets which in Christian symbolism represents the Day of Judgement and resurrection. Such angels could be depicted as leading soldiers to war or to the afterlife or carrying scrolls which were a symbol of life being recorded officially to indicate the honour being noted officially at the heavenly level.

Also important on the Cardiff Memorial is the use of the wreath held by the soldiers. Modern viewers are more likely to immediately link the wreath with the notion of death as it is commonly used as a floral tribute to the dead in funerals. What we are actually doing by using the wreath in this context is signifying a belief in victory over death, that is, the belief in the existence of an afterlife, but we can also see it used as a symbol of victory in sporting victories such as motor racing and Olympic competitions. As death and victory come together in the use of this symbol in the commemorative war monument, we are led seamlessly into accepting the connotation of victory in a 'just' war and death as not only an unquestionable consequence of war, but something that can be overcome.

The significance of objects is relatively easy to map and their ideological use in the commemorative war monument is not complicated to establish, however, there are more complex images in some monuments. Perhaps unexpectedly, the examination of a more modern monument provides evidence of a more obscure use of an ancient symbol; the commemorative monument to the Royal Signal Corps (Figure 5.5) demonstrates this obscurity.

This is the monument erected to commemorate deaths of members of the Royal Signals Corps in the National Memorial Arboretum in Staffordshire, England. The National Memorial Arboretum was first established in 1997 on a site of about 150 acres of land, and at the time of writing it is home to about 160 dedicated war memorials. According to its website, the Royal Signals Corps is currently '. . . engaged in operational duties across the globe', confirming that they are a contemporary fighting unit, set in this twenty-first century context, the memorial to their dead seems a bizarre image to use. The iconological symbolism of this monument provides the key to the selection of the figure. It is based on the emblem of the Royal Signals Corps: a representation of the Greek figure Mercury.

Mercury was the winged messenger to the gods and appears in winged sandals carrying a caduceus in his left hand.[1] In this memorial 'Mercury' is shown in a flight-type pose, wearing a helmet. Many traditional depictions of Mercury feature a helmet, but usually with wing-like feathers on either side, presumably enabling flight, later the Roman depictions featured no feathers on the helmet, whereas the helmet in this war memorial is featured with a single feather-like attachment on the left side; resulting in a helmet that is much more akin to feathered military headgear than those originally depicted in images of Mercury. The result is a 'militarized' Mercury, far enough removed from the image of a real soldier to glorify their image, but

FIGURE 5.5 *The Royal Signals Corps monument at the National Arboretum.*

with military connotations to enable the viewer to interpret the monument as a commemoration of war instead of an ancient Greek mythical figure. We see similar devices at work in the war memorial at Ashton-under-Lyne (Figure 5.6).

This monument features a wounded soldier exchanging a sword for a laurel wreath with a figure of Victory. By the time WWI was taking place soldiers no longer used swords, but the sculptor J. Ashton Floyd chose to use the sword rather than the more realistic pistol or rifle. We have seen how the sword has been used by the Greeks to signify justice, but Cirlot (2002) suggests that the Romans believed that because of its association with Mars, iron was capable of warding off evil spirits, but

FIGURE 5.6 *The monument at Ashton under Lyne.*

Source: Copyright David Dixon. This work is licensed under the Creative Commons Attribution-Share Alike 2.0 Generic Licence. To view a copy of this licence, visit http://creativecommons.org/licenses/by-sa/2.0/ or send a letter to Creative Commons, 171 Second Street, Suite 300, San Francisco, CA 94105, USA.

that its primary association is of receiving and giving a wound; resulting in meanings of liberty and strength gained through the presence of the sword (Cirlot, 2002:323). We can see that the message of strength is reinforced in the presence of lions at either sides of the memorial. The lions were used particularly in Victorian commemoration to symbolize the power of god. Here the lions guard against evil spirits but their presence also points to their faith and respect of the courage and faith of those they guard. The watch of the stone lion is eternal as is the place of those spirits they guard in the history of the nation. Of course we imagine lions would not be used to guard the tombs of pacifists who objected to the war.

Representation of soldiers on monuments

Much of the meanings of monuments are communicated through the selection of physical features chosen for the representations of soldiers; particularly in the monuments that not only commemorate the WWI, but also in newer commemorative war monuments. Moriarty (1995) referred to these 'soldiers' cast in bronze, marble and stone as depicting 'Greek gods' and belonging to a 'pure' race. This is seen in the examples of the Cardiff Memorial (Figure I.1), the Abertillery monument (Figure 5.7) and the Portsmouth monument (Figure 5.8) designed in different decades, yet sharing similar features.

Typically, the represented participant soldiers in the memorials share faces of perfect symmetrical proportions, square jaws, long slim noses and almond-shaped eyes, their faces can never be considered either plain or unattractive. Locks of hair are carved consistently. Bodies of the soldiers were also often perfect and muscular as seen on the Cardiff Memorial in the introduction. Physical proportions are similarly perfect, they are often tall and slim and, where flesh is uncovered, their bodies are represented as perfectly proportioned, muscular and lean. Such figures can be compared to the soldiers depicted in documentary photographs of WWI who were often malnourished and ill. Novels written by front-line soldiers (Remarque, 1987; Sajer, 2001) speak of constant hunger and dysentery.

The figurative representations of the soldiers create physiognomic stereotypes (Van Leeuwen, 2001:96) that cause the illusion of a common ethnic identity and a race that exists within the nation that shares only desirable physical features. The efforts to create the illusion of the nation as a homogenous group is discussed by Billig (1995) who argues that notions of a homogenous national identity are commonplace in the media and are based on false stereotypes. The practice of racial homogenization here allows the young working-class men who died in squalor, mud and suffering often sleeping in rat-infested trenches containing body-parts of their friends to be represented not as ill, malnourished or desperate but as perfect physical specimens also connoting reverence in the fashion of those placed on pillars by the Romans and Greeks, placing them not in an immediate time frame

FIGURE 5.7 *The WWI monument at Abertillery.*

of death and suffering but one of ancient eternal time as in the realms of the Greek gods fusing this with the nature of nation.

The common denominator in the represented physique of the soldier in the war memorials is strength; this is evident in the muscular bodies and strong, square jaw lines of the soldiers. This fictitious racial stereotype works well to create the myth of ethnic nationalism, giving the appearance of the required strength to its military force; a strength that is needed to enable it to fulfil wider political aims of conquest during war. Theories on the relationship between warfare and nationhood can help to elucidate on the wider role the commemorative war monuments play in creating and maintaining a particular relationship between an individual and their

FIGURE 5.8 *Monument to a WWII soldier in Portsmouth.*

government's military establishment. But this is, of course, never represented through actual concrete accounts of what that relationship was but through symbolism.

The importance of military recruitment to the survival of the nation is discussed by Posen (1993) who argues that warfare is made possible through promotion of nationalism. Posen is one of the few authors to examine the link between nationalism and the military. He argues that not only does nationalism increase the intensity of warfare, but:

> . . . it is purveyed by states for the express purpose of improving their military capabilities. (1993:81)

A crucial point made by Posen is the egalitarian appearance that nationalist ideology manages to promote through its military recruitment from all social classes. It has to be said that it is difficult to argue that the military is solely an elitist instrument of domestic repression when the opportunity to belong to the army is open to all sections of society and, theoretically, the opportunity to rise to higher ranks is open to those who enter at the basic level. Indeed, when looking at the way the British army is promoted in the media through advertising campaigns and within their own marketing literature, we see that the training and skills which the army offers to recruits are foregrounded as the main advantage of British army life; training and skills that those with limited or no qualifications at secondary school level might otherwise find difficult to access in civilian life (Abousnnouga, 2005).

However, Posen forthrightly argues that elites trick the lower classes into thinking they are engaging in an egalitarian form of democracy by widespread military recruitment. He demonstrates how nationalism has been used by elites both to prepare citizens for possible wars and to intensify ongoing wars. He pinpoints the 'problem' faced by elites: how to maintain support of soldiers once on the battlefield when:

> . . . the problem becomes how to keep these dispersed, scared, lonely individuals risking their own lives, and cooperating to take the lives of others. (1993:84)

Posen further argues that through the sponsorship of cultural and ideological components of nationalism, citizens will be prepared and ready to take up arms and continue in battle and asserts:

> The more successful states are in achieving this goal, the more competitive they will be. (1993:84)

In his discussion, he claims that the promotion of nationalism is achieved through literacy and ideology delivered to the citizens through schools, media and indoctrination within the military. States, therefore, act purposefully to produce nationalism because of its utility in mass mobilization warfare, and nationalism is the answer to the problem created by a vast increase in deaths due to advancement of military technology; nationalism will provide more willing volunteers; more soldiers to commit to ever-demanding warfare. The representations of masculinity that we find in commemorative war monuments, such as those in Cardiff and Exeter, present such an idealized sense of positive self-identity for young male participant viewers that they can only serve to add to the nationalist ideological package.

We can also begin to think about what we are seeing here in terms of the recontextualization of social practice. We have substitution of the actual weapons used for ones which signify justice. Rather than artillery shells, guns and hand grenades we find swords and heraldry shields. We have substitution of the suffering front-line soldiers for perfect physical forms drawing on Greek imagery. We have addition of religious symbolism and Classical architectural forms connoting higher ideals of social organization and truth. These combine to change what was a squalid war of attrition into something noble intertwined with layers of mystical importance. While of course we wouldn't expect the viewing public at the time to take on these discourses and in the last chapter the evidence was quite the opposite. But over time it appeared that along with other forms of realizations of discourses of nationalism and celebration of war have helped to maintain its place in society as a reasonable social practice. In the introduction to this book we asked if instead of finding these monuments in our towns and cities we found those that ridiculed war, that reminded us of the exploitation it involved, or at least the effects on civilians around the world whose worlds are torn apart under the rule of the weapon and the military.

In this section we have dealt with the representation of soldiers in the monuments and we have also seen that other figures from Classical and Christian symbolism are present. What we have said nothing of so far is who is absent from these representations. One important aspect of the recontextualization of social practice is deletion. Here we ask if any elements of the actual social practices are absent. So far we have seen that enemies are for the most part absent except in symbolic form and only when the victor is represented in the form of a deity. This part of war, the people who need to be killed, is not represented. This has an interesting cumulative effect as monuments appear over time. The impassive soldiers are remembered as soldiers often holding weapons or with artillery or machine guns nearby where it is important to signal specific roles. We are told on inscriptions that they gave their lives for god and nation. But the killing, the process of the events that took their lives, is absent. In WWI, monuments that have set powerful precedents in British war commemoration needed to almost delete the actual war itself and replace it with ancient history and Classical high ideals and eternity. We will be saying more about this process as we carry out our discussion. But also omitted are civilians in the territories where the battle took place and those of the elite class who managed the war. Missing are the horrifically mutilated who poured back across to Britain throughout the war and who remained largely invisible in public life. Missing are the grieving parents, wives and children.

The meaning potential of pose

Borg (1991) comments that, in contrast to earlier war monuments that featured officers, representations of the soldier who fights and dies without questioning the necessity of war were increasingly featured in the British war monuments erected following WWI. Semiotic choices can be used not only to communicate ideas about the meaning of war and the identities of the soldiers but also about the ideas and attitudes those soldiers hold towards war. One way that designers accomplished this was through pose.

On the figures of most of the soldiers found on the monuments, facial expressions are impassive, showing no particular emotion. Historians relate this representation back to the Greek sculpture of the 'Soldier of Marathon'. He depicts a soldier from legend who ran the 42 km from Marathon to Athens to announce the Greek victory where he collapsed and died of exhaustion. He became associated with the essence of the virtuous hero who gives his life for his homeland. His figure became familiar in later Renaissance representations of courage, patriotism and stoicism, such as in Johan Tobias Sergel's *The Dying Othryades* (1779) and Jean Pierre Cortot's *The Soldier of Marathon Announcing the Victory* (1834). It is this same stoicism and impassivity that is used to represent the faces of the young working-class men who died in the mud of France and Belgium. Van Leeuwen and Wodak (1999) write of the importance of people's reactions in the recontextualization of social practice. Actual facts and details are substituted by feelings, emotions and attitudes. We can imagine the actual kinds of expressions and reactions that could in fact represent war more accurately. Remarque (1987) gives a sense of more appropriate expressions when he describes soldiers listening to a dying, wounded man lying in no man's land calling out all for several days for his wife.

On the Royal Artillery monument in Hyde Park, London (Figure 5.9), the soldier's facial expression is also stoic and impassive. His pose is also important and it is clear that much thought and discussion went into these. Soldiers were often depicted either striding slowly forward or standing as if waiting. Evidence from monument planning committees and government guidance shows that all suggestion of aggression or violence was to be avoided (Bourke, 1996). There was to be no reference to the brutality or callousness of war.

Many of these depictions of soldiers clearly draw on the Egyptian canon in the sculpting of powerful figures. Such works typically displayed strong arms, with muscles clenched, the jaw is strong and jutting forwards and feet are stable on the ground where one foot strides forwards suggesting purpose (Davis, 1989). In Figure 5.7, we can see this as regards the Abertillery monument. Here the soldier is not particularly muscular but has one foot placed in front of the other. Also, on the Royal Artillery monument (Figure 5.9) we find the impassive soldier standing feet apart unmovable and firm in his belief.

Other poses suggest confidence and ease. The monument at Abergavenny in Figure 5.10 depicts a soldier with his upper body leaning on his upturned gun, legs apart, with his weight on his back leg and using his front leg as a prop for the gun. The pose is casual as that adopted by

FIGURE 5.9 *The Royal Artillery monument in Hyde Park, London.*

a gardener leaning on his spade and stopping to admire the fruits of his labour. The pose functions to communicate the soldier's satisfaction and contentment, but the viewer is not specifically told what the soldier is contented with, is it the sense of achievement from killing he has had by the use of the gun or is it the sacrifice of his own life?

Figure 5.11 depicts a sailor, half-naked, trousers rolled up, feet bare, his large, muscular frame sitting astride a small boat that is oddly tiny in comparison to the sailor himself. He effortlessly guides the boat with only one hand, his right hand, his left hand pulling back on the line. From his face we see he maintains a watchful gaze, protecting from those who might harm us, dutifully absorbed in the task; on the same monument we also find that Victory is depicted in an energetic pose reaching upwards to heaven.

FIGURE 5.10 *The monument at Abergavenny.*

Often soldiers such as in case of the Abertillery monument appear almost childlike in their expression as their faces carry an artlessness and innocence. This is also of importance in this particular statue in terms of the act of the removal of the hat from the head. On the one hand it is symbol of respect to remove one's hat. But the bearing of the head in this way was also a Christian symbol of bearing oneself before god, also suggesting vulnerability and innocence. Bearing the naked head and also baldness has been considered in many religions as connected to humility. In this sense while this figure shows no fear and certainly no aggression and a certain ease as he steps forward, this is a slightly different representation to some of the more confident and solid soldiers found on other monuments.

Nudity too here is important as in the case of the sailor shown above. This symbolism is also part of Classical and Christian themes. Greek artists came to think that clothing and other objects were distractions from the true self that could be revealed in the body (Stewart, 1997). One repeated theme in Renaissance art iconography was that of the two aspects

FIGURE 5.11 *The Exeter WWI monument.*

of love: the divine and the earthly. The former, which was the superior of
the two, was to be depicted as naked in order to symbolize contempt for
all material things in the world (Hall, 1974:226). From this, nakedness
itself became associated with truth (Ripa, 1539, in Van Straten, 1994).
Nakedness in Christian symbolism also came to mean an awareness of sin.
Eve is often depicted as naked, the primal innocence of the Garden of Eden,
also symbolized being naked before god. Even in more recent monuments,
along with other Classical themes we find such uses of nudity. This can be
seen in the Armed Forces Memorial in Figure 5.12. A naked dead soldier
is gently manoeuvred by two colleagues while one other highly muscular
soldier without a shirt chisels an inscription and another points the way
through an open door.

The scene, according to the sculptor, draws on images from Homer's
Iliad and the *Trojan War* where the body of Patroclus was carried on a

FIGURE 5.12 *The Armed Forces Memorial at the National Memorial Arboretum.*

shield by fellow Greek soldiers back to the grieving Achilles, whose armour he had borrowed.

The figures of the soldiers in this scene follow the Classical conventions, although their musculature is given additional attention. Van Leeuwen (1996) refers to such representation of physical features as 'overdetermination'. This can be done both biologically and culturally, for example, through physical attributes or clothing respectively. Like overlexicalization in language (Teo, 2000), where we would find an abundance of particular words and their synonyms this kind of visual representation gives a sense of overpersuasion and is normally evidence that something is problematic or of ideological contention. In the case of this sculpture why is it that all of the soldiers have such overdeveloped musculature? In photographs of soldiers in ongoing wars we do not see such bodies. When we read the accounts of front-line soldiers (Remarque, 1987; Sajer, 2001) we are told of the constant hunger, food shortages, awful sanitation and terrible health of soldiers. This, rather than excessively healthy soldiers, is the reality of the chaos, disruption and suffering that is war. The overdetermination clearly reflects a need to overcompensate.

The process of recontextualization we are seeing here involves the abstraction of war into the realms of the Classical, the heroic and the mythical. Nation itself and its call to participate become fused into this abstraction of the higher ideals of the great civilizations of ancient history.

When viewers were first offered representations of dead soldiers on monuments, however, there was much unrest. When Charles Sargeant Jagger's Memorial to the Royal Artillery was unveiled in Hyde Park, London, in 1925; reactions to the inclusion of a dead soldier were mainly negative (Compton, 1985). The memorial has four soldier figures around its base, one of which is a dead soldier, fully clothed and partially covered by his heavy military coat (see Figure 5.13). When the monument was unveiled it caused controversy from the public who, due to censorship of images of war deaths, were not used to being confronted by images of dead soldiers.

FIGURE 5.13 *The corpse on the Royal Artillery monument in Hyde Park.*

Here, the viewer is confronted with a glimpse of a dead soldier who lies under a coat with no indication of how or when he will be buried. But we find few corpses on British monuments as the authorities and those on commissioning panels were keen to keep away from any overt references of death, preferring the impassioned soldier keeping guard.

Elevation and height

In *Reading Images* (1996), Kress and Van Leeuwen introduced a number of observations about the meaning potentials in visual design that we can extend to think about the height of monuments and how this influences interpersonal relationships with the viewer. In the first place we can think about the observations they made about the relationship between power and angle of viewing. In the case of photographs, they observed that images taken from a low angle force by the viewer to look upwards at the image, thereby affording a position of power to the represented participant in the image over the viewer or we could argue make the viewer feel as if they are looked down upon and therefore inferior or powerless. On the other hand where the viewer looks down on the subject of an image they feel more powerful, or they might sense the relative vulnerability of the subject. This is often used for example by photojournalists to depict children in war zones to connote innocence. We could imagine the effect of a photograph of three dirty children depicted looking down on us from a height.

There is another aspect to height that we can draw out by adapting Kress and Van Leeuwen's (1996) account of the meaning of page placement of elements – whether higher or lower on the page. Van Leeuwen (2005) has discussed the metaphorical associations of height with status, as in 'upper class'. We also associate height with 'loftiness' of ideals, although this can have a negative connotation where we say someone has their head in the clouds. The opposite of this is a person who can be said to be grounded and down to earth or the opposite of lofty ideals could be baseness. It is from these associations that Kress and Van Leeuwen (1996:193) suggest that we think of that which is placed at the top of visual compositions as the 'ideal', whereas that placed at the bottom is the 'real'. So in an advertisement a beautiful woman might appear in the ideal as the fantasy, and the product in the real at the bottom. From this we can think about statues raised onto pedestals as being placed into the ideal, as being higher than the real, the everyday. Figures of soldiers are typically raised up several metres so that the viewer is literally at their feet. Typically in WWI monuments soldiers depicted as Classical gods in peaceful yet determined poses were raised into the ideal realm, into fantasy. We can imagine the difference in meaning if we put a statue of a soldier either on a pedestal of 1 m or 10 m, or if they were placed at the ground level, or even in a small hole. As we will see, later statues have been placed at the ground level rather than raised upwards.

Of course in the case of material objects size itself can create height. And as well as angle and high/low we need to take size into account which also brings its own meaning potential. A figure of a human can be represented naturalistically as we might expect of an average person. Or they could be represented in miniature as in the size of a doll or even a toy soldier. In contrast they could be represented just slightly larger than life, or massively oversized.

The WWI monument figures were mostly slightly larger than life-size at about seven feet in height as can be seen on the Abertillery monument. They are therefore just larger than life. It would not do to have them slightly smaller and less significant, almost childlike and therefore weaker. We can imagine the effect in one of our town squares where a soldier who gave his life for his country is represented and god but who is only the size of a toy soldier. Even if his musculature is overdetermined and his expression impassioned this would not create a sense of force, respect and merger with the eternal Classical civilization populated with gods.

In contrast it would not be appropriate to find a soldier represented in the same dimensions as the monument 'The motherland calls' in Volgorad Russia, unveiled in 1967, which stands 85 m high and symbolizes the end of the battle for Stalingrad. In this case the monument is intended to symbolize the spirit of the whole of the people of Russia as opposed to individual soldiers. And, as Kruk, points out, such outsized monuments were typical of the Soviet Union with its cult of collective identity and of leadership. A soldier of this size in a city centre would indicate that we lived with a cult of the military. If we look around the world at very big statues we find these generally represent dictators. Kruk (2008) has discussed the outsized statues of Stalin in the Soviet Union that were meant to symbolize not so much the man himself but the collective Communist spirit. Michalski (1998:197) describes the use of such massive monuments as part of a 'ruler's cult'.

In terms of degrees of elevation WWI figures tend to be placed on plinths that allow them to stand roughly six feet above the ground as in the Abertillery monument. The plinths force the viewer to look upwards to the figure, creating a power relationship between them and the figure. The represented figures have to be physically looked up to. Conversely, if they were at eye level the viewer would relate to the figure as an equal, or if placed lower the figure would be looked down on as when looking at a child. Placing the figures literally out of reach gives them special status in the viewer/figure interactive relationship; the dead soldiers aren't engaged with the viewer as an equal, nor are they devoid of strength and power, instead they are elevated to the ideal; a place that commands respect from the viewer gained by the lifting of their heads upwards. In this sense we find the impassive yet innocent soldier in the Abertillery monument, who steps forward slightly without fear, slightly larger than life and idealized as we look up to him.

We do find shifting uses of elevation and height by monument designers over time as can be seen in the Abertillery monument (Figure 5.7) of a WWI figure, 'The Yomper' Falklands War Memorial (Figure 5.14) erected in 1992 and the Portsmouth monument dedicated to those who died in WWII erected in 1997 (Figure 5.8). The Abertillery statue is of a typical height for war monument sculpture, slightly larger than life-size; this way, when raised high on the plinth it appears as normal height, but slightly larger than life, from the perspective of the viewer.

The figure of 'The Yomper' departs significantly from the practice of life-sized representation. 'The Yomper', sculpted by Phillip Jackson and unveiled in 1992, takes its subject matter from images from the Falklands/ Malvinas Islands that were the subject of a power struggle in 1982 between

FIGURE 5.14 *'The Yomper', the monument to the Falklands War in Portsmouth.*

Britain and Argentina. Photographs of the soldiers carrying the Union Jack flag, walking or 'yomping' towards Port Stanley appeared in British newspapers at that time and are described by Boorman (2005:35) as one of '. . . the enduring images of the Falklands War'. Although 'The Yomper' does not stand on an elevated plinth, it is huge in proportion: about twice life-size. Its strength comes largely from its enormous proportions and reflects the political climate that surrounded the events in the Falkland/ Malvinas Islands in 1982.

By 1982 Britain was no longer a major colonial power in the world, yet when challenged for territory by Argentina, its government was able to respond with some considerable force, sending its army halfway around the world to demonstrate to Argentina its determination to hold on to the territory in the face of counter-claims by Argentina. The political mood was reflected in the press at the time, where the rhetoric was largely aggressive and jingoistic in nature. Although not raised into the ideal by means of a plinth, the imposing height of 'The Yomper' does raise the figure high into the ideal, and in doing so it embodies the nature of that particular war; it looms over the viewer, its size connoting continued power and strength of the nation, demonstrated by their military capability. In complete contrast to 'The Yomper' is the 'Soldier of WWII' by the artist Vivien Mallock (Figure 5.8).

After WWII there was no nation-wide movement in Britain to commission war monuments as there had been after WWI. Furlong et al. (2003) suggest that this was down to the much lower casualty figures in WWII, saying that this is the reason that new memorials were considered unnecessary. To commemorate the WWII dead, the names of the dead servicemen were usually inscribed on a plaque and attached to a section of the existing WWI commemorative monument in each city, town or village. But what we would also like to argue is that there was not so nearly so much political reason to foster nationalism in the same way. Much of this had been done through propaganda during the war and there was a sense of relief as the war was over and what had been established was a truly evil enemy who had carried our extensive bombings on the homeland had been defeated and invasion avoided.

Nearly 50 years having elapsed since WWII there was a revival in the construction of monuments to the servicemen or this war as many of the actual participants had begun to grow old. We will be looking at a range of these newer monuments in later chapters. One of these is Vivien Mallock's WWII soldier. Here the soldier is represented through a life-size model of a young man; head bowed, looking sad, tired and clutching a letter from home. This sculpture departs from the style of previous war monument sculptures in terms of size but mainly due to the angle it is viewed from. The height of this monument encourages the viewer to look slightly down towards the young soldier who appears to be not much more than a child. The relationship of adult to a child is enacted in the height differential between the figure and the viewer. This change in height profoundly impacts on the viewer/sculpture relationship; no imposing, awe-inspiring power is connoted, the viewer looks down at the seated soldier and in doing so is encouraged to view the soldier with tenderness and pity rather than awe.

The lack of celebration of victory is notable when considering the war it commemorates ended in victory. There is no Classicism, no reference to glorious ancient civilizations. The low plinth here places the soldier not in the ideal but in the real. At the time discourses of war had begun to represent soldiers not as idealized impassionate or artless heroes but as ordinary human beings. There was more of a focus on the experiences of the humanized soldiers as they were 'in action' overseas, than on the reasons for the conflict or the aims of the faceless enemy who makes them suffer. Instead of awe, viewers are encouraged to feel familiarity with this soldier and to see him as an individual. Its lack of elevation provides access that the viewer can even touch the figure removing the boundaries of the earlier monuments. Combined with the sad expression and pose of the figure the height differential between viewer and representation creates unequal power differentials between viewer and the represented soldier. We argue that this differential is achieved through a combination of facial expression, bodily pose and angle that have all combined to create a relationship akin to that of a child and an adult; which in turn encourages the viewer to feel tenderness towards the soldier. This view is supported by reported reactions to the statue by a viewer whose letter appears on the sculptor's website. Ted Reynolds wrote:

> . . . I looked across the road and saw the new statue of a wartime soldier that brought tears to my eyes. (T. Reynolds, in a letter to Vivien Mallock, online reference)

In another letter, the same writer describes seeing a woman weeping in front of the statue, her husband had been killed as a young soldier in the battle of Arnhem and the woman now frequently visits the statue and talks to it as if it were her husband. The statue obviously invokes strong emotions in some viewers, the writer of the letter is an ex-serviceman who fought in WWII; he relates to the statue that he says captures a familiar scene he has in his memory, whereas the woman imagines the statue as a representation of her dead husband.

It could be argued that these responses would be different if the represented soldier was depicted in a different stance or pose, such as that depicted in the Paddington statue. The soldier in the monument at Paddington Station, London (Figure 5.15), is also shown reading a letter from home, but standing tall, upright, rather than sitting with a bowed head.

FIGURE 5.15 *A WWI soldier at Paddington Station.*

When compared alongside each other it becomes apparent that the two statues communicate very different viewer/represented participant relationships. Although the situation is similar in both monuments, receiving a letter from home, it is the power differential created by the height and viewing angle that encourages a different relationship with the viewer. Even the rare representation of a dead soldier in the Royal Artillery Memorial at Hyde Park Corner, London, gives power to the soldier due to its elevated position:

As Kress and Van Leeuwen (2006) argue:

> . . . if a represented participant is seen from a high angle . . . the represented participant is seen from the point of view of power. (p. 140)

It may be that the emotional reactions of the viewers of the WWII soldier in Portsmouth are triggered by this inversion of power. We are used to seeing soldiers represented as powerful in British commemorative war monuments, when confronted with a powerless soldier we are forced to consider the reality that war can render the hero weak. Could it be that it is the possibility that his weakness will leave us undefended that frightens us?

We have seen that it is the choice of vertical angle that partly makes the monument to the WWII soldier in Portsmouth stand out among figurative memorials that feature soldiers, because it results in connoting vulnerability rather than strength. This latter departure from the connotative meaning found in traditional monuments points on the one hand to changing discourse of war and soldiery emerging in the late twentieth/early twenty-first century. However, in later chapters as we move on to look at a range of more contemporary monuments we do still find much evidence that war is nevertheless being at the same time legitimized in much the same way recontextualizing it away from the actual horrors that are its reality.

Conclusion

In this chapter we have begun our analysis of the way the monuments themselves communicate. This has permitted us to begin to show how the designers realized the kinds of communicative purposes established in the previous chapter – to draw the angry and restless working class population away from their bitterness about the war and the way it provided evidence of social inequalities and the abusive position of the ruling elite. We have seen how war and the participants in war are represented through Classical and Christian references to communicate high ideals and the destiny of the nation. What these ordinary working-class people did was not simply die in squalid pointless deaths, cast into the grinding machine of a colonial war by greedy rulers as is represented in the Stadler cartoons seen in the introduction to this book, but formed part of a noble and glorious higher level of being with the promise of reward by god. They themselves became part of the glory of the protection of the nation itself. Such was the commitment of these soldiers that they stand impassively totally immersed in the cause or artless and gentle, energetic and lively or powerfully guarding. We also began to think about the social relations created by these monuments by looking at the use of elevation by designers to place the figures of the soldiers high into the ideal. As we shall see in later chapters many of these semiotic choices change in more contemporary monuments. But what we shall also see in the next chapter is that studying use of other semiotic resources used by designers helps us clarify what it is that we are seeing communicated, to better identify where the social practice of war is being recontextualized.

Note

1 A caduceus is the staff, or wand, that Hermes is said to have used to separate two fighting snakes; hence its subsequent use as a sign of peace.

CHAPTER SIX

The materiality of monuments

In this chapter we move onto the meaning potential of the materiality of monuments. We look at the semiotic meaning potential of design choices of different kinds of stone and metals. We then move onto how monuments can create or foster interaction with those represented on them and finally on to the representation of action on monuments. We show that it is important to ask what figures are represented as doing as well as their appearance and positioning as considered in the previous chapter. At the end of the chapter we bring together the tools from this chapter with those from the previous chapter to analyse a monument that on first glance may be considered as anti-war. We show that a closer analysis, using the tools we have developed, suggests something quite different.

The meaning potential of materials

When designing a monument intended for use in an open space, artists must choose a material that is durable as they sit in open public spaces; initially, this constraint may appear to limit possibilities for analysis of the material as a semiotic resource. However, Kress and Van Leeuwen (2006) point out that the durability itself is a sign for the attitudes society has towards their heroic figures:

> It is no accident that the statues erected to commemorate heroic figures are made of durable materials, or that tombstones are still carved: the durability of the materials makes them usable signifiers for the meanings of permanent feelings we intend to produce. (p. 225)

War monuments have been produced in a range of materials that have very different meaning potentials. In the last chapter we were looking at monuments that were predominantly produced using bronze, such as the one at Paddington Station in London (Figure 5.15), the following two monuments are produced in different materials: marble in the monument at Cowbridge (Figure 6.1) and stone in the case of the monument at Almeley (Figure 6.2).

In the example at Paddington Station, despite the poignant action of reading a letter from home, the soldier appears sturdy; this is partly due to the characteristics of the material: bronze, is a naturally dark colour and heavy in weight. In addition, the sculptor has chosen to place the coat on the soldier's shoulders, letting it widen out at the hem; a feature that emphasizes the broadness of the soldier's shoulders. The appearance of the soldier wearing such a heavy garment with apparent ease seems to make this soldier appear strong to the viewer, but how do viewers

FIGURE 6.1 *The WWI monument at Cowbridge.*

interpret strength through materiality? Kress and Van Leeuwen (2001:75) explain this by relating appropriate material signifiers to humans' ability to match concepts on the basis of their physical experiences of the relevant materials.

According to Kress and Van Leeuwen's (2001) principle viewers interpret the soldier's strength metaphorically through a combination of the known heavy weight of the material and the dimensions of the garments, understood through their '. . . physical experiences of the relevant materials' (p. 75). Perhaps we can better understand this effect if we imagine the other two figures (Figures 6.1 and 6.2) cast in bronze instead of the white marble and stone and vice versa.

The memorial at Cowbridge is cast in white marble. This is a good example with which to explore Kress and Van Leeuwen's (2001) point regarding the flexibility and multimedial nature of semiotic principles and the importance of defining the key principles that lie at the basis of synaesthetic correspondences. The material selected here, white marble, has a range of experiential meaning potentials to the viewer; where 'experiential' references to a viewer's possible previous encounter with the material. The qualities of marble are cold, heavy and smooth. For many years its coldness was exploited in the food retail industry where thick marble slabs were traditionally used in small food retail outlets as counters and cutting blocks for cheese and cold meats.

However, the heavy and cold qualities of the material give way to its smoothness when drawing on its correspondence with Classical art. In this context marble lends antiquity to the meaning widening the meaning potential of the war monument. The use of marble goes back to the sculpture of much earlier periods: Ancient Greek, Roman and Renaissance art, such as that of Michelangelo, the Italian renaissance artist.

In the context of more modern public art, the choice of material gives extra support to the meaning potential of the monument when considered in conjunction with the pose of the soldier. The Cowbridge soldier represented in a pose that signifies mourning, physical strength and a show of might are not relevant to this action; mental strength here being a more important attribute. The use of smooth, white marble enhances this action, bringing elegance to the pose, whereas bronze would bring with it an unnecessary physical strength. It could be argued that by using this material the artist gives the soldier a link to much older civilizations, placing him in a tradition going back many centuries, and in doing so, naturalizes and legitimizes his place in society.

This link to ancient traditions is also connoted by the use of stone that has been used for centuries to create representations of nobility, kings and saints. Viewers draw on their experiential associations of seeing stone figures adorning ancient buildings, and that they also draw on their knowledge of their cultural practice which uses stone to create those buildings. This practice of building ancient castles and cathedrals in stone give the material a meaning potential of longevity and ancientness and ties it to the established dominant institutions of monarchy and religion. In addition, stone has an organic quality that lends a concept of naturalness and evolution to the object it forms. Comparing the stone and bronze soldiers also enables us to appreciate the association of physical strength that bronze gives to the soldier.

Kress and Van Leeuwen (1996, 2001, 2006) have highlighted the multiple qualities of materials; they note that once artists had a wider selection of materials available to them from which they could create their pieces the material itself became an integrated part of the work:

> . . . the material becomes a fully exploitable and exploited resource. (2006:224)

While stone carries strength in its use as a building material, it also has the ability to be carved easily into smooth, rounded shapes giving sculpted figures softness. The WWI stone soldier in Almeley (Figure 6.2) seems a much softer, gentler person than his bronze comrade in Exeter (Figure 5.11);

FIGURE 6.2 *The WWI soldier at Almeley.*

this is partly due to the pose and facial expression, but the material also brings its share of physical softness to the meaning potential of the image, although part of this will come from the Classical references to higher ideal and high thinking that this material can bring.

In choosing bronze to cast their statues, the war memorial artists have brought extended meanings of strength and power to the soldier and to war. By rejecting white marble or stone they background meanings related to other human characteristics: purity, beauty, softness and elegance. They could also have chosen to cast the soldiers in aluminium, for example, like the famous statue depicting an archer 'The Angel of Christian Charity' in Piccadilly, London. This was the first public statue in the world to be cast in aluminium, although the fountain on which the statue sits is cast in bronze, the artist chose aluminium to cast the naked winged archer.

Clearly, a winged archer must be light to enable effortless flight; consequently a heavy bronze would not suit the representation, the light weight of the aluminium harmonizing with the object. Unsurprisingly then, the use of aluminium was not taken up by the war memorial artists. Had they chosen aluminium there may have been a sense of lightness and fineness; altering the meaning potential of the object into a light, fine soldier.

We can also draw out the meaning potential of these materials by thinking a little more about what would not be appropriate and why. Treated stainless steel could be durable but this would not bring the same connotations of timelessness that can be brought by bronze or stone. And, along with metals such as titanium, steel suggests something created by factory process as opposed to that which was forged or carved by hand. And it is this level of human involvement, craft and care that must be signified. Perhaps one of the most durable materials that create problems for waste disposal is certain plastics. But this would again communicate factory or scientific-based processes and not hand-made. Additionally plastic suggests something cheaper as a commodity. Other monuments around the world have used different materials but clearly the meanings were very different. For example, the Minnesota five-story high Iwo Jima monument erected in 2002 to commemorate the savage sacrifice that war requires of life includes a steel silhouette of the classic photograph of the soldiers hoisting the flag. This is positioned over a realistic mural of Iwo Jima with real boulders at its base. Here clearly the connotations here are not related to eternity nor durability, but use an iconic image associated with determination along with a brutal war scene to tell something of the horror of war that is endured by soldiers which has tended to be a theme more typical of American war monuments.

The Korean war-veterans memorial erected in 1995 in Washington depicts 19 stainless steel soldiers walking over a landscape that resembles the rice-paddies of Korea. Again different meanings are created for a war that was more of a modern war and less easily drawn into the meanings of Classicism and ancient bronze furnaces. In terms of pose and figure type these soldiers are also less idealized and portrayed walking slightly stooped with their capes blowing in the icy Korean wind. In this sense both of these American monuments seek to represent setting in a way that the UK monuments do not, even in the case of more recent UK monuments. What is important in these US monuments is where the soldiers fought and the conditions in which they did so. Particularly in British WWI monuments location and conditions are completely abstracted and substituted for impassioned expressions, forceful poses, Classical architecture and materials that connote the past and eternity. The US monuments rather communicate the endurance of war even if, like the British monuments they silence the broader social effects of war on the local communities, the effects of weaponry on bodies and the arms industry that supplies them.

One other important aspect of materiality is solidity versus hollowness. We will be dealing with this meaning potential more in later chapters. But we will mention it here briefly. The WWI monuments represent the figures as solid 3D objects. Other statues, as we have seen, can involve different choices. The Minnesota Iwo Jima monument uses a 2D outline of the soldiers raising the US flag on the Island. While other monuments have rendered this scene in 3D in this case it appears enough to index the iconic image as a way of signalling the identity of the scene. And these 2D soldiers are placed high into the ideal, floating over the mural. We will see in the following chapter on the representation of women on monuments that there are degrees of 2D–3D realization as elements can be represented in-between. And certainly it is clear that 2D representations have not been favoured as appropriate to commemorate soldiers whereas, for example, members of the gentry were happy to be represented for posterity in oil paintings. Clearly though such a genteel and fragile representation would not be suitable for the communication of eternity. And we can imagine the very different physical presence of a painting which lacks the physical presence and solidity of the bronze or stone statue.

But what we do not find on WWI monuments is hollowness. The monument of Oscar Wilde, for example, that stands outside Charing Cross station, London, is hollow. This suggests vulnerability, transparency and complexity, suitable for representing the complex character of Wilde. Such representations, however, would not be suitable for the commemoration of soldiers unless this meaning was intended. Such an image of a fragmented transparent soldier might be more fitting for anti-war design that pointed to the way the soldier was fragile and used. In our chapter on contemporary war monuments we do find one example which does suggest more fragility in the Merchant Seamen's WWII Memorial in Cardiff Bay. Here we related this to changing discourses of war and a humanization of the soldier.

Speech acts and gaze

Human gaze behaviour is complex. Either fixing or avoiding one's gaze can signal extreme emotional states, just as it does among animals, but in its simple form gaze among humans is a cue to our verbal interaction, as Morris (2002), biologist and anthropologist, says:

> It is, in fact, the evolution of speech that has made eye contact such a significant and useful human signalling device. (p. 107)

Adapting semiotic features of Halliday's (1985) theory of speech acts, Kress and Van Leeuwen (1996, 2006) show that we can think more systematically about the way that non-linguistic communication can create different types of relationship between image and viewer that we can draw upon to think about monuments. When we speak, Halliday argued, we can do one of four basic things: offer information; offer services or goods; demand information; demand goods and services. In each case there is an expected or alternative response possible. Kress and Van Leeuwen (1996) thought images could fulfil two of these: 'offer' and 'demand'. So images can be seen by viewers as referencing actual acts of interaction in talk.

Both speech acts and image acts can be realized by 'mood systems'. For example, in speech, commands can realize the imperative mood as in 'Don't do it!' Offers can be realized by the indicative mood as in 'You won't like this'. And we can indicate our attitude through other cues such as tone of voice and posture. In images we can find both demands and offers realized visually along with the form of address. In an advertising image an attractive person might look out at us promoting a particular banking service. This has two functions. On the one hand this creates a form of visual address – the viewer is acknowledged. On the other it produces an image act meaning that the image is used to do something to the viewer. This is what Kress and Van Leeuwen (1996:124) describe as a 'demand image'. It asks something of the viewer in an imaginary relationship, so they feel that their presence is acknowledged and, just as when someone addresses us in social interaction, some kind of response is required.

The kind of demand, the mood of the address, is then influenced by other factors. There might be a slight frown that is unwelcoming and maintains a social distance. There might be a warm smile as in the case of the advertising image, along with an open posture. In real life we know that certain kinds of demands require certain kinds of responses. If someone smiles at us we must smile back or risk offending them. Of course in the case of the advertising image we know that there will be no consequences if we even stick our tongue out at the woman selling the banking services. But for Kress and Van Leeuwen we still recognize the demand.

In the case of war monuments the figures do not look at the viewer. The interactive relationship between the viewer and the figures is restricted due to the tendency of the figures to gaze upwards, downwards or away into the distance, making eye contact with the viewer impossible from the usual viewing angle.

The following three examples illustrate the effects of gaze: the first example, in the monument at Paddington Station, London (Figure 5.15), we see the figure reading a letter from home; the second in Exeter (Figure 5.11) features several figures, all of whom look into the distance and the third, situated in Maesteg (see Figure 6.4), has the figure looking straight ahead. In the case of the Maesteg example if we take the bayonet he is holding into account, we could say he is engaging eye contact with an imaginary enemy.

It is clear that the artists are making a choice in not engaging with the viewer, but what does this say about the relationship we, the viewer, are meant to have with the soldier? The figures demand nothing of us. They simply offer themselves for our viewing. If a civilian looks out at us from a war-torn city in a news-photograph they share their grief and pain with us. The demand is that we respond in some way, with pity, and even with our money if the image is a particular charity for war victims. The soldiers on these monuments are not asking us to respond to their suffering, their horror and their squalid deaths. Consequently, the viewer is a mere voyeur separated by the social distance created by the lack of eye contact. We are not encouraged to 'ask' the represented soldier about his experiences; nor can we ask the wider questions about the point of war or his opinion on that war.

The viewer is led to see their relationship with the soldier in a particular way, not quite as an individual they would readily interact with as they would with a relative, or a friend, but as someone who exists outside of their realm of interaction, as in a person depicted looking off frame in a news photograph. This has continued through to contemporary monuments.

We can imagine the oddness of being looked at by all the soldiers walking bleakly through the paddy fields in the Korean veteran's monument. If they did what facial expression would be possible and appropriate? What if the soldier on the Cardiff monument looked out at us from his mini-acropolis? In this case they might be asking questions of us, as to why they are there, why they died and why are we still alive. But these figures are also in a kind of sleep mode. They are generally often almost trancelike in a realm between life and death typical of Christian symbolism.

The implied gaze, however, can be a powerful tool on the monument. We can see this in the 'Shot at Dawn' Memorial at the National Memorial Arboretum (Figure 6.10). This monument represents the soldier with his eyes covered completely; it helps us to appreciate the importance of the eyes being visible to the viewer in artistic representation of figures. The covering of the soldier's eyes removes the opportunity to have an interpersonal relationship with the viewer on any level; he stands there alone in his terrifying world. The monument was erected to commemorate the 'Shot at Dawn' events: cruel executions of WWI soldiers by their own army. As will be demonstrated in the discussion of this monument in a later section, the connotations brought to the meaning potential by its other elements do not, however, lead the viewer to criticize these events.

Interpersonal interaction can also be influenced by the way monuments are constructed with regard to allowing degree of proximity. We deal with this specifically in Chapter Eight where we look at more contemporary monuments which are designed to 'implicate' those who visit them as part of a learning experience. We also see this in the design of the Portsmouth monument in Figure 5.8. But WWI monuments generally used a range of devices to precisely create social distance. This could be achieved simply by height in the case of the Abertillery monument (Figure 5.7). But in other cases, as in the Cardiff monument (Figure I.1) the figures are separated from the viewing space by stone borders which were also surrounded by flower beds. And as we find in this later chapter there has been a shift towards soldiers being placed in the everyday in much more intimate rather than remote relationships with the viewer. In so many ways the figures on the WWI monuments were idealized and remote, hovering in a mythical realm between life and death where they fuse with ancient and glorious ideas and times. And while earlier monuments were given borders to keep people at a social distance so later ones began to seek to draw viewers with their boundaries and walk among them.

Transitivity on monuments

In this section we begin to deal with what the figures of war monuments are depicted as doing. One of the elements of discourses as well as participants, places and ideas, some of which we have begun to deal with, are sequences of activity. Transitivity in linguistic analysis refers, broadly, to who does what to whom, and how. This allows us to reveal who plays an important role in a particular clause and who receives the consequences of that action. A transitivity analysis can show us who is mainly given a subject (agent/participant) or object (affected/patient) position. As we explained in Chapter Three, Halliday (1978) identified six classifications of verb processes. Particularly useful here are: material verbs where there is a result or consequence; mental processes where people sense things or think things; behavioural processes which depict psychological or physiological actions; existential processes where someone or something is present. Of course in actual war the micro details of verb processes would involve material verbs of killing and destroying where the soldiers were the agents, if unwilling ones. It would also involve soldiers and civilians being in the affected/patient position of being the victims of attacks and wounding. It would most certainly involve mental processes of terror and hysteria. We can look, therefore for the way that analysis of transitivity reveals processes of recontextualization.

The huge war monument in Newcastle (Figure 6.3) by the sculptor Sir William Goscombe John offers a good starting point from which to explore transitivity. The theme of this monument is recorded as being the raising of the four battalions of the Northumberland Fusiliers in response to the call to war (Borg, 1991) and according to the information held by the national archives (Your Archives, The National Archives, online reference) it was commissioned privately by Sir George and Lady Renwick to also commemorate the safe return of their five sons from war and Sir George Renwick's 50-year anniversary in public life.

The sculpture's main feature is a large crowd scene, a procession of life-size figures can be seen; said to represent the volunteers who had joined the forces and now enthusiastically going off to war. Other figures such as women, children, drummers and a representation of the mythological winged Victory can be seen floating above the group blowing a horn which is the symbol of the Day of Judgement.

According to Borg (1991) this memorial represents the 'patriotic confidence' with which Britain entered the war. This is a singular representation of military recruitment in WWI. After an initial enthusiasm that brought about a million volunteers forward, other measures, such as changing the age limits for entry into military service and conscription had

FIGURE 6.3 *'The Response', Newcastle.*

to be introduced to compensate for the decrease in volunteers; resulting in an army numbering nearly five million (Dewey, 1984). And in fact it is well documented that the British government had great difficulty recruiting from the North East of Britain and had to send soldiers north to close down printing presses that were highly critical of what they described as a colonial war (Curran and Seaton, 1977). Nevertheless, the sculpture manages to realize its singular message of enthusiastic, voluntary military service through a number of material and behavioural processes.

This monument gives the viewer a clear sense of a collectivized group moving forward as one. It achieves this by packing the figures closely together and positioning them as if they are moving forward towards their right, or the left, as seen by the viewer. This gives the impression that the whole community responded to the call to arms together without hesitation. Most men are already wearing uniforms and carrying guns, connoting military service, enacting the behavioural process of a readiness to fight. Looking more closely at the group we find its members are carefully individualized with their distinctive features and postures each telling its own individual story. For example, we find two figures at the front of the procession shown drumming, leaning forward suggesting they are eager to move into battle. Others are seen with their arms around women or children, depicted as fathers in the process of protecting them from the imagined enemy who typically is not shown. In this way, while we are presented with the collective readiness to go to war; to fight, maim and kill, or be maimed or be killed, we are also shown that these men are prepared to make individual personal sacrifices in leaving their children.

The monument manages to communicate both collectivism and individualism. It depicts an enthusiasm for war and at the same time suggests a rationale for war: the protection and defence of one's family. We have seen how it presents a collectivized and individualized view of the 'response' of people from the North East as willing and eager participants in war, but we are told by historians (e.g. Curran and Seaton, 1977; Dewey, 1984) that the 'response' to the call to war in the North East, and indeed in other parts of the country, included a certain amount of resistance. Imagine if someone had designed a monument called 'The Conscription' that depicted a line of very young men being forced to join the army or face a jail sentence if they refused. What bodily postures and material and behavioural processes would have to be included?

The material process of protecting and defending can also be seen in the memorial at Maesteg (Figure 6.4), this time the soldier is positioned on the battlefield indicated by his fallen comrade.

Here the soldier is shown in the process of defending his injured friend from further attack by the enemy. He stands with one foot forward suggesting purpose (Davis, 1989), yet, in contrast, while his pose and the presence of the gun suggest his readiness to fight, the expression on

FIGURE 6.4 *The WWI soldier at Maesteg.*

his face remains calm, even content; there is no evidence of a mental process of aggression in his face. The sublime expression affords him a dignity.

We see another individual soldier willing to defend colleagues on the war monument at Oldham (Figure 6.5).

Designed by Albert Toft and unveiled in 1923, the topic of the monument is said to be a scene from the trenches (Borg, 1991). The image features healthy, muscular soldiers in bright, vigilant poses. The pyramid formation allows the positioning of the soldier at the top of the mound. Looking at his pose: arms down at his sides; casually holding the gun held in his right hand

FIGURE 6.5 *The monument at Oldham.*

and one leg bent at the knee, we see a confident, unthreatened stance. If he were to have stood at the top of a WWI trench in this way a sniper would have shot him immediately, but the relaxed, fearless pose of the represented monument soldier allows connotations of infallibility. The presence of the mud, denoting the trench, brings an extra layer to these meanings than would not exist if the figure was positioned directly onto the plinth; even with the most basic historical knowledge of trench warfare, the viewer is able to infer the great danger in the situation. The behavioural processes here as the soldiers energetically keep on the lookout suggest energy as opposed to inwardly looking soldiers turning introspective to survive the horrors of trench life where one-third of all deaths were from disease which takes the number to around three million.

The willingness to fight an unseen enemy is frequently connoted in the memorials through behavioural processes, although not always in the same format as we can see here in another Sir William Goscombe John sculpture in Llandaff, Cardiff (Figure 6.6).

This monument is unusual in that its two represented child participants are not being protected, but sent to fight. Positioned near a school, it shows two young boys, one of whom is wearing short trousers, standing on either sides of a robed female figure. She is intended to be a personification of Llandaff (Borg, 1991), her clothing connotes ancient, mythical figures and the shield she carries connotes protection.

Both boys are carrying guns and stand with one leg slightly forward in confident, yet relaxed, poses appearing as if alert and ready to leave. Although they have guns, they aren't yet in military uniform, suggesting they are about to leave to join the war. The female is carrying a shield in her left hand that is held up in a position which suggests she is motioning the boys forward; presumably into the war and battle. Her right hand is raised in front of her. It is said that she is blessing the two boys (Borg, 1991). In Christian symbolism the hand pointing upwards represented the reward for the righteous and ascent into heaven. In this sense the boys are classified on the monument as part of Llandaff given meaning by the central element in the form of the personification. It is the community itself

FIGURE 6.6 *Llandaff, Cardiff.*

that fuses with the figure who leads them reminding them of the heavenly rewards for those who are ready to go.

Kress and Van Leeuwen (2006:79) suggest that visual representations can adopt narrative structures or conceptual structures. In narrative structures participants are represented as engaged in some kind of activity as we saw above where the soldiers are keeping watch. In conceptual representations social actors are represented in terms of attributes. In this particular monument we can think about the children as being represented as part of a narrative where they are called to act righteously and ready to leave. At the same time conceptually they communicate through their attributes, both through pose and facial expression, but also as they are classified through their standing on the same plinth as the personification and therefore connected into the same mythical realm.

Bringing mythical figures, iconographic symbolism and children together to enact behavioural processes of protection and enthusiastic participation in war is seen again in an extreme form in the monument that stands in Richmond-upon-Thames, London. Unveiled in 1923, by the army officer and sculptor Captain R. R. Goulden, this monument relies on a number of iconographical symbols and behavioural processes that combine to celebrate sacrifice. The representation is of a partially naked man shielding two children; he carries a torch in his raised left hand and a sword in his lowered right hand while he stands among thorns that are serpent-shaped and twist around his feet, going up between his legs and falling over his right shoulder. Conceptually the male figure carries attributes of his nudity, being naked and vulnerable before god, but also an indication of truth through it being an indication of contempt for all material things. The torch he carries in his left hand was also used in Greek mythology to symbolize truth, literally lighting the way through darkness and therefore metaphorically revealing truth through the obscurity of confusion and lies.

The now familiar material process of protection is enacted with the presence and posture of the children. Their facial expressions point to mental processes telling us how they feel about the soldier they cling to. The child standing to the front of the sculpture looks up in awe of the soldier, while the child standing at the back hides behind the sword in fear, an act that suggests the child looks to the soldier for protection. In certain war monuments ancient mythical symbolism gives way to later theocratic ideological positions. It is interesting to observe the blending of such ideological positions with representations of the concept of self-sacrifice for the nation as the images serve to illustrate Smith's (2001) comments on the practices of nationhood.

Smith (2001) commented that commemorative ceremonies that glorify the war dead lead us to view the nation as 'a sacred communion of citizens'; a process that accords with an interpretation of nationalism as a 'surrogate religion' (Smith, 2001:35). We have seen how this is possible in the examples of commemorative monuments that use behavioural processes to construct a 'communion of citizens', but what of sacrifice of life? The commemorative war monuments were built to commemorate the deaths of those who fought. How do commemorative war monuments communicate the concept of sacrifice of one's life during war for the nation?

The large cluster of serpent-shaped thorns on the Richmond-upon-Thames monument, representing the entanglements of war (Borg, 1991), twists its way around the feet of the male figure, travelling upwards between his legs and draping itself around his body. Thorns connote pain, according to Cirlot (2002) the rose-bush emphasizes a number of opposites that include pleasure and pain and it also relates to the symbolism of the cross. The serpent has appeared throughout history in a variety of forms and has a complex range of associations, but the encircling serpent, such as the one we find in the Richmond-upon-Thames monument, signifies the principle of evil (Cirlot, 2002).

There is also a story in Greek mythology of the friendship that was created between a lion and Androcles after he pulled a thorn from the lion's foot (Macdonald, 2009). Thorns symbolizing punishment appear in the Bible; the most common of these stories is the Christian story that tells of the crown of thorns that Jesus Christ was made to wear as he died on the cross; many images depict a Christ with blood running from the wounds that the thorns had made around his head, the face of Jesus is usually depicted as sad, but viewers of those images easily understand that he is suffering by the presence of the thorns and the nails in his hands and feet.

The male figure in the monument at Richmond-upon-Thames shows no sign, in either his facial expression, or his body posture that he is feeling any pain, but in reality thorns twisting around naked flesh would be unbearably painful. So the viewer reads the image of the thorns in his flesh that connote pain, with the sublime expression on his face that connotes mental processes of serenity – the classic impassioned soldier of Marathon impassioned expression – and the behavioural act of protection and understand that the soldier has overcome physical discomfort to triumph for his cause.

There is a wider symbol of sacrifice; the male figure in the memorial is almost naked from the front apart from the thorn branch draped around him like a loin cloth, this is an image that, in part, resembles common images of Christ on the cross, bleeding from the wounds made by the thorns around his head. The representation in the war monument tells us that not only has the male overcome the pain of war and triumphed, but also that he has willingly and painlessly sacrificed his life; just as Jesus Christ did according to Christian belief. These themes can be seen represented more explicitly in the following example from Dover (Figure 6.7) that was again designed by the sculptor R. R. Goulden, who was born in Dover, and unveiled in November 1924.

FIGURE 6.7 *The monument at Dover.*

The elements that connote Christ's sacrifice are brought more readily to the viewer in this example. The body is much leaner than the muscular soldiers that commonly appear; notice how the rib cage stands out on the torso. The soldier is represented wearing a loin cloth, as found in images of the crucifixion, again a difference from the crucifixion images of Christ and this representation is the position of the thorns that, as in the Richmond-upon-Thames monument, are positioned around the feet and connote pain, as we saw in that monument the thorns relate to the rose bush, and according to Cirlot (2002) symbolize a triumph over physical constraints.

The symbol of truth is seen in the nakedness features here, as it did in the Richmond-upon-Thames example, but the most obvious emblem of religious ideology here is the cross that the soldier is holding upwards towards the sky. Here the cross is in flames, which, according to Cirlot (2002), has significant symbolic meanings. He outlines the use of fire in a number of pre-Christian societies and its relation to the '. . . solar symbolism of the flame' (2002:105). Fire was considered to come from the sun, the giver of life through its power to enable growth of food sources. This idea then develops into the symbol of eternal life that extends to the notion that transcendence of fire is necessary to achieve purification and regeneration, '. . . purification is the necessary sacrificial means of achieving the sun's triumph' (2002:105). The sacrifice of life, as Jesus' sacrifice on the cross, is necessary to reach a pure, eternal form of life. So, in the commemorative war monument at Dover we have a justification of death in war as not only a purifying triumph over an evil enemy, but a necessary act to achieve immortality.

The Christian notion of sacrifice, often fused with Classical styles and themes predominates in many WWI monuments; this is also the case with one of the major contemporary war memorials, although the symbolism used here is slightly more obscure. The Armed Forces Memorial at the National Memorial Arboretum in Staffordshire is 'a living memorial' in the sense that it is constantly being updated with the names of soldiers who have died on duty in ongoing wars or who have been killed in terrorist action; 119 names were added in 2009. Standing on a high mound, it is made up of huge circular shaped walls, an obelisk, two large sculptures and a stone wreath in the centre. This monument is also revealing in terms of what the figures are depicted as doing which in itself has become iconic for contemporary support for soldiers and war heroes.

The two sculptures are group scenes that are intended to be seen in sequence and read as a narrative (The Armed Forces Memorial Sculpture, online reference). At the core of their subject matter the sculptures have the death of soldiers and their resurrection. At the same time they incorporate the role of the family in the process of war and sacrifice (see Figure 6.8a, b).

These two monuments are part of the 'Armed Forces Memorial' at the National Memorial Arboretum, sculpted by Ian Rank-Broadley and dedicated in 2007. The description of its narrative by the sculptor state that both Greek mythology and the Christian religious story feature in the sculptures (The Armed Forces Memorial Sculpture, online reference).

The first scene (Figure 6.8a) is said to be based on the story of Achilles and Patroclus, as set out in Homer's *Iliad*, which tells the story of the battle between the Greeks and the city of Troy, during the Trojan War. In the battle Patroclus was killed by Hector; after his death, Patroclus' body was carried from the battlefield on Achilles' shield and held aloft. The story continues that Achilles was so distraught after the death of Patroclus that he refused to part with his dead body until an apparition of Patroclus appeared to him asking him to cremate his body so that he

a)

b)

FIGURE 6.8a, b *Part of the Armed Forces Memorial at the National Memorial Arboretum.*

could enter Hades; the home of the dead in Greek mythology (Holoka and Weil, 2003).

This idea of life continuing after death is continued in the second sculpture (Figure 6.8b). This figure symbolizes the Christian belief in life after death and the sacrifice of Jesus Christ. This piece is meant to give a resolution to the soldier's sacrifice, signified by the gap in the doors being pointed to by a soldier; these doors lead to paradise where, in keeping with Christian belief, the soldier will come back to life after his death on earth. In addition to being part of the narrative of resolution, the doors have been designed to act as a practical conduit of the sun, enabling them to participate in the annual remembrance ceremony. The architect Liam O'Connor is said to have created the gap in that precise position in order to allow the rays of the sun to shine on a stone wreath in the centre of the structure at the exact hour of remembrance each year: 11'o'clock on 11 November (The Armed Forces Memorial Sculpture, online reference). The visitors of the monument are also informed that this is the same as at Maeshowe in Orkney where the setting of the winter solstice sun casts a light into the inner chamber of a 5,000-year-old burial site. In this monument too, the sun's rays are likewise caught on the eleventh hour of the eleventh day of the eleventh month. Such symbolism serves to provide not only additional interest to tourists, but it also serves to implicate war into some broader mystical scheme – further layers of abstraction.

The scenes in this monument are depicted in the Roman Classical narrative fashion where some of the characters and interaction are more naturalistic and others highly symbolic. In the first sculpture the viewer is presented with a scene of three groups: in the central group we see the dead soldier being held aloft on a stretcher, not simply carried but held aloft into the ideal to be celebrated. To some extent here we see a scene from a battlefield as comrades carry one of their wounded. But this takes on a symbolic element due to the way he is carried. To the right and left of this central group we see the dead or wounded soldier's family engaged in the process of grieving; on the left we see his wife who holds up her arms towards the body with his child clinging to her and on the right we see his father comforting his grieving mother on the ground. In the Roman narrative tradition this fusing of scenes from different times and places is not problematic. But it is of note how due to the longer tradition of such Classical references in British war commemoration that this is not seen as an oddity.

Of course this scene could be made coherent were the battle to have taken place on British soil. But what is important here, which is distinctive to the WWI monuments is the representation of grief and loss. The notion of sacrifice, while here represented through symbolic elements, ceases to be realized through impassioned service for nation in the realms of Classical ideals, but by placing it into the concrete reactions of pained wives, mothers and children. This is part of the process by which soldiery, in the later part of the twentieth century and into the twenty-first century has become something everyday where the public are encouraged to align more directly with the actual experiences of ordinary everyday soldiers. Here soldiering is not explained as part of the service of greater ideas and god, although this association has not disappeared completely, but through a more naturalistic sense of what these young men go through on our behalf, even though in the wars they fight we may never be told why they do so, nor who really their enemies are nor what they want (Moeller, 2009).

Of course, an alternative interpretation of the presence of the grieving family is possible; it could be that their presence helps the monument to communicate the message that war has destructive effects on the family; criticizing rather than legitimizing the war process. However, this interpretation is less likely when considering the resolution to the event as portrayed in the second monument. The primary agent in the second sculpture is the figure on the left of the scene who is engaged in the behavioural process of directing the central group towards the open doors, indicating the path of resurrection for the dead soldier. The central group is made up of the dead soldier and two of his colleagues: a female and a Ghurkha soldier. On the right there is a figure of a highly muscular soldier who carves the name of the dead soldier on the wall, this act replicates the actual process of inscribing the names of dead soldiers on the inside walls of the monument at its centre which lies through the open doors.

This inclusion of the material process of inscribing completes the journey of the dead soldier for the viewer; telling them that the soldier will be resurrected, thereby negating his death, and reminding the viewer that he will live forever in the memory of the nation by means of his name having been recorded on the National Armed Forces Memorial.

It is possible to view the inclusion of the processes of pointing the way towards resurrection and the recording of the name of the soldier as a feature that may have allowed the subject of the soldier's death to be presented in a form that the viewer can accept more readily as a resolution to the conflict and to the act of sacrifice. This was not the case when Charles Sargeant Jagger's Memorial to the Royal Artillery (Figure 5.13) was unveiled in Hyde Park, London, in 1925; reactions to the inclusion of a dead soldier were mainly negative (Compton, 1985). The memorial has four soldier figures around its base, one of which is a dead soldier, fully clothed and partially covered by his heavy military coat. When the monument was unveiled it caused controversy from the public who, due to censorship of images of war deaths, were not used to being confronted by images of dead soldiers.

In their participation in war, the soldiers have to face death as well as bringing about the deaths of others; whatever else it may involve, it is undeniable that war involves killing. However, while we have seen examples of a soldier's death almost barely represented in the Royal

Artillery Memorial at Hyde Park, we do not see the material process of killing anywhere in the commemorative war monuments. Nor do we see who the soldiers we commemorate kill. There are simply no recipients. This is an interesting exclusion. Given the extensive effort put into demonization enemies during conflicts we might ask why commemoration of soldier should not involve celebration of the material processes in which they participated. As we saw in Chapter Four committees specified that there should be no reference to fighting or aggression in the concern to bring the public together through nationhood. The act of war in relation to an enemy is thus suppressed with a view to foregrounding the values and ideas of the nation itself where the impassive giving of the soldiers points to the worthiness of the nation.

In fact the only depiction of killing in the war memorials is found in the form of symbolic representations depicting Classical figures as in the monument at Mountain Ash (Figure 6.9). The Mountain Ash War Memorial was designed by James Harvard Thomas and completed by his son George after his father's death in 1921 (Turner, 1996:744). The opening ceremony took place on 5 June 1922 and was attended by the usual list of local official elites of civil, military and religious sectors. As if to emphasize the hierarchical nature of these ceremonies the order of procession ends with a curt notice:

> The General Public are warned that they will not be allowed to take up any position on Memorial Site until after the Procession arrives. (From a copy of the original details of proceedings of the unveiling ceremony supplied by the Public Library, Mountain Ash)

In their article on the unveiling ceremony that took place on 5 June 1922, the local newspaper, *The Aberdare Leader*, described the memorial as:

> The bronze statue is a magnificent female figure of Victory holding forth a graceful palm. At her feet is a nude figure of the Evil One: the whole subject being emblematical of 'Right over Might'. The inscription carved on the granite runs as follows – 'the Great War, 1914–1918'. Sons of this town and district. Let this of you be said – That you who live are worthy of your dead. These gave their lives that you who live may reap a richer harvest ere you fall asleep. (*The Aberdare Leader*, Saturday, 10 June 1922)

The female figure here is robed and, although not winged, it is clear she has a resemblance to Nike the Greek god of Victory. She holds a dagger in her left hand that is raised above a naked, fallen man. We have no visual clues as to the identity of the fallen man; he has no uniform so he could be the enemy, the relief panels below the main sculpture featured four service members: a soldier, a sailor, an airman and a nurse. It is often

FIGURE 6.9 *The WWI monument at Mountain Ash.*

the case that slightly more naturalistic representations of members of the different armed forces are classified as the same being treated equally yet under a personification of Victory which is therefore placed in the ideal as compared to their real.

The main figure in the Mountain Ash monument is rare in terms of the process it represents: killing and the triumph expressed in the way she holds the dagger. But we still do not find the figure in the material process itself. And the elegance of the robed figure itself negates the brutality of taking a life. Of course here the figures represent the personification of Victory and the personification of evil slain and therefore symbolize the war rather than depicting the acts of which it comprised. We will examine the use of such personifications on monuments in the following chapter. But here this representation preserves the image of the soldier as dignified protector relieving the viewer of having to contemplate the horrors of battle.

The few monuments that do represent death either allow the viewer to take a controlled peek at the physical sacrifice of the soldier, as in the Royal Artillery Memorial in Hyde Park, or they resolve the difficult subject of death with an ideological confirmation of the soldier's resurrection, as in the Armed Forces Memorial in the National Arboretum. The viewer is never allowed to consider victims of war in any realistic manner. Another excellent example of representation of war as victimless is the monument at Carmarthen.

This monument, designed by sculptor Sir William Goscombe John, provides the viewer with two views of warfare: injury and the soldier's imperviousness to injury. It features a soldier wearing a medical bandage around his head and although the bandage signifies injury, this message is overridden by other communicative channels: a relaxed body posture; a composed facial expression; a heavy, strong body, the latter is also metaphorically understood by the viewer through the use of bronze material.

If we contemplate the monuments' role as part of a wider, banal military recruitment tool we can understand the possible reasons for such mythical, as opposed to realistic, representations of the dangers of war to the individual. Billig (1995) argues that the difference between recruitment to fight for the modern nation in comparison with medieval war is that during medieval times recruitment to war depended on the cooperation of feudal barons, whereas in the modern period recruitment to the military is sought directly from the people who are urged to fight for their nation. Billig also comments that whereas fighting under the command of the medieval land-owner was compulsory, the majority of modern-day military recruitment is done on a voluntary basis. These comments provide a useful elucidation of possible motivations for such mythical, positive representation of injury during war. Billig (1995) argues further that the maintenance of the idea that war is necessary, and inevitable, is crucial to the survival of the nation; because it is in this way that future recruitment to participating in war on behalf of the nation is ensured.

Modality

One final observation we wish to make about the monuments in this chapter draws on Kress and Van Leeuwen's (1996) concept of visual modality which involves the way that representations are close to or further away from naturalistic truth. On WWI statues there is generally a decrease in articulation of detail of clothing and faces of the figures of the soldiers and other figures which changed to greater degrees of naturalism in more contemporary monuments. For Kress and Van Leeuwen this would mean that truth or 'modality' is lowered and that therefore these are not realistic representations. Of course this would seem obvious. But we have to take the next step and consider in what ways the detail has been reduced. In some statues detail is smoothed away to give a beautiful roundedness as seen on the figures of the Cardiff monument seen in the introduction. The faces are without furrows, with smooth, slightly unfinished features. We can imagine the other end of the scale which might be found in the harsh details of faces shown in documentary photographs intended to reveal actual people in real moments of time. Where detail is smoothed out we have metaphorical certainty and idealization as opposed to full naturalistic modality where we have complexity and greater moral ambiguity. The young men who died in the mud of a colonial battle where they had nothing to gain personally are therefore represented as abstractions. We could imagine the effect were these soldiers represented in high modality.

We can see the shift to higher degrees of modality in both the Yomper monument seen in Figure 5.14 and on the medical officer in the Armed Forces Memorial seen in Figure 5.12. Here facial features are much more pronounced as are the details of clothing and equipment. So too are the poses more naturalistic as opposed to the more poetical poses of the Classical figures and those of some of the WWI figures that show bright enthusiasm and energy as in the Oldham monument shown in Figure 6.5. However, notably the figure in the 'Shot at Dawn' monument (Figure 6.10) is represented in lower modality through the detail of his features clothing and even body proportions. In such cases this strategy can serve to reduce the difficulty in looking at the scene for the viewer. But more broadly the increasing naturalistic modality of the figures on more contemporary monuments is again part of the shift to soldiers as less idealized and more everyday where they are like the viewer with human fears and ordinary pleasures and families. What we show in Chapter Eight, where we look at more contemporary monuments, however, is at the same time as finding a move towards greater naturalism we also see a shift towards different kinds of complex symbolism and abstraction.

As well as reduction of naturalistic detail monument designers have also used blurring of surfaces. We find this, for example on the Will Lambert project for the Revensbrück Concentration Camp. Such blurring of surfaces can have the association of blurring of certainty and knowledge. We could imagine the effect had the soldier of WWI been represented in high modality, or with blurring. How would a realistic soldier have appeared positioned among Classical architectural forms and Christian symbolism? Advertising images often require low modality images in order to symbolize a simplified world where the products are more easily able to communicate the kinds of idea and values that the advertiser seeks to load onto them. So too in war monuments a naturalistic representation of a soldier would sit awkwardly in a largely symbolic environment.

But importantly on monuments we find that modalities can be mixed. On the Armed Forces monument we find that the soldiers nursing the Christ-like corpse are represented in high modality. Yet she finds herself among the muscular god-like soldiers. We could ask why she is not in this scene also topless and represented with excessive musculature. Of course her role is neither sexual, nor mythical here, as she represented the everyday female involvement of caring in the services. In this way this monument

FIGURE 6.10 *'Shot at Dawn' at the National Memorial Arboretum.*

combines older traditions of Classicism, with more contemporary realism, where soldiery is something ordinary.

Anti-war commemoration

In this last section of this chapter we bring together the observations of this chapter along with that in the last to look at one monument that could at one level be seen as bringing a slightly more critical view of war. In Britain there are no anti-war monuments as such. In 2001 a memorial 'Shot at Dawn' was unveiled by Gertrude Harris, the daughter of Private Farr, one of the soldiers who had been executed by the British Army in WWI. Until that point there had been no public commemoration of the executions. Ostensibly, the monument can be considered to be a negative comment on the behaviour of the British Army towards over 300 of its soldiers in the WWI. Many were young boys, some of 16, suffering from shell-shock and nervous disorders murdered to set an example to others where their own fellow soldiers were forced to act as firing squad. The executions were used to control the soldiers' behaviour; the names of the executed were often referred to by the officers on parades, acting as a terrifying warning to those who may be thinking of deserting or refusing to carry out orders (Arthur, 2002). But a closer analysis of the monument reveals a less than critical stance towards the memory of the events (Figure 6.10).

Designed by Andy Decomyn, it stands in a far corner of the National Memorial Arboretum. It is modelled on a young soldier, 17-year-old Private Herbert Burden, who was executed by soldiers of his own army at Ypres in 1915. It is placed at the head of over 300 wooden stakes on which the names of the other soldiers who were executed are inscribed. According to the guide, the designer has arranged the stakes in the form of a Greek theatre '. . . symbolising the tragedy that these events signify' (The National Arboretum guide book). And the designer points out in his design notes that this was to commemorate the pardoning of these men. Not, it is of note, to commemorate the viciousness of the regime that carried out such punishment.

The artist chose to sculpt the statue from white cement resin material. The colour here acts to connote the innocence of the soldiers, many of whom suffered from shell-shock and were unable to function in the terrifying environment of the trenches. The same material also communicates softness and lightness as opposed to the weight and immovability of bronze and the eternity of stone. The softness also suggests something that gives and yields as opposed to being durable and resilient.

The use of wooden posts to commemorate the 306 men who were shot is also of note. Had these been of bronze or stone this would have created very different meanings. There is not the sense of weight, importance, eternity and immovability. Wooden stakes additionally do not require the same kind of effort or personalized manual skills of forging bronze or the delicate skill for sculpting stone in the Classical styles. We can draw out the difference here by comparison with the soldiers represented as bronze pillars on the New Zealand monument that we discuss in Chapter Eight. In this case the pillars bring connotations of the solid and the permanent. They are angled to suggest a dynamic and forceful posture. We can imagine how even the symbolic wooden stake might be angled or fashioned in order to communicate shell-shocked young soldiers being shot as examples by their own friends who would also risk punishment if refused to do so. The use of stakes presents a far less challenging, less demanding, image to the viewer, than a figurative representation of 300 soldiers all tied and waiting to be executed by their own army colleagues.

The firing squad too are represented not in high modality but furthest into the realm of symbolism as six Fir trees. Trees are often used to symbolize nature more broadly, the environment, recycling or the cycle of renewal. So the agent who killed those terrified young men suffering from shell-shock is not symbolized by something terrible but by something that embodies the natural. If the representation of the firing squad was in high modality, which could have been achieved by representing the firing squad and the others awaiting execution as soldiers instead of stakes and trees, and these were fashioned from a metal such as black iron we could imagine the difference in meaning. Placed in public places this could commemorate the crimes that the state can commit against its own population. But of course such representations are not possible, clashing with the ideal of the soldier who serves and gives. Soldiers' novels of WWII (Burgett, 2001) similarly speak of ranks of men being instructed to walk across open ground in the face of machine gun fire and mortars. Here human life has no meaning as compared to objectives and deadlines (Figure 6.11).

The use of the trees to represent the firing squad also changes the kinds of transitivity that we would have found in the actual situation. There are no guns pointing at the soldier, no people to take responsibility for the action. The tree is often a symbol for acts that sit in harmony with nature as opposed to the firing squad which destroys and is cruel. But the tree in its form makes the representation of transitivity difficult. As we saw in the New Zealand monument even straight bronze pillars can be made to look as if they are attacking through angle of positioning. Trees simply stand and grow. Kress and Van Leeuwen (1996) also suggest that in images transitivity can be indicated by the presence of 'vectors'. These are the pictorial versions of the kind of arrows we find on diagrams to represent direction of movement. So in images these can be represented by pointing fingers, or by direction of gaze. In monument design a vector could be used to indicate the direction of fire if the form were not a tree, which makes the addition of elements so difficult. And what this also does is

FIGURE 6.11 *The 'Firing Squad' as represented on the 'Shot at Dawn' Memorial.*

suppress the actual experiences of those who were forced to comprise the firing squads.

The soldier himself stands in an erect posture, with no sign of the quivering shell-shock symptoms accounted by historians, blindfolded with his hands tied behind his back and his hair neatly combed. He is represented as one and a half times the usual human height. In this sense he is slightly larger than life as was the case with WWI figures. This has the effect of making him appear slightly more powerful and much less vulnerable had he been slightly smaller than life-size.

Another feature worth further examination as regards modality lies on the front of the soldier's chest. Here the designer has placed a perfectly round disc-shaped pendant; this represents the piece of white cloth, or white envelope that was attached to the soldier to aid identification of the target, the heart, for the firing squad. In reality the cloth or paper would have been irregularly shaped, not a perfectly circular-shaped disc as represented in the monument. This disc appears as if it had been mass produced in a factory, rather than a hurriedly torn off strip of cloth or paper in a squalid and hasty process carried out behind the doors of any real system of justice.

The features and clothing of the soldier are represented in low modality. Features are rounded and undetailed, cartoon-like. On the one hand this serves to shift the representation away from the naturalistic and documentary. We can imagine the difference in meaning where this figure is represented in high naturalistic modality with full features, details, texture of clothes, hair and skin. The roundedness and simplified form also serves to create an impression of neatness and order that did not exist; it regularizes what, according to historical accounts, was a hurried, brutal military practice. There is no sign of the rough physical experience of trench life or being caught in battle, nor of the psychological damage soldiers are said to have suffered.

We can imagine the difference were a massive bronze statue of a naturalistic soldier being shot by a horrific looking cruel firing squad to commemorate the way that the state can truly abuse the lives of its citizens in war was positioned in the centre of towns and cities. As with the Arthur Stadler cartoon we considered in the introduction to this book this could be one part of the way that our public spaces become infused with discourses that ridicule war, its brutality and consequences and all that it stands for as opposed to those that are largely celebratory.

The 'Shot at Dawn' monument figure wears a blindfold, as many executed soldiers did, removing the gaze from the represented figure and taking away the opportunity for the soldier to interact with the viewer and make demands of them. This covering of the eyes makes this an 'offer image' allowing the viewer to focus not on the soldier himself, his feelings and how he wants us to react to this – perhaps bring help, understand the madness in which he find himself – but on the event itself.

Over 300 soldiers were executed by the British Army in WWI, many for 'desertion' or refusing to follow orders to go over the top. The irony of the story of Private Herbert Burden, the subject of the 'Shot at Dawn' monument, is that he had not run away from the battle, but had innocently left his post to go to comfort a friend who was stationed nearby (Anon, BBC news, online reference). Most of these soldiers were young boys who had joined the army before they had reached the official enlistment age, as in the case of Private Burden who aged 16 had lied about his age to join the Northumberland Fusiliers. For these young boys in particular, the horrors of trench warfare were unbearable and it was commonplace for soldiers to be found incapacitated, disoriented and wandering around aimlessly. We now understand the majority was most likely to have been suffering from post-traumatic stress disorder, a psychiatric injury, but this medical diagnosis was not available at the time. Those sent to the medical huts and diagnosed with 'nervous' conditions would soon find themselves returned to the front, so men of all ages would commonly try to get discharged from the trenches on physical medical grounds.

Arthur (2002, 2009) provides a comprehensive account of experiences of WWI soldiers, many of whom testify to the extents men would go to in order to be excused from duty. Once they were off the battlefield, wounded men in medical facilities would pick at their healing wounds to postpone their discharge and subsequent return to the front. Captain Maberly Esler tells that one medical hut was full of soldiers with wounds to their hands; leading the doctors to conclude that the men had lifted their hands above the trench deliberately to get wounded and sent to the medical facility (Captain Maberly Esler in Arthur, 2002:89). Such accounts of unwilling and terrified soldiers are common in the novels written by soldiers themselves but not something that is included on war monuments.

Conclusion

In this chapter we have added a further layer of understanding of how and what war monuments communicate by looking at their materiality and what kinds of actions are represented on monuments. We are beginning to see that three-dimensional communication as well as using range of iconographical and iconological symbolism draws on a range of semiotic meaning potentials that are based on experiential associations. In this chapter we have also seen the way that designers can use material to infuse the idea of sacrifice with a sense of immovability, eternity and destiny. We also saw the process of idealization that could take place of soldiers through the reduction of modality. Combining these kinds of observations with those from the previous chapter we were then able to show how these allows us to look more critically at a monument that may on first glance appear to be dealing with war in a less celebratory fashion. As we apply these tools to more monuments across the following chapters their use in facilitating more systematic observation will become more apparent.

CHAPTER SEVEN

Women on war monuments

One notable feature of WWI monument is the use of women. While later monuments represent women more frequently and in different ways these early designs, while favouring representations of men, had very specific uses for women depicting them in the form of protected wives and daughters, or mythical figures personifying actions, places and values. In each case these representations played an important part in the recontextualization of social practice, in substituting actual reasons for the men to go to war, suppressing the actual anger and powerlessness felt by women, deleting women's actual roles during the war and also replacing the actual actions of the nation, and its struggle with another, for abstractions.

While women's role in WWI was not in the form of official military personnel, they did play a crucial role in the war. In the first place women were seen as one tool that could be used by the state to urge their male relatives and neighbours to go to war and were directly addressed in government propaganda posters. Although women had not yet been allowed to vote, the authorities claimed that a woman had a duty to her country to persuade her husband, brother or son to fight for the nation. An example of one such poster addresses women via a series of questions based on fear of invasion and guilt, finally asking 'WON'T YOU HELP AND SEND A MAN TO JOIN THE ARMY TO-DAY?' (Grayzel, 1999:64).

In the second place women carried out a large-scale and dangerous role in arms factories during the war. With so many men leaving their jobs to join the military, a chronic shortage of labour emerged; this shortage was made worse by the introduction of conscription for men in 1916. Women, mostly working class, were urged to fill this gap. Braybon and Summerfield (1987) note that the unemployment figure for women in October 1914 had dropped to 139,000, the figure for the previous month had been 190,000, by December 1914 it had gone down to 75,000 and to 35,000 by February

1915. As these figures suggest, hundreds of women went to work in the munitions factories, risking losing their lives to bombing raids, toxic poisoning and accidental explosions. Indeed, many women lost their lives while doing their work; a fact that was recognized in contemporary media reports such as the one in the *Manchester Guardian* in 1916, paying tribute to the munitions workers in 1916, the writer of the article marvelled at their '. . . courage . . . and . . . perfect discipline . . .' (Calkins, in Cook, 2006:238).

In the third place, as we discuss in a later section in this chapter, women in large numbers worked as nurses on the front lines experiencing the same dangers of artillery barrages as men (Doerr, 2006; Maddrell, 2007). Many of these women pioneered medical treatments which were to prove highly influential in modern medicine.

But what we show is that none of these actions and roles are represented on monuments. And even much later where more contemporary monuments have begun to represent actual roles carried out by women these still largely communicate meanings that serve to soften and humanize warfare. We begin by looking at the representation of women on WWI monuments then moving on the progressively more contemporary examples.

Women representing the Home Front

One frequent use of women on monuments is to represent the nature of war as protection of the home front. Women would be shown cowering beneath or behind powerful soldier figures. One example is the monument at Port Sunlight in Cheshire (Figure 7.1).

This monument was commercially sponsored by the company Lever Brothers to commemorate the loss of their employees – although this was done during the time of fear of workers' movements described in Chapter Five. The monument is comprised of a Celtic cross placed on an octagonal plinth that has relief panels depicting members of various services: ambulance men, wounded soldiers, gunners, sailors and anti-aircraft personnel. The main sculpture sits above on the plinth and is comprised of three soldiers: one wounded and crouched low; another with his gun at the ready; a third with his bayonet fixed. There are also two women, one of whom seems to be trying to reach the wounded soldier, the other crouched low protecting some of the six children represented in the sculpture.

As with the Cardiff monument, the figures on the Port Sunlight monument are viewed in a circular pattern. According to Borg (1991), this monument draws on a tradition of ancient, continuous narrative found in both ancient Greek art and the paintings of the Renaissance period which could fuse both real and symbolic elements and compress both time and space. This means that in the scene we can find the soldiers fighting at the

FIGURE 7.1 *The Port Sunlight monument in Cheshire.*

Source: Copyright David Dixon. This work is licensed under the Creative Commons Attribution-Share Alike 2.0 Generic Licence. To view a copy of this licence, visit http://creativecommons.org/licenses/by-sa/2.0/ or send a letter to Creative Commons, 171 Second Street, Suite 300, San Francisco, CA 94105, USA.

front impassioned and certain where the children stand huddled behind them as if being protected physically by their presence. And the woman, in a role as carer, tries to reach out to the wounded soldier. In this narrative we find no enemy and we do not see the conditions in which the soldiers lived – it is well documented that elites felt it best to allow the soldiers to live as poorly as possible in order to foster their fiercer instincts. And through the continuous narrative the involvement of the soldiers is clearly represented as one of protecting the vulnerable, the women and children, and not as protecting the interests of the elite in a colonial war over territory and resources in the Middle East. The role of such monuments was to foster this former image in the minds of restless working classes who had begun to widely question the purpose of the war.

Representations of women in uniform

As well as having civilian paid employment opportunities for the first time, the onset of war in 1914 led many women to form military-style groups. Soon after war was declared, a Women's Emergency Service (WEC) was formed; this eventually became the WVR (Women's Volunteer Reserve). These women based themselves on military hierarchical lines, wearing military-style khaki uniforms and drilling on village greens (Grayzel, 1999). The wearing of the khaki uniform was a source of much criticism from both men and women who regarded it as an act that brought ridicule to something that was essentially sacred. Their argument was that as women would not be called to fight on the front line, the uniform would never be stained with blood, nor would it ever form their shroud after the sacrifice of their lives, as it would with male soldiers (Grayzel, 1999).

Male reaction to females wearing the military uniform is reported to be in contrast to the reaction evoked by the uniform of the VAD (Volunteer Aid Detachment) that had 74,000 nurses, two-thirds of them female, working both at home and abroad (Watson, 2004). The nurses' uniform symbolized care for the wounded or dying soldier; supporting him, not competing with him, attracting both admiration and respect. It is in this context that we see occasional tributes to nurses in WWI monuments.

The stone statue of the nurse on duty is part of the Hereford war monument (Figure 7.2). She does not occupy the monument alone; in keeping with the WWI war monument tradition, she shares the monument with a soldier, a sailor and an airman. Her uniform is carved in relative detail, she appears ordered and tidy with her hat perfectly in place and her bodily pose connotes the carrying out of nursing duties, efficiency and reliability. But the activity depicted is not one of dealing with pain and terrible injury and fear but where she carries utensils. Her facial expression is one of focus.

Also of note in the form and style of this monument is in the first place that Christian symbolism is chosen over Classicism. Those who give their lives in the act of nursing and caring are not placed into the same kind of realm of glorious ancient civilizations and gods as are the soldiers themselves. In the second place the figure of the nurse is of stone rather than of marble with its Classical connotations. And the stone does not

FIGURE 7.2 *The WWI monument at Hereford.*

communicate the same kind of weight and durability as the alternative of bronze.

We see a similar representation in Figure 7.3 in the monument at Mountain Ash.

The pose of this nurse is one of modesty and duty, with her hands clasped neatly and primly in front of her body. Her facial expression is one of kind openness and passivity, suggesting she is content with her role, as opposed to the facial expression one might find in a nurse engaged in the act of dealing with thousands of horrifically injured soldiers each day on the front lines. We can imagine both the kind of expression and pose that

FIGURE 7.3 *A nurse featured on the WWI monument in Mountain Ash.*

might better fit in this case, one that indicative of a wealth of strength and courage. Many of these front-line nurses were in fact leaders in the pioneering of new medical techniques and treatments for wounds (Doerr, 2006; Maddrell, 2007).

Nurses in the VAD served both in hospitals at home and at the battlefield hospitals near the front lines in France and Belgium. While abroad, their lives were at risk from shell attacks and sniper fire as they raced to collect the injured soldiers from the battlefield. Just like the male soldiers on the battlefield, they too suffered the symptoms of 'shell-shock': a nervous disorder brought on by the loud shells flying past their heads.

Some of the nurses had mental breakdowns resulting from the pressure of dealing with the horrific wounds presented by the soldiers on the wards, medication to treat them was insufficient and the sheer workload entailed in their role put the nurses under considerable mental strain. Bagnold's (1978) account of a VAD's work in a London hospital describes in detail the horrific wounds on the men who had been sent home from the front.

The level of modality is also important in this representation. On the one hand the figure is represented somewhere in between 2D and 3D. The viewer is not encouraged to look up at this figure in awe nor to walk around and contemplate it. The surfaces of the clothing and face are rounded, simplified and idealized. And she is represented against a blank background. She is represented not in a narrative scene of any sorts but conceptually in terms of her attributes, her full formal uniform, pleasant appearance and gentle pose. Along with the soldiers as Classical gods and protectors she forms one of the participants of the war. Within the military itself there was in fact much respect for these women some of whom were buried in military cemeteries and awarded medals (Watson, 2004).

The tendency to reserve the more agentive roles in war commemoration to men and to represent women as passive is one feature of the monuments that helps us to understand the way that their primary aim was the promotion and protection of the nation-state. This idea can be explored by comparing two real examples of notable female figures from the medical profession who participated in WWI.

The first example is the remarkable achievement by a Scottish doctor by the name of Elsie Inglis, who, after a successful career as a doctor in Scotland, had the idea of providing a fully equipped hospital unit staffed by women to support wounded soldiers either at home or abroad. After a struggle, she managed to secure funding for the first hospital in France: this was the beginning of the Scottish Women's Hospitals (SWH). Dr Inglis later led teams of doctors and nurses deep into Europe, establishing field hospitals in Serbia and Russia among other sites. Leneman's (1994) account of the life of Elsie Inglis reveals remarkable feats accomplished by the doctors and nurses of the SWH. The women showed tremendous skill and courage, working in hard environments; some collapsed under the strain suffering mental breakdowns, others died from the diseases they encountered. Their advancement in treatment contributed greatly to the limited knowledge of the age (Crofton, 1997). The skills they developed in the treatment of the effects of gas, burns and gangrene at the hospital in Royaumont, France, led the way for other medical centres to follow.

Elsie Inglis died of cancer before the war ended in 1917. Her stunning achievement was not recognized in a public memorial, there is a memorial hospital in her name and a plaque to her memory in St Giles Cathedral, both in Edinburgh, but, at the time of writing there is no public sculpture commemorating to her war contribution. Would it have been different if she had died at the hands of the enemy? This was the way our second example, Edith Cavell, died.

Edith Cavell was a nurse from Norfolk who served in military hospitals and clinics on the front line in Belgium during WWI. As well as training other nurses and nursing wounded soldiers, she also actively helped many British and French soldiers to escape into Holland from where they could find their way home and be redeployed into military units. Information regarding these activities made its way to German military command; she was caught, arrested and tried at a German court martial. Britain and American authorities were aware of the story of her arrest and trial at the time, while Britain felt it could not intervene to get her released, American authorities did try to persuade the Germans to consider saving her life for humanitarian reasons. However, the German military found her guilty and she was executed by a dawn firing squad in October 1915.

By the time her dead body was brought back into Britain by train, the public had been well informed of her situation and hundreds came to each station on the route to pay their respects (Souhami, 2010) and the government gave her a state funeral (Souhami, 2010). Her death at the hands of the enemy gave the British government the opportunity to conduct a rousing propaganda campaign that highlighted the inhumanity of the enemy and urged people to join the military to fight brutality. Souhami credits her with helping to double army recruitment figures in Britain. Nevertheless, the interesting point in relation to commemoration is that, unlike Dr Elsie Inglis, Edith Cavell has public memorial monuments dedicated solely to her; the most notable is the memorial designed by Sir George Frampton in St Martin's Place, near Trafalgar Square, in London (Figure 7.4).

We can contrast this representation of Edith Cavell with those found in the typical commemorative war monument representations of nurses, such as the one in Hereford. First, instead of the expected nurses uniform, she is wearing a long dress and a full-length wide coat with huge sleeves, this style of garment is found on statues of the mythical figures such as the 'Victory' we have seen represented in other monuments, connoting both the Classicism of the Greek period, and to the modern viewer the wide sleeved robes worn by judges and barristers, servers of justice, when in court. She is also positioned against a Classical-style obelisk as opposed to the Christian styles seen above for the nurse. Cavell is embraced within the eternal higher ideals of the nation.

In the early twentieth century, women who entered public space were bound to be judged negatively in some way whether they were: deemed to be taking jobs that rightfully belonged to men; pretending to be as skilled as men in expecting equal pay; trying to become soldiers but not offering themselves for sacrifice on the front line, even though they were not permitted to do so; or behaving in a sexually immoral way by volunteering to leave the home to do war work of any kind. Only patriotism was recognized as a 'moral' reason for taking employment; personal benefit was seen as an immoral motivation.

FIGURE 7.4 *Edith Cavell.*

Even the nurses were not exempt from moral judgement. Darrow's (1996) description of the role French nurses played in WWI paints a consistent picture that displays hostility to nurses based on similar suspicions held by British society towards its female military volunteers. Nurses in France were portrayed as morally dubious, scheming, husband-hunting or seeking erotic pleasure from seeing naked, defenceless soldiers' bodies, she notes:

> Anything women did to contribute to the war, even nursing
> its wounded heroes, was suspect. (Darrow, 1996:106)

The absence of the uniform in the Cavell monument also demonstrates ambivalent attitudes of men towards women's role in the war and how clothes define women in society. Furthermore, Edith Cavell's death at the hands of the enemy was a sacrifice of life that women were officially not allowed to give, preserving the sacrifice of life for the nation as a male-only right presents a conflict for commemorative monuments; a conflict that is resolved with the lifting of Edith Cavell into the realm of the mythical women of ancient Greece. As a notable victim of 'the enemy' Edith Cavell became a symbol of the cause for war. Her transformation from the everyday nurse to the mythical, robed figure connotes grandeur; in turn this lends legitimacy to the ideological position taken by the nation, thereby reinforcing the justification for sacrifice. A nurse's uniform, it seems, could not be considered a sufficient vehicle for the connotation of sacrifice for the nation-state. Also, notice how she stands in a regal style pose, not like the dutiful pose of the nurse in the Hereford monument, again connoting grandeur; her firm stance shows neither servitude, nor vulnerability as we saw in the representation of ordinary nurses.

The words 'humanity' and 'dawn', at the head and foot of the inscription respectively, tell the viewer that she, or the nation, is a symbol of humanity and in doing so implies the enemy as 'other' who showed a lack of humanity in the act of her dawn execution. By connoting mythical figures, Edith Cavell is transformed from the nurse into the nation, reminding men of the reason for their own sacrifice; in this case not the vulnerable women at home, but the nation itself embodied by the female.

Women as personification of the nation, emotions and concepts

Women were nevertheless very important for monument designers and appeared frequently as Greek and Roman gods, personifications of ideals and places and as mythical figures representing the spirit of local communities.

The conflict in attitudes towards women's participation in war and the practice of personifying the nation in female form is combined in the following examples from Aberystwyth (Figure 7.5) and Finchley, London (Figure 7.6), showing a naked woman. These monuments stand out as they represent women not as the vulnerable, but as the spiritual ideal.

The monument at Aberystwyth was designed by the Sicilian sculptor Mario Rutelli and unveiled in 1923. The length of the obelisk is decorated with palm fronds. In Greek mythology the palm was a symbol of military victory and in the early Christian age became a symbol of victory over death as acted out in the sacrifice of Christ. According to Cirlot (2002), it

FIGURE 7.5 *Part of the WWI monument at Aberystwyth.*

is also an emblem of fecundity; this explains its common use with female figures.

The obelisk is topped with a winged figure of the Roman goddess Victory. She is poised on an orb, holding a laurel wreath in her right hand; all familiar symbols of triumph and peace. In this case, therefore, the nature of winning the war is personified through a goddess. Through this reconextualization the actual nature of what that Victory was and what it involved is substituted for a symbolic figure from Classical mythology. The pointless battles where hundreds of thousands of young men were killed on each side as small amounts of territory were won and then immediately lost by each side, young men forced to simply walk into machine-gun fire, are substituted by a graceful, leaping Classical figure. We will discuss shortly while these figures of women were found so appropriate for such personifications, as opposed to male mythical figures.

The Aberystwyth monument has another naked woman at the base of its column representing 'humanity' rising out of the entanglements of war, although she is commonly referred to as 'peace' (Borg, 1991). She is depicted as being the in process of freeing herself from thorns; thorns carry their own connotations of punishment and pain, as discussed in the analysis of the Richmond-upon-Thames example, from Greek and Christian allegory. The pain of the thorns is intensified by their impact on naked flesh. The naked form itself has its own Greek and Christian-based meaning potential as discussed in the previous chapter where we looked at its relation to truth and being naked before god.

The woman uses both hands to push herself forward from the thorn bushes; the pose allowing the viewer to feel the effort she makes to free herself. Her naked flesh is surrounded to the hip by the thorn bush and, as in the Richmond-upon-Thames male figure; her facial expression shows no pain. Her physical strength, connoted by her endurance of the thorns, is emphasized further by the exaggerated muscles that feature on her body, arms and legs.

This biological 'overdetermination' (Kress and Van Leeuwen, 1996) reflects an important overcompensation and conflict in the representation of the female form as a persona; representing 'humanity', she is portrayed as strong enough to endure whatever humanity encounters, especially war, but she is at the same time to some extent the female who reminds the viewer why war is fought. She has long, swept-back hair, very unlike the styles worn by the Classical figures, although her body shape is similar to that of the Classical sculpture the Venus de' Medici she is slimmer and her breasts are pronounced. She resembles a woman drawn in fantasy art where artists combine heightened sexualization with bodily strength to represent female warriors. Despite her physical resemblance to a Classical figure she nevertheless also represents a less symbolic, everyday woman. The overdetermination of her physical features that connote strength, sit in juxtaposition with the overdetermination of the physical features that connote femininity: exaggerated curves and long flowing hair.

Unlike the male figure in the Richmond-upon-Thames monument she carries no sword, so we cannot associate her with battle or having an active role in the meting out of justice through objects. Nor does she protect children, so we are unable to associate her with battle through behavioural process of being the agent of protection, nor participation in actual processes of fighting a war of attrition.

Although the whole monument is set above the viewer, within the monument itself the naked woman is placed a long way beneath 'the ideal' position of the Victory figure and is set in 'the real' (Kress and Van Leeuwen, 1996, 2001), standing upon a base that has bronze reliefs showing the Aberystwyth coat of arms and the Welsh dragon, so fusing the commemoration with a more regional form of nationalism, also used to distract from collective workers movements.

The physical location of the woman on the monument, that is positioned well below the towering Victory figure but close to the symbols of local and national identity, combine with her contemporary appearance to connote her greater proximity to everyday society while Victory is a the top of a high column. The female represented participant in the Aberystwyth monument carries within her three identities: she is humanity; the nation and the struggling female that war is fought on behalf of all. All this is present without any acknowledgement of the sacrifice made by women in WWI.

In the art of ancient Greece the naked female body was celebrated as a thing of beauty, athletes often ran with little or no cover on their bodies to celebrate the attainment of the perfect, accomplished human being (Greer and Lewis, 2004). Initially, following the traditions of the ancient Egyptians, Greek sculptors represented only male bodies but later moved on to the female naked or half-naked body, Greer and Lewis (2004) comment:

> Greek sculptors achieved an idealization of feminine strength
> and serenity that paralleled the earlier idealization of the
> male body. (p. 94)

This practice changed under the influence of Christianity, as Loverance (2007) says, the early Christian artists struggled with the identity of the naked female in art, seeing Eve as a naked, evil temptress. Initially they did not adhere to the Greek tradition of 3D representations of the naked, beautiful woman. However, this early Christian attitude changed to one that associated nakedness with truth and a rejection of the material world (Ripa, 1539, cited by Van Straten, 1994). So, earlier practices were soon resurrected in the work of the Renaissance artists who attempted to replicate the ideals of the ancient Greeks in their work. Hence, once again the female form was represented naked and as a thing of beauty. It is in such representations that we find the origins of the forms found on the war monuments.

We find a different representation of the female body in the monument in Finchley, London (Figure 7.6). Designed by Emile Guilaume and unveiled in 1927, the monument, called 'La Delivrance', was described by Borg (1991:103) as the '. . . only statue in London to be sexy'. The shape of this woman's body differs from that of the woman represented in the

FIGURE 7.6 *The WWI monument at Finchley, London.*

Source: Image reproduced from www.geolocation.ws/v/E/2622964/statue-of-la-deliverance-henlys-corner/en. Photographed by David Howard © 2007.

Aberystwyth monument in that the curves are less defined, giving a more athletic appearance to the figure. The pose also suggests athleticism with the head and arms raised upwards, legs tight together and the delicate balance on the balls of the feet. Again we find the mythical figure of Victory but here as athletic and energetic.

The apparent readiness to move onwards and upwards is typical of the art of the then new century, rather than the idealized yet natural forms that have been discussed so far, artists experimented with the body as a symbol for a utopian future (Michaud, 2004). In the first few decades of the twentieth century among some avant-garde European artists there was a shift away from idealizing the naturalistic body towards representing the body in order to reveal inner spirit and attitudes. The human body became a symbol for a utopian future (Michaud, 2004). Artists experimented in different, sometimes clashing directions. More rigid and athletic postures were one of these shifts. La Deliverance shows Nike not in the usual impassive pose but as the collective athletic body ready to move ahead. This use of the athletic body to represent inner attitude was of course later taken in ideological extremes in Soviet and Nazi art (Bown and Taylor, 1993). Again, drawing on Van Leeuwen and Wodak (1999) we can think of this in terms of the ways that actual motives and sequences of activity are abstracted and substituted.

In the example at Bridgend we referred to in Chapter Five (Figure 5.1), we find another representation of a woman's body as the personification of the nation. The figure known as 'Britannia' goes back to Greek mythology's 'Athena', the daughter of 'Zeus', from whose opened head she was born, fully equipped for battle. A goddess of war and wisdom, among other things, Athena was widely associated with defensive wars, from which she always emerged triumphant; she was usually depicted carrying a spear or a shield (Hard, 2003). This mythical resource is drawn upon in the Bridgend commemorative war monument as Britannia carries the objects of war: a sword, a banner and wears a helmet.

Britannia has her origins with the Romans. Britain, like many European nations at the time, drew on Greek and Roman mythology, based especially around the figures of Athena/Minerva the goddess of war, also capable of strength, restraint and strategy, for a national emblem. Others goddesses used were Germania, Helvetia and Polonia. The personification of places as well as emotions (love, fear), ideas, concepts (war, victory), natural phenomena (sky, rivers) among other things, was a key feature of ancient Greek art. All of these were depicted as women. This trend continued through Roman into Christian art and since the emergence of the nation-state has been an important resource for the representation of war, the nation-state and its objectives.

Stafford (1998) provides a number of observations that allow us to understand a little more about why these female personifications were used by the nation-states. On the one hand it is telling that in Greek society, when women were so subordinate to men, that the qualities deemed so important by Greek men were represented in female form (p. 43). Her explanation for this is that in male-dominated societies extremes of both good and evil tend to be represented in female form or as 'other'. She says:

> While the fact that women have such a low profile makes the female form a practically suitable vehicle for abstract ideas in search of an

> incarnation psychologically their desirable form conveys the desirability
> of the abstract values they embody. (p. 53)

Such representations of the nation and the national spirit draw out the paradox of the actual denial of the role of women in cultural production and the national enterprise (Rodríguez, 2006). Yet most importantly the use of this feminine personification is a crucial component of the substitution of an abstraction for the actual intentions of the colonial powers of WWI and the war of attrition they were prepared to carry out in order to realize them.

As well as her link with warfare, stories also refer to Britannia's beauty and her encounters with various males who were attracted to her; she is said to have beaten off their advances, killing them in the process (Hard, 2003; Harris and Platzner, 2003). This fearless, wise, sexually desirable woman evolved into Minerva in ancient Rome and, via Roman occupation of the British Isles, became the symbol for the British nation. Rodríguez (2006) sums up the widespread cultural practice of the adoption of the female to symbolize nation as:

> Within patriarchal discourse, women are considered
> biological reproducers of the nation, and are thus
> constructed in traditional nationalist discourse as symbolic
> bearers of the collectivity's identity and honour: the icon of a
> mother symbolises in many cultures the spirit of the nation . . . (p. 3)

In the Bridgend monument Britannia stands against an obelisk, Christian symbolism is used in the form of the cross, the wreath of bay leaves and the palm; symbolizing sacrifice, victory and peace. The foundation of Christian ideology, sacrifice, is connoted by the pose Britannia strikes with her bare leg forward, reminiscent of the image of Jesus Christ on the cross. We see in this example how sacrifice for the nation is legitimized by recontextualizing what actually took place through deletion of horror, abuse of life by the elites and the role of women through a number of resources that specifically add meanings that suggest a collective act of nation, where the differences in terms of who fought and died, who lost loves ones and who profited by the war are concealed by the abstraction of the national personification who is both strong and bears feminine traits.

The personification of the nation is also seen in slightly different forms in the monuments at Weston Super-Mare and Bridgwater, but these monuments specifically symbolize the connection between nation and expanding territoriality; expanding outside the legitimate limits of the nation-state. In the Weston Super-Mare monument there is a figure of a winged victory that stands with outstretched arms on an orb; symbolizing the world. She holds an olive branch in her hands; symbolizing peace (Cirlot, 2002). The 'world' is, significantly, placed under the feet of the figure, a position that connotes power and control over the object, and that which it symbolizes.

Within the context of the war monument, the message symbolized by the olive branch tells the viewer that peace is achievable by war and relates this not just to immediate peace and release from the conflict itself as the lower figure in the Aberystwyth monument depicted. Here the conflict and the Victory are placed in terms of territory and power. This linking of the British nation and the rest of the world is taken further another example situated at Bridgwater.

The designer of the Bridgwater monument John Angel called his winged figure 'civilization', although she is known locally as 'The Angel of Bridgwater'. Angels are usually depicted upright, or in flight, so it is of interest that in John Angel's representation she is seated on a throne in the manner of a mortal queen. This seated physical position gives her a worldly, rather than supernatural, quality; achieved by the connotations of a royal ruler seated on a throne. 'The Book of Law' rests in her lap, guarded by two angels. In her right hand she holds an orb, symbolizing the world, that is surrounded by four figures representing the four corners of the earth and holding a banner that represents its unification.

In this small section of the sculpture the viewer sees that their nation has control of the earth; not too far from the reality of the time as Britain's colonial empire in the twentieth century was still vast enough to warrant the notion that that the sun never sets on its territory. The relation between these territories and their ruler was, of course, one of inequality, however, the monument naturalizes and legitimizes the ideological position that views the nation's claiming of external territory through war as a given; this point is made clearer by examining the other symbols in the monument.

Under the feet of the seated figure there are four grotesque images: a monstrous head, a skeleton, a figure holding its head in its hands and figures in combat. These images are said to represent the atrocities of war and are cited by the designer as being representations of: bloodshed, corruption, strife and despair. In this composite image the horrors of war are acknowledged, so could we argue that in representing the horror of war, the monument condemns the practice? Crucially, the 'atrocities' positioned under the feet of the figure are therefore represented as being kept under control by the feet of the nation. The ugliness of war is not completely avoided; instead, war is presented as something that the nation has to keep at bay. At the same time, the fact that the atrocities are acknowledged in the monument warns the viewer that war is a necessary evil in order to keep the world civilized, which, as we see connoted by the presence of the book that is guarded by divinity, is attainable through the implementation of this nation's laws.

Moving to the back of the monument, the viewer sees the angels' wings forming a canopy that shelters a small group of figures said to represent: Labour, Education and the Home.

Protected by the angel, these figures serve to remind the viewer of the reasons for war: to preserve 'the cornerstones' of civilization. The inclusion of the figures representing civilization and the symbolic representation of the world plays an important role in the wider communicative potential of the monument.

As a final example we find a mythical/legendary figure used to personify a locality. Here what is of interest is the way that grief and the war are interwoven with existing local stories and persons as a strategy to naturalize them and infuse them with ideas and values related to belonging and longer histories of the character of the place. We find this on the WWI monument at Merthyr Tydfil (Figure 7.7).

Designed by L. S. Merifield and unveiled on Armistice Day in 1931, the monument features two women and one man. The central figure is a robed 'St Tydfil'. According to legend she was a king's daughter who had been

FIGURE 7.7 *The WWI monument at Merthyr Tydfil.*

killed by pagans in the fifth century (Breverton, 2000). She stands within a central Portland stone screen, on top of a base that supports several objects: a helmet, crossed swords, a ram's head and garlands. According to the artist's description (Monument Records, Merthyr Tydfil Library) these objects represent 'an altar of sacrifice' as discussed in Chapter Six. Here the choice has been to represent St Tydfil on top of the urn itself which takes a Classical form as does the broader altar in which this is positioned. St Tydfil has her arm raised which in Christian symbolism communicates the reward of the righteous and the ascent to heaven.

To her right is a man representing a local miner (Monument Records, Merthyr Tydfil Library) standing with his head bent down and gesturing towards the ground – miners were not themselves required to go to war. The woman on her left, also standing and gesturing towards the ground with her right arm, with her left arm she supports a baby, a blanket wraps around both their bodies. Dark (1991:138) describes the figures as having been sculpted with 'particular intensity', but what features inspire Dark to make this comment? The inclusion of these two figures addresses the miners who would have lost brothers or sons and the women who would have lost husbands. These were considered as unstable times by government and national and local capitalists. Such statues attempted to place the deaths of local men as part of local lore, a personification of the community in the form of St Tydfil who leads the mourning of the local people.

The bodily pose of the two figures: lowered heads and gesturing towards the ground, communicates grief as if pointing to a spot on the ground as a grave. But this is not desperate grief of broken people as the poses are nevertheless upright and dignified, perhaps with the suggestion of respect.

Representations of the roles played by women in WWII monuments

We now compare these earlier monuments, erected at a time when Britain was an imperial power, personifying the nation and its goals in the female form, with the representation of women in contemporary war monuments. These contemporary monuments have been erected in a post-colonial period, in the late twentieth and early twenty-first centuries; this change in status removes the option of representing woman as a personification of the nation that conquers the world. Before examining the monuments themselves to reveal which of the alternative representations modern artists have selected, a contextual overview of the extent and nature of the role women played in WWII is provided in the following section.

When WWII started, women again played a major role at home in replacing male employees in the workplace. This time the government did not rely on poverty and a sense of national duty to lure women into employment. Instead they conscripted women into employment under 'The Control of Employment Orders', which meant that civilian men and women could be ordered to work anywhere in the country, miles away from their homes, unless the women had children under the age of 14, or were married. In these cases they would usually be allowed to remain at home, or if deemed suitable, given work closer to home.

Women also took the place of men in agricultural roles in the 'Land Army', as they had in WWI and some joined the VAD. Taking voluntary work into consideration, an estimated 80 per cent of married and 90 per cent of single women were contributing to the war effort in 1943. The pay inequality issue persisted in WWII, some women protested against the unfair conditions; Braybon and Summerfield (1987) cite an example of women striking against the unfair pay differential between male and female wages (73 shillings and 43 shillings, respectively). The women were publicly condemned for striking; eggs and tomatoes were thrown at them and they were accused of '. . . letting the country down' (Braybon and Summerfield, 1987:176). Similarly, in Bristol contempt for females employed as bus conductresses, a person employed to go around the bus collecting fares and giving tickets, was shown when men gathered to throw stones at the trams while calling for their dismissal (Beddoe, 2000). The expectation that women should relinquish their employment in favour of the returning male soldiers can be traced back to WWI official discourses, as Noakes (2006) points out, the largest union representing women workers in 1918, the National Federation of Women Workers, supported their relinquishing of their employment.

Women also joined military groups that were set up during WWI, these were: WAAC (Women's Army Auxiliary Corps), WRNS (Women's Royal Naval Service) and the WAAF (Women's Auxiliary Air Force). Their involvement in military roles, although eventually accepted, were deeply resented by many and was always presented as a temporary situation that would end as soon as the war ended and men returned to reclaim 'their' roles in the workplace. In the military units the women did a variety of jobs, both at home from the age of 18 and on the front from the age of 20, including: clerical work, driving, telephone and signal operators, coders and decoders, mechanics to name a few (Calkins in Cook, 2006). Their role in intelligence through the map-making process was crucial. Maddrell's (2007) accounts of the role females played in wartime geographical intelligence shows not only the wide extent of their contribution, but also the extent of the lack of recognition for their contribution to the discipline of Geography.

In contrast to WWI there was a marked increase in the militarization of women in WWII; it is reported that 640,000 women had served in the three 'auxiliary' services: the ATS (Auxiliary Territorial Service Category), WRNS and WAAF (Mellor, 1972, cited by Doerr in Cook, 2006). Although they were not officially engaged in battle as their male counterparts were, many lost their lives in battle situations. The heaviest loss for the WRNS was in the sinking of the Aguila in August 1941. It had been torpedoed while sailing in a convoy from Liverpool – 21 Wrens were killed in the attack (Crabb, 2006). Crabb (2006) lists the known numbers of women lost as: 225 British women on British service ships and 222 on British Commonwealth service and mercantile women during WWII (pp. 214–30). He also lists nine known memorials to the lives lost on ships, but notes that 'only a few' are dedicated solely to women.

The three auxiliary services reported a total of 624 female fatalities, with many more wounded or taken prisoners of war (Mellor, 1972, cited by Doerr in Cook, 2006). This figure does not include the deaths while serving in the Special Operations Executive (SOE) – they parachuted 50 female agents into occupied Europe. Some disappeared completely, 15 were captured by the German army, tortured and, apart from three, were executed (Doerr in Cook, 2006:243). In a key role working as an intelligence officer in the British secret service, Vera Atkins liaised with the French resistance in occupied France. She recruited over 400 agents, 39 of them women. Thirteen of the female agents were killed; some executed by their German guards after being captured and tortured (Cook, 2006:34). According to McIntyre (1990:151) women were as vulnerable to bombing as any soldier, sailor or airman, not only because they worked in targeted locations, such as munitions factories, but also because of their military involvement; 400 women in the ATS died while on active service between 1939 and 1945. It is against this background that we analyse the few commemorative war monuments dedicated to the women who participated in WWII which have for the most part been erected relatively recently.

The most prominent memorial to the women of WWII is the monument erected in Whitehall, London, in 2005 (Figure 7.8). The design had been selected from 12 entries in a competition that was judged by a group of people occupying high status positions in the world of art. The designer states that his inspiration comes from the memories he holds of his mother's employment in the manufacture of munitions (John W. Mills, online reference). The monument is described as depicting the contribution made by all women to the war, not just the military personnel.

The monument is in the shape of a cenotaph – an empty tomb – and cast in bronze. Although it is said to be the largest bronze sculpture in the City of London, at 22 feet, it is not as high as Lutyens' stone cenotaph to soldiers that also stands in Whitehall which has an overall height of 35 feet. The north face of the cenotaph gives details of the unveiling; the south face of the memorial has the following inscription:

This Memorial Was Raised To Commemorate
The Vital Work Done By Nearly Seven Million Women
In World War II.

FIGURE 7.8 *The monument to the women of WWII in Whitehall, London.*

Void of human figures, 'the tomb' has a further function: it acts as a wardrobe, providing an unusual visual synecdoche. On each face of the monument there are clothes pegs on which hang various types of clothes worn by women in wartime. A closer inspection of the way in which the clothes hang from the pegs reveals their low modality representation. They hang in an unnatural shape suggesting they are almost half occupied by a ghostly presence. The uniforms, 17 in number, hang in shaped poses, as if they have headless, armless, legless bodies inside. The sleeves are at jaunty angles facing towards the pockets, giving a frivolous feel to the imagined activities. Their shapes are cartoon-like though low modality with reduced articulation of details. They are therefore simplified and idealized.

This monument is reportedly not appreciated by all ex-WWII female military personnel; many of whom worked hard to campaign and raise the money for the erection of a monument specifically to women. These women have protested that the monument has no meaning, with its lack of human images it fails to do justice to the memory of the females who contributed to the war. A former member of the WRAC who helped to raise funds for the commemorative war monument commented on the design:

> It has a frieze of hats and coats around it which means
> nothing to anyone. What the heck does it mean? We want
> some say in the design. It is for us and it's our money that has
> paid for it. (Lillian Edwards quoted in the *Wilmslow Express*,
> 13 August 2003)

The act of hanging up the uniforms connotes an end to the activities; an end to the war. In reality the end of the war also meant an end to many women's jobs; an image corresponding with their actual employment role rather than their sacrifice. Lillian Edwards' dissatisfaction with the design is understandable when considering the expectations she might have based on her experience of viewing the kinds of monuments already discussed where soldiers are represented as powerful impassioned Classical figures placed into eternity. On this monument the fact that the representations are void of human figures suggests that the role females played in the war is more important than their sacrifice. In a sense, in celebrating their employment role the monument denies their sacrifice. It suggests something temporary despite the use of the traditional bronze to connote weight, solidity and ancient tradition. We can also see that the clothing has been placed appropriately in the 'ideal' well above the gaze of the viewer. But it is the clothing which has been hung up that is now idealized – clothing realized through lower modality emphasizing softer rounder forms.

The darkness of the cenotaph itself loses the power of the brighter stone with its fake block effects typical of the Classical styles, to connote the glorious civilization and high ideas of the men's monuments. At least on the Armed Forces Memorial discussed in Chapters Five and Six (Figure 5.12) while the woman soldier is depicted in a caring, nursing role, there is some greater sense of material process. A semiotic study of monument design would have indicated the many mistakes made here. Of course, as we shall see in the following chapter, contemporary monuments tend not to follow these same patters as we have seen for WWI. But we can place the disappointment of the women who raised the finds for the monument against some of these raised expectations.

In addition, the verbal component in the form of the inscription is remarkably simple in comparison with the 'sacrifice' and 'glory' found in inscriptions that usually commemorate the role played by male soldiers; focusing on 'work', albeit 'vital' work done by absent females, excludes the notion of sacrifice.

One monument to the WWII women that does feature a figure is the one at the National Memorial Arboretum seen in Figure 7.9.

This monument is one of two at the National Arboretum that was designed by sculptor Andy Decomyn who used his wife as a model for the statue. The monument to the WWII ATS women at the National Memorial Arboretum features a woman in uniform seated on a low plinth that places her at eye level to the viewer. The ATS is described as a 'Cinderella' organization by Braybon and Summerfield (1987) and was the only military group to use khaki uniforms; the WAFS wore light blue and WRNS wore dark blue. Apparently, they had an unglamorous, even 'immoral' reputation among both males and females; its members being widely associated with a lack of education and skill (Braybon and Summerfield, 1987; Summerfield, 1997; Grayzel, 1999; Watson, 2004). However, about 212,500 women served in the ATS by 1943; 335 of them were killed and several more wounded (McIntyre, 1990).

FIGURE 7.9 *The memorial to the ATS at the National Memorial Arboretum.*

The colour of the concrete and cement material chosen for this monument is white. It is not the common choice for war monuments that, as we saw earlier in this analysis, is bronze connoting strength, weight, durability and ancient hand-based techniques of forging, although the resin used here is described as being able to withstand acid rain and is vandal resistant (National Arboretum Guide, p. 54). Nevertheless this form gives a sense of moulding rather than the more epic processes of carving and forging and appears softer, gentler and more giving.

The white colour chosen for the design is also important in the way it communicates. In symbolism, white is associated with purity and cleanliness and also with optimism and truth as opposed to darker colours which can suggest darker solemn moods and obscurity. This also serves to reduce the level of modality that could have been raised by the use of full colour palette to represent the woman more naturalistically. This is something that is the case through all monuments, however. The full colour palette can suggest liveliness and fun as well as naturalism. In monuments the single colour of bronze or stone is more moderate and stayed.

The modality of the figure is also reduced as the body parts such as the eyes are exaggerated. Her hat and head are overly large and out of proportion. She appears almost as a cartoon.

The pose of the figure finds her sitting at an angle, her head looks slightly over her right shoulder in a classic photo pose, her legs are drawn together, close to her body and the pose is recognizable as a characteristically feminine way of sitting. According to Argyle (1975) females take up less space than males and tend to draw their limbs to the body, while males spread out into the space around them, this posture was typical of those found in the commercial photographs of females commonly found in the WWII period. Her demeanour is almost coy and does not remotely connote battle or bravery as commonly found in the representations of males in commemorative war monuments.

This idealized image of woman has no trace of death or wounding, nor of agency. There are no material processes represented here, only 'sitting' and 'smiling'. Nor is the monument raised on a pedestal to suggest we look up to the ATS soldiers in the ideal.

The monument arguably simply reinforces conventional notions of femininity: as an object to be visually caressed, cared for and protected. This voyeuristic relationship is further defined by the element of gaze. From an interactive viewing perspective the monument follows the now established pattern; the represented participant makes no eye contact with the viewer resulting in the lack of engagement.

Conclusion

In this chapter we have applied the analytical concepts from earlier chapters combining these with contextual information to continue to show how these can draw our attention to features and forms that enhance our ability to describe what we see. These allowed us to think about the iconography of monuments where women are represented as Classical figures personifying concepts and nation. And it allowed us to think about the way that the same figures were represented differently at different times as we looked at postures and materials. They also allowed us to reveal the way that even where women's actual participation in war has been represented that this is through reduced modalities and caring roles or as symbolizing the Home Front. But in all cases material and iconographical semiotic choices are different to those found for the representation of the role of men in war, even though in the case of men it is never clear what they themselves actually do. But we do not tend to find women represented in bronze standing solidly and impassively appearing as Classical gods.

CHAPTER EIGHT

Changing discourses of war

In this chapter we turn out attention to the changing discourses of war
as they are realized on the war monument. On the one hand we find the
changing role of the war monument in a shift towards the tourism industry
as part of heritage trails and a move away from commemoration to history
as learning and experiencing. On the other hand discourses of war have
themselves changed. While many linguistic analyses of war discourses
found in political speeches suggest that these have remained largely the
same over centuries, perhaps it is at the visual level where this change
can be documented. Wars, as in WWI and WWII, were formerly fought
between large national, more or less equal enemies, taking place on font
lines with large armies organized around formal structures and aligned
to industrial production of weapons and resources. Official reasons given
for participation in these wars were documented by the likes of Graham
et al. (2004): to fight an evil enemy, a common cause, a greater calling
such as god or truth, while behind these wars, as in WWI, could lie issues
of competition over resources, territory and colonies.

But war has changed. Smith (2001) points out that enemies no longer
have clear links to official states. They are not structurally organized in
the manner of Western state armies and act within the people, attacking
only when beneficial to them. Such enemies cannot be beaten with
traditional military technology and organization. In WWI and WWII the
military objective was the defeat of Germany. In later conflicts terms like
'peacekeeping' and 'humanitarian' are used. Yet these are more activities
than outcomes. And the actual outcomes may even be impossible to see,
such as what kind of political system may finally arise in Iraq, which
of course is problematic in terms of gaining wider public support. But
for Smith, while discourses of war may have been modified to match
this change, there is still a public, political and institutional sense that

traditional industrial-based warfare can work. In the United Kingdom such is the power of the rhetoric of Britain's success in the two world wars, wars defeating an equal might enemy, one where the homeland was defended in a war away from the homeland, free of military occupation, that still provides the basis for the discourses of war that are most widely disseminated. When 'our boys' are paraded at national sporting events, there is still the idea that they will go overseas and defend our interests against evil threats.

It is into this context that war monuments have continued to be built, one where war is different, yet not fully understood but where public support for them is still important and remains an important site for the promotion of national identity. In this chapter we look first at some of the visual designs of contemporary monuments and how these have changed, looking at the discourses that they communicate. Second we turn our attention specifically to the inscriptions found on monuments over time with a view to the way the kinds of presuppositions, identities and actions have changed as discourses of war have changed. Here we begin with some older WWI inscriptions and then move on to more contemporary ones. In each case we consider the relationship of these to the changing visual discourses.

The Wootton Bassett war monument

At the time of writing the British Army was deployed in over 80 countries (British Army, online reference), engaged in all kinds of military activities, including participation in conflicts as part of NATO. While the majority of Britain's war monuments date from the WWI period, due to the sheer need to foster nationalism, the late twentieth and first decade of the twenty-first centuries have so far also been a very busy period for war monument building. As well as contemporary wars these frequently commemorate specific groups involved in earlier wars and also wars that have formerly not been commemorated such as to the men who went to join the international brigades in the Spanish Civil War unveiled in Swansea 2011. We begin our analysis with one of the monuments to the contemporary conflicts, with a monument (Figure I. 2) unveiled in 2004 in a busy shopping street in the small town of Wootton Bassett in the South of Britain. What is particularly interesting about this monument, as well as its design, is the process that led to the monument being erected that involved the public at many different levels, including local councillors, shop-owners and school children. We begin with this story.

On the surface the development of this monument appears slightly more democratic where it is more usual that they are processed through official government committees. But a closer look reveals something very different which draws even local children into the discourses of war.

At the time of writing, this small town was of particular interest in the national media as it was to this location that the bodies of the dead soldiers who had fought in Afghanistan were being initially repatriated. The existence of the new monument and the narrative behind its appearance was not missed by news reporters.Wootton Bassett would soon play in the repatriation of the bodies of the war dead from Afghanistan to nearby RAF Lyneham. From 2001 to 2007 the bodies of military service personnel were publically repatriated through the streets of Wootton Bassett from RAF Lyneham. These public repatriations soon became a common news feature as the bereaved families and members of the general public, some of whom had travelled several miles, lined the streets as the coffins went by. These events form contextual layers to the meaning of the Wootton Bassett monument as it has become a symbol of not only military sacrifice of life, but a departure from traditional, restrained public displays of grieving that were previously predominant in Britain.

Wootton Bassett previously had no war memorial and the British Legion, the association for former soldiers, had been pressing for one for many years. In 1997 a14-year-old female army cadet, connected to the Legion, started to collect signatures for a petition to have one made. Local council members and the Mayor became involved, such appeared to be the public support, and fund-raising began. The story had been a convenient one for local news media as a local girl was showing plucky respect for an older generation.

A number of objections to a monument were made by one councillor who took an anti-war position but these were easily silenced with the support of the majority of councillors and the local media and there was a call to generate funds for the building of a memorial. Part of the given evidence for the monument's popularity with the public was that even a Muslim kebab shop owner had contributed, in fact the largest single amount to the fund of £1600.When £20,000 had been raised, a public competition was started that called for local people to submit designs. The majority of these came from local schools, from where the winning design was chosen. The committee narrowed the choice down to eight and local people were able to vote for the winner through a ballot held in the local library. The winning entry was a globe held by one hand that was designed by a 15-year-old boy from a local comprehensive school. However, when the design was sent to the manufacturers for costing, the committee were advised that having the globe supported by one hand was a weakness that may be a health and safety hazard; acting on this advice, they decided to adapt the design to support the globe with four hands. The manufacturers also recommended the use of bronze, which would suffer a colour change when placed in the elements but would not deteriorate and decompose. Correspondence among the records show that the selected design was commonly read by the people involved in the committee as a 'frail world' that has to be cared for and handled carefully.

The commissioning committee made the additional recommendation that the globe in the chosen design would be placed with the Falkland Islands facing towards the local Royal Air Force base to acknowledge the role of the base in the Falklands War. The statue was then unveiled by the Mayor and was marked with a parade of British Legion and army cadets, a fly-past by a Hercules jet from airbase and the singing of a hymn 'I vow to thee my country' and the English National Anthem. The unveiling ceremony differed very little from those of the post-WWI unveiling ceremonies in the 1920s with themes of militarism, religion and nationalism all included.

In sum, the Wootton Bassett monument came into existence through official institutions: the local Member of Parliament, RAF Lyneham, the British Legion, the local council, schools and local library. It was then presented as a monument that had its origins in the feelings of local people. But the question could be asked as to which sections of the population this reflected. One interviewee suggested that those who voted for the monument were mainly retired people visiting the library. Historians have noted that at the unveiling of many of the WWI monuments crowds would shout their objections, aware on one level of the question of the grotesque waste of life that was being swept aside through absurd nationalistic imagery. Yet these monuments, through the representations of the news media, in classrooms and other official institutions, easily become accepted as the voice of the people. These objects make a claim to house our memories and identities, to signpost in our public what ideals, values and identities we commonly cherish and seek to celebrate. We analyse the monument itself under headings to draw attention to different semiotic choices made in the design.

Iconography

Much of the meaning of this memorial is created through its iconography of the globe and the hands that hold it. There are four hands holding the globe up. This is a common image found in advertisements that reference climate change and environmental issues. It is used to symbolize unity between people and the planet and points to the way that the health of the planet is in our hands. Of course in this case such images themselves conceal and recontextualize the actual origins of climate change in global capitalism and rampant consumerism and the actual concrete solutions that are required and by whom. The same process of recontextualization is taking place here as regards war. The discourse of war being realized in this case appears to be one associated with the unity of people and planet. War is connected to our role in taking care of the planet. The globe does in fact occur on many of the Classical war monuments, although these were rarely represented in full and generally provided a platform for the figure of Classical god Victory reaching upwards towards god, sword in hand. Also here something is thought about whose hands these are – presumably the hands of 'our' soldiers. And this has become obscured in war discourse. Who is doing the policing and why and why in turn some terrible regimes are not policed and remain invisible.

The globe itself is as significant to the nation in the twenty-first century as it was in the colonial period of WWI. As links with the rest of the world strengthen through capitalist structures, so the interests of the nation increasingly depend on other parts of the globe. Economic ties inextricably bind them together, just as they did during the empire building days of the colonial powers. A difference between colonization and globalization is that the colonial powers took world resources by overt shows of force and occupation, whereas globalization 'takes' resources, ostensibly at least, through corporations who often require military backing. There are those who would argue that colonial powers are still at force; twenty-first century elitist discourses of 'war on terror', put forward as a rationale for military engagement, are often countered with discourses that claim that wars are actually being fought not for security but for the control of a region's natural resources.

Form and space

This is not a massive monument. A truly massive globe would have given the sense of military fanaticism or would have shifted the symbolism too far away from the military message to one of adoration of the planet itself. The monument uses the standard bronze, which is used to connote eternity and which gives the rougher texture now associated with monuments. While the surface is shiny it is also rough, and suggests something less designed and polished and more natural and organic.

Of course steel, or aluminium, could have been used but were not. For one part their brighter colours would have connoted modernity, technology and science as opposed to timelessness. The lack of detail and blurring on bronze sculptures also reduces modality and helps to give a sense of that which is symbolic rather than documentary. The hands, in contrast, are much larger than natural human hands. Much smaller hands would have suggested difficulty in supporting the planet. A very large hand would have suggested controlling or the power to manipulate the planet or could have suggested that the planet was already safe in our hands rather than requiring our further efforts.

Size and height

The globe is placed into the ideal, but not too high. We can imagine the effect were it 20 m up. The pedestal itself is simple and square in shape.

None of the Classicism of the earlier WWI pedestals is present, where there was a preference for pillars or geometric shapes that suggest the obelisk. The simplicity points to a sense of modernity and therefore a suggestion of contemporary issues. This combination of semiotic resources realizes a discourse that is very much aligned with that of humanitarianism that now defines much military activity such as in the occupation of Iraq and Afghanistan. Throughout the first decade of the twenty-first century the public became familiar with the news media representation of 'our boys' and the protection of vulnerable citizens from fanatics. Yet the names of the soldiers on this monument are from WWI and WWII. Smith (2001) was concerned about the British public and institutional lack of awareness of the way that war has now changed. This monument communicates something of activities of peacekeeping but nothing of the costs of this and the complexities of the situations that lie behind these. In the fashion of the WWI monuments the micro-processes of war are recontextualized. Soldiery and war remain positively evaluated even if in contemporary conflicts their meaning has completely transformed. The reasons for soldiers being in Afghanistan, the conflict associated with Wootton Bassett, and the aims of the conflict, are deleted.

The Australian WWII monument

In the following monument we also find the use of the environment to bring together connotations of nature and nationalism in a contemporary war monument commemorating soldiers from Australia who died in WWII that stands in Hyde Park, London (Figure 8.1). In this case we begin with an analysis of the monument itself and then go on to consider information about its commissioning and design.

The Australian war monument comprises a long curved wall, containing over 200 tonnes of granite, taking up a large section of the corner of the park and costing nearly AUS$10 million to build. The wall curves around the corner of Hyde Park and also curves in height, being about 4 m in the centre and lower at each end, forming an amphitheatre. A further layer of panels lean irregularly against the wall and several stone blocks are placed irregularly in front of the structure within the curve. Names of the places from where Australian soldiers were enlisted are written randomly across the blocks with the names of 47 battle sites superimposed over these.

Iconography

Unlike the WWI monuments we find no Christian or other religious iconography. The design borrows from the megalithic Classical style, but with its curve and slope and plaques leaning against the main wall it also

FIGURE 8.1 *The Australian War Memorial, Hyde Park, London.*

draws heavily on the tradition of installation art. Like many contemporary monuments we not only find hints at Classicism but also important departures from this style. Much iconographical work is done by the place names of Australian towns and battle areas that are, in the tradition of monuments, written in a slender Times New Roman font, signifying tradition and elegance. Clearly we could not use Ariel or Courier, which would carry different connotations (Van Leeuwen, 2005). Water in the form of fountains that cascade water over the plaques is used to symbolize purity. The inscription on the monument itself explains that:

THE FLOW OF WATER OVER THESE NAMES EVOKES MEMORIES OF SERVICE, SUFFERING AND SACRIFICE.

It is of note for understanding the recontexualization of war and the fostering of nationalism that service, suffering and sacrifice are to be signified through the flow of water and so rendered themselves as pure acts. Purity has been a constant theme in war monuments. In WWI monuments soldiers would walk or stand with their hat removed. The bare head was associated with lack of sin and being able to bear all before god. Clearly the purity of the soldiers themselves and the morality of the motivations for their actions are still an important part of the discourse of war commemoration. The granite used for the wall is itself a green variety of granite brought from Australia, which the designers suggest connotes the essence of the Australian bush. Such connotations and symbolism are typical of these monuments erected partly for the purposes of tourism (Karp and Lavine, 1991). On the central plaques in the wall we find a range of nationalistic and military emblems.

Form and space

The wall takes up a lot of space creating the amphitheatre, which itself has meaning potential. The monument could be much smaller or discrete. It could have been comprised of just a few blocks, or a small semi-circle, enough for one person to walk into. The scale of the monument is interrelated with the Australian Government's concern to promote the country as an international player in its own right, shifting further away from its association with being a colony. In his inauguration speech the Australian Prime Minister over-lexicalized (Kress, 1989) the nature of Australia as a nation in its own right, suggesting that here lies an awkward or contestable matter. Many of the American WWII monuments in France are also characterized by such large constructions. It appears that this has symbolic importance in terms of marking a presence in other non-national territories. There is a clear association of space with significance, which has added importance when commemorating in a space away from the homeland. We could imagine the reversed meaning were only a small match-box sized space occupied.

Size and height

There is also meaning potential in the height of the monument. Four meters is about twice the human size and the names of the places and battles are placed just above head height. The meaning would have been different had the wall been 10 feet in height or had it been placed below ground level for us to look down upon. We can again draw on Kress and Van Leeuwen's (1996) account of the nature of the ideal and real in compositions. WWI monuments tend to have either pedestals or at least large steps raising the whole structure off the ground and into the ideal. In the case of the Australian monument, typical of newer designs, the base is at ground level. It is not raised at all away from ground level. In this case the monument is much more grounded, even if part of it is raised higher than human experience. Clearly war has become less idealized and more on our everyday level. Particular semiotic choices in size and height can also be explained through more recent changes in British Government policy as regards these kinds of public art and displays. Karp and Lavine (1991) describe a drive where public displays, such as in museums have to be lively and people-friendly places that 'implicate' audiences. As part of this process, war monuments become not only sites of mourning but also of learning and may even tend towards the quasi-artistic and curious, with instructions on how to understand complex symbolism. Newer monuments often point out that they are arranged so that they catch the sun's rays on a certain day, or that they align with certain stars, or face a city far away. All this, say Karp and Lavine, is about the veracity of the experiential. This Australian monument is designed to 'implicate' with overt symbolism a sense of being part of the landscape.

Curvature and angularity

Curvature as opposed to angularity is also important in the form of the wall. There is curvature not only in terms of the form of the amphitheatre itself but also where the wall is higher in the middle than it is at the ends. We can bring out the meaning potential of this choice of semiotic resources if we imagine the effect were the wall was simply a flat square. The meaning potential of angularity versus curvature is where the first is associated with rationality and the second with emotions, the organic and femininity. While Classical WWI monuments used curvature there was also an emphasis on straight lines and pillars. The Australian monument is characterized much more by curvature and therefore the emotions and the organic. The organic nature of the monument is also communicated by the lack of symmetry that characterized the Classical monuments. The Australian wall is not symmetrical but ends with different heights, and rather than dominating the landscape with its own space follows the contours of the park up the gentle slope. The designer of the monument said that the form was to suggest the sweep of the Australian landscape and the openness of the people.

Regularity and irregularity

The organic and non-rational signification in the form here comes also from the meaning potential of regularity versus irregularity. Whereas the Classical statues emphasize symmetry and order, the Australian monument emphasizes irregularity. The Australian monument uses plaques that appear as if they have been laid precariously against the main wall. Stone blocks positioned in front of the wall are done so as if without precision. Irregularity can have the meaning potential of not following rules. In extreme forms and depending on how it is combined with other features it can mean playful, or even chaotic. This potential is clearly realized in this case. We find lack of regulation. Against the much straighter, although organically curved wall containing the iconography of the nation, we find the much less planned and unregimented blocks that appear as unfinished, as incomplete. The association here again is with something organic and spontaneous rather than regulated and ordered, informal rather than formal. The act of war is not so much official but of the ordinary people and connected to the earth itself.

Solidity

Above we found that WWI monuments used the meaning potential of solidity versus hollow having the metaphorical association of certainty and ease of understanding rather than being able to see beneath the surface, the workings and possibly the vulnerabilities or fragility. In the Australian monument we do find some lack of solidness as we can see into the gaps where the plaques are leaning. Combined with the lack of order this semiotic choice helps to communicate more fragility and humanity. The form of the amphitheatre itself suggests something open, where we are able to enter and experience.

The commissioning of the Australian monument

Further crucial information about the semiotic resources used in this monument comes from the process of its commissioning and planning. Is this monument simply a case of the collective mourning of ordinary people? Just as WWI monuments would be commissioned by committees of ruling elites, so monuments like this one come into being as a result of series of committees, often at the government level. Westminster Council, which manages Hyde Park, is approached each year by many more groups with proposals for monuments than it can possibly accommodate and has established a number of committees to manage the situation (City of Westminster, 2004). Specific documents available from the council provide guidelines on the process of initiating and developing monument proposals. This appears on the surface to be a fairly democratic process. However, the Westminster policy states that works should not offend: 'The purpose of public art is not to shock or outrage the passer-by, but to add to the interest, richness, beauty and vitality of the street scene or public place' (City of Westminster, 2004b:4). Clearly this would mean that we might be less likely to find designs that are highly critical of war.

The Australian monument was in the first place commissioned by the Australian government. With the go-ahead from the Westminster Council they commissioned leading national artists and architects to produce potential designs. They were instructed to represent the 'national spirit', which of course is a highly conservative idea that involves essentializing the complexities of identities that lie within national boundaries and across history identity. It invites national myths where somehow the essence or soul of people can be found in the landscape itself (Jaworski and Thurlow 2010).

It is clear that the Westminster Council has been keen to foster works that create favourable links with different national governments. Other monuments in the park follow this pattern. The New Zealand War Memorial, positioned just across the park and unveiled in 2006, was developed by Ministry for Culture and Heritage in consultation with the Ministry of Foreign Affairs and Trade. Such cases indicate kinds of interests and power behind the semiotic landscapes around us and point to which voices have the power to create public representations of war in our societies. Indeed we must ask what gets excluded through the kinds of projects that are considered a useful contribution to the tourist and culture trail and that do not offend. Indeed, Kirshenblatt-Gimblett (2006) points out that the discourses of heritage that underpin such representations are generally diplomatic, conservative and celebratory. However, such monuments can guarantee large number of nationals visiting their national shrines, bringing possibilities for links with other kinds of both cultural and material consumption (Dicks, 2003; Housely and Wahl-Jorgensen, 2008) and international trade.

In sum, the Australian War Memorial is typical of this genre of tourist interest sites that aim to 'implicate' the visitor. Discourses of war merge with cultural mythology and symbolism about national character, and also those of artistic trends and innovations. For the Australian Government this monument serves in the first place to promote its own world status as a nation-state. In this process, war is realized through discourses that in contrast to the WWI monument communicate something much more organic, where attitudes to it appear to fuse with the shape and colour and majesty of the landscape and manner of an essentialized people. Nevertheless this is uncritical and carefully selected for realization by a series of official government committees.

The New Zealand WWI and WWII monument, London

In Hyde Park, London, we find the monument to the New Zealand dead in the two world wars titled 'Southern Stand' (Figure 8.2). Designed by the sculptor Paul Dibble and architect John Hardwick-Smith, the monument was dedicated by the Queen in a service held in 2006. The monument is comprised of 16 vertical, bronze, cross-shaped pillars standing at different heights in semi-grid formation on a slope. Each pillar, referred to by the artist as 'standards' (Ministry for Culture and Heritage, online reference) is engraved with a mixture of emblems from New Zealand life and environment, such as flora and fauna, literary references and military

FIGURE 8.2 *The New Zealand War monument.*

references in the form of poppies and Defence Force emblems. According to the artist, the forward lean of the 'standards' give them a 'defiant pose' (Ministry for Culture and Heritage, online reference).

Machin's (2007b) comments on connotations of movement and determination created by forward leaning shapes are relevant here as they confirm the artist's perspective on his decision to tilt the pillars forward. Despite this connoted defiance and determination, the representation does not appear so aggressive as it might if the pillars, or 'standards' were representations of actual soldiers, just as we saw in the use of trees as the representation of the firing squad in the 'Shot at Dawn' monument in Chapter Seven. The symbolic representation reduces the modality of the aggression that would be connoted if 16 soldiers were placed walking down the slope as opposed to 16 pillars. This is an important use of semiotic resources to communicate the attitudes of the soldiers as they move in disciplined formation, all striking the same angle of pose, united in spirit and purpose – the hardness of the material also playing an important role in communicating the force of their presence. This is of note in terms of the way that mental processes can be signified through behavioural processes that are themselves signified through forward leaning shapes.

Each pillar is capped with a cross that illuminates at night. The designer explained that they are arranged in the shape of the Southern Cross constellation and indicate the compass direction that will direct lost New Zealanders towards home. From the daytime viewer's perspective the connotations of warriors created by the shapes and position, capped with a cross denoting religious denomination realizes the meaning that the warriors are acting with divine legitimacy. As with the Australian monument, there is no challenge to a nationalist ideological position that might be held by the host country.

As the New Zealand monument rises from ground level and is spaced out on the ground, the viewer is invited to mingle with the formation; to go in close. The pillars also carry facts and general cultural information about New Zealand, for example, the 'iconic' New Zealand fern leaf and 'traditional' Maori carvings. This helps also to dilute the sense of the aggression as it connotes 'learning', 'education' and 'cultural inter-communication'. The monument was in fact developed by the Ministry for Culture and Heritage in consultation with the Ministry of Foreign Affairs and Trade. The designer spoke of the monument allowing British people to learn something of the relationship between the two countries. Yet the discourse of war and nationalism remains. A soldier's identity remains bound up with ideas of nation and heritage. And what exactly do we learn about the relationship between the two countries? The formation of the pillars, according to the designer, also resembles that of the New Zealand All Blacks rugby team when they perform the *haka*, their pre-match ritual. Discourses of nationalism, reified ancient history and sport are all seamlessly drawn upon. As is more typical of contemporary war monuments, Classical symbolism and idealized soldiers are replaced by abstractions and layers of symbolism.

The Merchant Seamen Memorial, Wales

The Merchant Seamen Memorial unveiled in 1997 is interesting both through its design features and in terms of where it is placed telling us something about why viewers may now come to gaze upon these memorials. The memorial was commissioned in 1994 by the Cardiff Bay Arts Trust. This was part of a broader plan to regenerate the Bay area including the construction of a tidal barrage to make the Bay lake area permanent rather than being tidal. There was also a plan to attract more wealthy people to live in the Bay area as new apartments with waterfront views were developed. Formerly the Bay area had been highly multicultural and inhabited by a largely poorer section of the Cardiff population. The design itself was chosen after a competition and warded to Brian Fell whose father had been a merchant seaman. We first look at semiotic choices found on the monument and then go on to discuss the context where it is positioned, among other tourist, heritage and shopping sites (Figure 8.3).

FIGURE 8.3 *The Merchant Seamen's monument.*

Iconography

The monument combines the frame of a boat as if run ashore with a face on the hull of the ship. It lies flat in a circle which carries the inscription. Here we find a return to classism – a broken statue from the Acropolis or a Roman courtyard. A face rendered in perfect clean lines and symmetry as in Classical sculpture. Like the Classicism of WWI statues, the face is restful, asleep, an absence of suffering, where sleep in Christian symbolism communicates the realm between life and death. We do not find a gaping mouth and empty half open eyes of a corpse, nor evidence of pain, fear or injury. Nor do we find the face pressed and flattened into the ground but rather resting easily and gently. But unlike earlier monuments, the solidity of stone and the raising into the 'ideal' through pedestals is not present. So while we find the high ideals of Classicism and the impassioned, peaceful face along with the symbolism of sleep, this is placed in the real, in the everyday. And while there is a circle around the monument containing the inscription this does not form a border. This is an object which we can explore by touching. And many children immediately climb on the monument as their families walk along the water front to see attractions or enter shops and cafes. In

WWI monuments the figures were placed both in the ideal and framed away from everyday life.

Roundness and angularity

Roundness can mean 'smooth', 'soft', 'gentle', 'emotional'. It can also mean 'fluidity', 'ease' and 'organic'. In contrast, angularity tends to be associated with 'harsh', 'technical', 'masculine' and 'objectivity'. These may be positively or negatively evaluated. In some of the monuments, we find a stress on roundness. The Classical architecture of the Cardiff Memorial while using clean lines emphasizes curvature. The Merchant Seamen monument, while partly representing a ship is particularly round in its form bringing meanings of softness, gentleness and ease. While the destruction and sinking of a merchant vessel would have been a violent and terrifying act here all of this is removed.

Solidity versus hollowness

Van Leeuwen (2005) suggests that if we can see the core of 3D objects, this may suggest vulnerability, or accessibility indicating a degree of openness or transparency where we are able to see the internal goings-on. For the most part statues of soldiers are represented as solid. They are not vulnerable, and we are not encouraged to look beneath the surface. This may seem an obvious observation since of course most public monuments are solid. But this is precisely because they are generally used to depict solidity of character, a single uncomplicated view of a figure to be revered, rather than analysed. In the case of the Merchant Seamen monument we do not find solidity. We are able to see inside and it is made of relatively thin metal sheeting. A boat could have been represented giving a more solid durable form. In this case the Classicism of the monument, unlike that of the WWI monuments is not combined with solid immovability. The fragility of those involved in the war is communicated.

The setting of the Seamen's monument

What we would also like to draw attention to in the case of this monument is the context where it appears. The monument is placed within the dockside development of Cardiff Bay. The Bay was a project financed with £500 million of public money (Dicks, 2003). Other monuments can be found at the Bay commemorating the ethnic diversity associated with the area – people who would be now excluded after gentrification. Along with this are examples of cultural heritage in the form of a plaque with poem written by a local poet. The Welsh National Opera and the Assembly building also stand in the Bay. Alongside this a range of bars, restaurants, shops and markets regularly appear with some kind of ethnic theme. Surrounding the Bay are luxury flats, the BBC Dr Who exhibition (the series is filmed in Cardiff), Techniquest, a kind of science activity museum for children, a Ferris wheel and an old-fashioned merry-go-round. Dicks (2003) argued that the development overall is typical of a trend in urban development where 'cultural quarters' are created that bring together shopping, performance and exhibition. For Dicks (2003:7), this is a form of cultural display 'geared towards the cultivation of the model consumer, rather than the model citizen'. In this sense the Merchant Seamen Memorial falls into part of this tourist-consumer experience.

We can ask therefore what kind of gaze is brought upon this monument. We have thought throughout this book about the way that these monuments come to appear to house our collective ideas, values and concerns as they are placed in the squares of our villages, towns and cities. In such cases they often sit alongside other civic and public buildings. In the case of the Merchant Seamen's monument the commemoration of war sits alongside a range of other cultural exhibitions and opportunities for consumption. The viewer sees the monument in their role as the tourist/consumer. Housely and Wahl-Jorgensen (2008) argue that in this kind of gaze all becomes a sight for consumption. War is not presented to us as something to understand and certainly not to criticize and in a sense it becomes more a cultural marker of the tourist value of the Bay itself as much as the deaths of soldiers and the process of war. Cohen (1988) has argued that things in heritage become cultural goods, part of something that must be profited from in the tourism/leisure industry. The monuments must be part of the marketability of the whole of the Bay area. And tourist destinations must have markers that set them apart from other destinations. In the Bay area we find other symbolism used to represent the history and heritage of the area that also links with the meaning of the monument. The Welsh National Opera house is formed in the shape of an upturned Celtic boat. The Welsh Assembly building is built from authentic Welsh slate – more symbolism of the nation lying in the landscape itself. The history and heritage of the area here does not include the more recent history of South Wales ravaged by global capitalism and its loss of coal mining and the resultant massive unemployment levels and associated poverty and other social problems. History and learning in this symbolic sense are not about actual concrete situations but abstracted and symbolize broader concepts of belonging to a timeless ethnic essence and ancient mountain rock forms. The subsequent reliance on heritage tourism for economic survival will not be included as part of the heritage trail. War commemoration becomes one more aspect of that history symbolized.

What cannot so easily be commodified and made marketable is not likely to be reproduced in such heritage trails. These kinds of monuments also play into the processes described by Karp and Lavine (1991) above.

Public displays of this nature must be lively, people-friendly and encourage 'learning'. This fuses with the idea that the tourist experience has associations of self-betterment and learning (Rojek and Urry, 1997). As we visit the Bay we can also learn about its history and the identity of Cardiff. But these are always selective and positive. So these war monuments house emotions and feelings but as part of larger settings of tourism, leisure and consumption.

War monument inscriptions

In this section we turn our attention to look at the discourses communicated by the inscriptions on war monuments. In the early 1960s Barthes (1977:39) had argued that images are 'polysemous' – that they are a 'floating chain' of signifiers where the viewer can choose some and ignore others. It was the role of words and captions to 'fix' this floating chain and to 'hold the connoted meanings from proliferating. So the meaning of images would be controlled through captions. In the case of monument we might say therefore that the material design choices are such a floating chain which could be controlled and fixed by inscriptions. We do not see it quite that way. We would argue that for both the material design and the inscriptions it is the readers/viewers who anchor the meaning. Both the material objects, we have shown in the last few chapters, and the texts embody a meaning potential (Halliday, 1978), or a set of possible meanings. Which ones of these will depend on who reads, when, when and for what reason. We have seen that designers of the monuments have visually used iconography, form and materials which they believe have the cultural resonance to communicate specific discourses. Inscriptions do not anchor a free flow of signifiers but are one more semiotic tool through which discourses can be communicated. As we show in some ways the linguistic discourses have changed less than the visual discourses.

In this section we use Fairclough's (2003) approach to uncovering ideological implicitness and assumptions in texts. What we look for in the inscriptions are the kinds of taken-for-granted ideas, identities and values that are represented. Such agreed-upon assumptions are especially important in the communication of national community identities. Just as the material objects sit in our public spaces housing our collective ideas and values, pointing to what we cherish and celebrate, so too must the language communicate what it is that 'we' believe and what is common sense to us.

Fairclough (2003) says of the relationship between ideology and assumptions:

Assumed meanings are of particular ideological significance – one can argue that relations of power are best served by meanings which are widely taken as given. (p. 58)

Fairclough outlines three main types of assumptions:

- *Existential assumptions:* assumptions about what exists
- *Propositional assumptions:* assumptions about what is or can be or will be the case
- *Value assumptions:* assumptions about what is good or desirable.

We will be looking at a range of inscriptions first from WWI monuments and then more recent monuments for the kinds of assumptions they carry.

Of course we could take the inscriptions as simply appropriate to the expression of grief and commemoration of the loss of loved ones. Raivo (1998) claimed that nationalism, the ideology of belonging to the nation, was an essential part of war remembrance. But looking more carefully at some of the assumptions contained in these inscriptions helps us to think about this differently, to draw out the ways that more than simply remembering is taking place here, but rather a process of implication and recontextualization. In the case of the following inscription on the war monument at Colne, Lancashire, we find the following case of implication:

AT THE GOING DOWN OF THE SUN AND IN THE MORNING

WE WILL REMEMBER THEM.

ERECTED TO THE MEMORY OF THOSE WHO MADE THE SUPREME SACRIFICE.

GREAT WAR 1914–1918.

LEST WE FORGET.

On the one hand this inscription ties the act of remembering it with the realm of nature and natural cycles of life as in sunrise and sunset – the propositional assumption as to what will take place. This bonding of nation and ethnic identity with broader cosmic process and with nature itself is well documented (Jaworski and Thurlow, 2010). The soul of a nation and people is thought to reside in its most rural areas such as mountains and rivers. The idea of sun rise and sun set over the realm of the nation is also important as in the indication of the way that the act is fused into this cycle. Of course other daily routines could be mentioned: when we go to work and return in the evening perhaps. But this does not bring the same sense of natural rhythms and epic beauty.

The Colne inscription also does its ideological work for the promotion of a sense of community through the use of the active tense that requires an agent; this is achieved by the inclusion of the personal pronoun: 'we'. Had the passive tense been selected, the inscription would have read 'THEY

WILL BE REMEMBERED' & 'LEST THEY ARE FORGOTTEN'. 'WE' represents a community; it suggests a consentient group of people who will all remember dead soldiers in the same way; an 'Existential Assumption' in Fairclough's (2003) terms; one which implicitly refers to the community of the nation.

More explicit assumptions can be found in inscriptions such as the following on the Royal Artillery Memorial in Hyde Park:

IN PROUD REMEMBRANCE OF THE

FORTY NINE THOUSAND & SEVENTY SIX

OF ALL RANKS OF THE

ROYAL REGIMENT OF ARTILLERY

WHO GAVE THEIR LIVES FOR KING

AND COUNTRY IN THE GREAT WAR

1914–1919.

The Existential Assumption at work here lies in the line 'who gave their lives'; a phrase that closes down alternative discourses that otherwise may reflect the reality of the lives of the mainly working-class soldiers who joined the army voluntarily to escape poverty in 1914 and 1915, the conscripted soldiers who had no choice in participating from 1916 on, the post-traumatic stress disorder sufferers who were found curled up on the ground shaking with fear, the three million who died from disease on the front and those who were walked to their deaths into machine-gun fire. The notion of 'pride' too is used to bring a sense of the collective response to the act of 'giving'. At the time of writing one of the authors saw a news report related to a local man who had been involved in WWI in a particular role. The commentary provided a background with some archive film of the war with soldiers going 'over the top' (that in fact showed training footage). The commentator spoke about the actions of the soldiers in terms of the national pride still not forgotten for what these brave men did as they gave their lives to defend their country. On these monuments it is often the case that those who 'gave their lives' in later wars and conflicts are often added. Wars, despite their differing natures and reasons fuse together under this discourse. Not only are our understandings of former wars hampered but so too are our understandings of contemporary ones. In the view of Smith (2001) one problem in dealing with contemporary conflicts is that they are very different than the former ones. Yet as linguists have shown us, the dominant discourses used to represent each one are basically the same. Here these inscriptions provide the same fusing of meaning for all conflicts.

Assumptions about the intentions of the soldiers are also made quite clear on the inscriptions as in the case of the memorial at Weston-Super-Mare:

THESE DIED

THAT WE MIGHT LIVE.

The soldiers died for the survival of the collective. The novels of front-line soldiers do not represent the views of soldiers (Sajer, 2001) as being of this nature. Their motives are to survive, often primarily to find enough to eat, living in terror at what might next happen. Sajer describes how early in his army career he felt a sense of national pride which soon evaporated as he saw the first corpses of the enemy and then turned into horror at the insanity and routine cruelty of what was taking place. As time passed his main preoccupations were to fight hunger and illness.

Of course it is important to understand the relationship of the inscription to the physical monument as can be seen in this example from the Llandaff War Memorial:

LLANDAFF REMEMBERS HER OWN SONS

AND THOSE OF THE CATHEDRAL SCHOOL

WHO GAVE THEIR LIVES IN THE GREAT WAR

NON SIBI SED PATRIAE.

More didactic in tone, the inscription tells that the boys of the town and the school gave their lives for their country. However, the context adds a layer of meaning to this line. This memorial features images of two boys and a female personification of the town who is 'witnessing', or directing the boys to war. The physical location of the memorial is also significant, sited as it is on the village green in between the school and the cathedral it stands on the route where boys would be marched from one building to the other every day. These contextual features are significant layers of representation that add meaning to the whole; as such this memorial not only supports Kress and Van Leeuwen's (1996) comments on the significance of context and the inter-relationship of the materiality of meaning of surface and inscription, but it also exemplifies Fairclough's (2003) point on the theoretical value of identifying assumptions within texts:

> Certainly one cannot simply look at a text, identify assumptions, and decide on textual evidence alone which of them are ideological. (p. 59)

Another existential assumption on the Llandaff inscription is that all the men who died were 'sons'. The notion of sons again communicates natural and physical bonds to locality and we find the same on other monuments which may use this at a national level such as 'sons of Wales'. Such ideas of community at every level have been critically dealt with by anthropologists for many years and can be found well expressed in the writing of Anderson (1983). Billig (1995) too was interested in these subtle and mundane everyday ways that the idea of an imagined 'us' is forged. Yet within this imagined community at the time of the commemoration great socio-economic issues were at stake. The war was over, millions of working-class young men had died and survivors returned to poor conditions, poverty and no state help, aware of the successes of worker movements abroad. Sons here suggests something deeply cherished by the town or nation compelling survivors to feel fused with the community and nation.

We also, of course, find clear references to religion. For example, the text that accompanies the memorial at Oldham reads:

DEATH IS THE GATE OF LIFE

1914–1918

TO GOD BE THE PRAISE

1939–1945.

These few lines carry the cornerstone of religious ideology in their existential assumptions of the existence of an afterlife. The nationalist ideology is in the inclusion of the dates, which make reference to the two World Wars fought on behalf of the nation. If we were to see just the inscription, without the accompanying visual representation of the soldiers defying death in 'the trench', we could argue that the nationalist message is still achieved. The key is that the visual components of the monuments allow the viewer to *feel* the experiences metaphorically in a way which the written discourse, in the form of inscriptions, alone cannot achieve.

In this monument visually and materially we find handsome and well-uniformed soldiers (documentary images of WWI soldiers in the trenches show them mainly with make-shift and random clothing along with dishevelled and worn-out uniforms) striking energetic and unlikely poses, positioned high on a pedestal. Materially we find heavy bronze and stone with Classical references. Here war is represented not as humiliation, suffering, nor killing and maiming. The reasons for the war are not directly present. Linguistically we are told that being killed in the war is also part of a greater scheme of things. Death is not simply a gristly and pathetic end as a soldier dies of typhus in the mud of Flanders or is forced at gunpoint to charge a machine gun across a large stretch of open land, nor to listen at night while dying and horribly wounded men trapped in no-man's-land called out for their wives. Rather it is connected to god and eternity. The Classical references, religion and the material associations of stone and bronze place this beyond ordinary mundane meanings of body and pain.

We analysed the Mountain Ash war monument in an earlier chapter where we looked its combination of obelisk, the personification of Britania and the Christian alter: the fusing of the glorious eternal civilization with its higher ideas along with Christian worship. The monument carries several inscriptions addressed to different audiences. These point to the debt incurred by the soldiers' sacrifice and a willingness to reciprocate by the living. Reciprocation of the sacrificial act is specifically referred to in the inscription of the monument at Mountain Ash.

TO THE GLORIOUS DEAD

THEIR NAME LIVETH

FOR EVERMORE

FOR IN THEIR PASSING

THEY HAVE CONQUERED DEATH

AND THROUGH THE YEARS SHALL

SHINE THEIR UNDIMMED YOUTH

WHOSE DAUNTLESS COURAGE

WAS THE LIVING BREATH

OF FREEDOM AND CHIVALY

AND TRUTH.

The Value Assumption in the first inscription relates to the sacrifice of life for others; the deification of the dead: 'GLORIOUS DEAD' carries the assumption that dying can be positive in the right context. The Existential Assumption in the second stanza is related to sacrifice and the existence of an afterlife: 'THEY HAVE CONQUERED DEATH' carries the assumption that the soldiers live on spiritually despite their physical demise. The text expects the viewer to accept the premise that dying for others is highly valued and that life continues on some other level. 'THEIR UNDIMMED YOUTH' also points to eternity of the youth achieved rather than its cruel waste. Visually and linguistically we find a sense of the local youth placed into eternity characterized by higher values through their worthy acts. The nation itself symbolized by the personification of Britannia and the Classical values this brings stands against the obelisk above the urn in the ideal above the inscriptions that sit in the real.

A third plaque speaks directly to the living:

SONS OF THIS TOWN

AND DISTRICT

LET THIS OF YOU BE SAID

THAT YOU WHO LIVE

ARE WORTHY OF YOUR DEAD

THESE GAVE THEIR LIVES

THAT YOU WHO LIVE MAY REAP

A RICHER HARVEST

ERE YOU FALL ASLEEP.

The Propositional Assumptions relating to what may or will happen: a better life for the survivors of the war when it is over. The inscription on the Mountain Ash Memorial guides the viewer through a particular ideological process: the honouring of sacrificial acts; belief in an afterlife; sacrifice is made for fellow citizens; war ensures better life for the living and a debt is owed to those who sacrifice for you. For Rowlands (2001), this is a memorial that satisfies the requirements of its function in its acknowledgement of the debt of reciprocation. Again we have reference to natural rhythms and the soul of the community through reference to the harvest. Of course other daily rhythms could be used but they are not.

While nowhere in the text do we see explicit mention of dying for 'King and Country' as we have seen in other inscriptions, nationalist messages are implicitly entwined through a series of assumptions about communal belonging and causal effects of an individual's behaviour on others in the community. In addressing its message to the 'SONS OF THIS TOWN AND DISTRICT', the text is a verbalization of Smith's (2001) definition of a nation: '. . . a named human community . . . having common myths and a shared history . . . common rights and duties for all members' (p. 13). Here all have shared concerns and aims and there are no divisions of social class. The frequency of these meanings in the inscriptions of monuments is a classic case of overlexicalization and overpersuasion pointing to the underlying anxieties of the ruling elite.

The inscriptions of the contemporary monument

While the WWI monuments drew on assumptions about god, the giving of lives, eternity and sons of communities, more recent monuments do not. What they tend to do is either be much more minimal or provide additional information relating to other symbolic and mystic meanings of the monument.

The Armed Forces Memorial commemorates soldiers since WWII. Earlier in the book we looked at its representation of a combination of continual narratives where the mother and wife weep as highly muscular

Classical-style soldiers carry a dead comrade high on a stretcher. The inscription is:

THEY DIED

SERVING

THEIR

COUNTRY

WE WILL

REMEMBER

THEM.

While the monument is itself quite abstract the inscription uses less symbolic language than the earlier monuments with no reference to religion or to the afterlife. Here this is accomplished only at the visual level where the dead soldier lying on the ground represents Romantic paintings of Christ and where the Classical elements connote the greater tradition of higher ideals, truth and eternal time. The monument visually represents life after death and we see the Christ-like figure on the ground and the muscular soldier chiselling his name into the walls of eternity. We also find a symbolic door to the afterlife. Also we no longer find lives being given, but the notion of dying while in service to the nation. And again here we have the 'WE' and the propositional assumption that we 'WILL' remember them. At the visual level here we find religious notions, eternity, high ideals and Classical figures. At the linguistic level we find nation.

In the inscription the act of service being described is an interesting one. There is the assumption that these deaths were done as an act of serving the nation and not simply as these people needed a job and career. Recruitment material for the British Armed Forces heralds adventure and also being taken care of and having friends rather than serving one's country as reasons for signing up. The authors have collected material and followed recruitment campaigns in the poorest areas of Cardiff in South Wales, UK. It is from such areas where the majority of soldiers are recruited who otherwise have little opportunity for an interesting career but who have little self-confidence and thus need the promise of being cared for. Yet this reality is recontexualized to one of serving when they are later killed in conflicts they will most likely, as the public at home, do not understand.

At the time of writing the Olympic Games in London were just coming to an end. Soldiers had provided security at the games and a member of the commentary team on one television station commented that she would like to thank them for the job they had done before they go off to other lands to continue to serve and protect us. Such 'service' unproblematizes and simplifies the reasons for military engagements that may or may not represent the best interests of all, or any, of those of us watching. Of course, the Olympic Games are times when nationalist and ethic discourses are rife so this should be of little surprise. But monuments here are certainly one way that such discourses are maintained, serviced and naturalized.

The Armed Forces Memorial also carries other information in linguistic form provided on the brochure which guides visitors around the site. Representing the door to the afterlife the monument has a small gap forming part of one of the scenes. Visitors are told that as well as being part of the narrative of resolution they are positioned in the precise position in order to allow the rays of the sun to shine on a stone wreath in the centre of the structure at the exact hour of remembrance each year: 11 'o'clock on 11 November. This date is given as important since at the same in a 5,000-year-old burial chamber at Maeshowein Orkney the setting of the winter solstice sun casts a light into the inner chamber. Such symbolism serves to provide not only additional interest to tourists, but it also serves to implicate war into some broader mystical scheme – further layers of abstraction. We saw too above how the Australian monument provided reference to its symbolism on the inscription itself telling viewers that water symbolizes the sacrifice and bravery. The New Zealand monument in the form of the cross provides symbolic references to configurations of stars to guide lost New Zealanders home.

Other monuments rely much more on the visual realm for more complex references. The Wootton Bassett monument has the following inscription:

LEST

WE

FORGET.

There are no linguistic references to the peacekeeping communicated visually by the monument. But we still find that a 'WE' is addressed. And exactly what we might forget is not specified but articulated through the form of the monument itself. Placed in the shopping street this claim to common psychology, its claim to house our shared feelings and values, is presented as everyday and natural in the manner of buying daily bread. Yet who and what shall we not forget is not expressed.

Interestingly, in the case of the Yomper monument commemorating the Falklands war we find no reference to nationalism while the massive figure itself certainly represented a time of heightened nationalism and celebration of the military.

TO COMMEMORATE ALL THE ROYAL MARINES AND THOSE WHO SERVED WITH THEM IN THE SOUTH ATLANTIC DURING THE FALKLANDS WAR OF 1982.

Such a massive and assertive soldier would have sat uneasily perhaps with linguistic references to god and nation. Michalski (1998) has spoken of such large monuments often being related to the cult of leadership or of the military. In this sense connection to nation linguistically may have been inappropriate perhaps connoting a military state.

The inscription on the New Zealand monument analysed visually early in the chapter is as follows:

whatever you do
Remember you have the
Mana, the honor and
The good name of the
Maori people in your
Keeping this night.
Do you duty to the last,
and whatever comes
never turn your backs on the enemy.

This inscription is cited as being from a Chaplain, Reverand Wainohu who gave this talk before soldiers attacked at Gallipoli in 1915. Important here is also the form of the inscription. The other inscriptions we have looked at use variations of Times New Roman with slim, formal letter shapes. They are also always organized with centred paragraph orientation so that both edges of the text are jagged but symmetrical. Machin (2007b) has discussed the associations of this alignment with formality and status, as opposed, for example, to texts where one side has straight edges or where both sides are ragged, yet not symmetrical, which is often used to connote informality and creativity. The inscription above is on the one hand aligned with straight edges to the left. It is not a formal text in this sense. It is neither sombre nor self-important. Although the text is presented in short lines almost as a poem and therefore something heartfelt, as opposed to longer lines typical of other written texts that are intended mainly to inform. Also the font itself is informal mimicking a hand-written, personal style. The text itself assumes a coherent and unified Maori people who all have the same kind of honour. There is a sense of the duty and honour that is involved at not retreating from an enemy, to stand and face them. Accounts of Gallipoli suggest the same kinds of cruel lack of regard for human life found in WWI more widely. But in this case the inscription has a number of roles. Soldiery has become less idealized. The act of commemoration with this informal voice is different from the mightier voice of the WE seen above related to the gates of eternity, glorious dead, harvests and sunsets. But this inscription helps to place the monument into the realm of cultural heritage, a romanticized and reified ethnic past.

Visually the act of war and the identities and feelings of those who fought it is represented by forward sloping bronze pillars decorated with iconic features and shaped like the Christian Cross. The figures, in the form of *Haka*, move with certainty in close and rigid formation presumably towards an enemy who is absent from the scene. The crosses themselves resemble star constellations. Themselves they provide a visual spectacle. In line with government policies on public display it provides opportunities for learning. The inscription too forms part of this curiosity and places the experiences of the soldiers into the same realms of ethnic identity and tradition. So these war monuments house emotions and feelings but as part of larger settings of tourism, leisure and consumption. As in the case of the Merchant Seamen's monument we find history and cultural heritage but rendered as ancient, eternal and mystical (mana as an ethnic form of honour). These mark out who we, or the collective, are through symbolism, abstraction and certainly not through more difficult aspects of more recent ancient history.

Conclusion

In this chapter we have shown that analysis of the details of the semiotic choices made in more contemporary war monuments, and placing this analysis alongside contextual information on commissioning and design, reveals something of the changing discourse of war in Britain also about the new uses monuments have been put to as part of the heritage and tourism industry. Some of these monuments still draw on Classical features and Christian symbolism. But there is a shift to abstraction and other kinds of symbolism to do with reified ethnic identities, heritage and even sport in order to communicate national identities. While the idea of soldiery as sacrifice and serving the nation is still apparent soldiers are now much more humanized and representations have shifted in some instances away from the power and might of the state represented through massive Classical structures, but through more organic and informal references. And perhaps as war itself has become less easy to understand and represent though older discourses and as it can no longer simply be justified through the call of the nation and its place in the world, so representations have shifted to the more complexly symbolic, even mystical, and abstract. And war and nation have merged with other banal symbols of nationhood such as sport and reified ethnic identities. Acts of soldiery become also local identity markers alongside other historical symbolism such as the more ancient elements found in Cardiff Bay. War is not so much a reality, but a set of celebratory and safe icons of place and people.

Conclusion

The 'call to arms' (Graham et al., 2004), or the legitimization of warfare, by the nation-state has been studied extensively in CDA. This body of literature reveals creation of an exaggerated polarity between us and the people of the enemy which Billig (1995) describes as being continually fostered at mundane, banal everyday levels in things like sport; providing a underlying sense that we are somehow essentially different to others on the basis of political boundaries generated since the seventeenth century (Gellner, 1983). Or the enemy are orientalized and represented as uncivilized, overemotional, irrational and untrustworthy. This literature also tells us that this call to arms comprises a sense that 'we' fight for a greater good, whether this be god or democracy. When we see war visually in news media, we see soldiers keeping watch and peacekeeping, we see bombardments but without the consequences of these. Such discourses of war as 'humanitarian', as 'peacekeeping' and as keeping an orientalized enemy in check, are also disseminated by movies and computer games. In sum, this works to help to legitimize and naturalize war. The ideological effect is that war becomes part of the taken-for-granted background of our lives and a normalized social practice for nation-states as they seek to perpetuate themselves.

The questions as to *how* social practices such as war are recontextualized through language have lain at the heart of the tradition of CDA. Such studies (Wodak and Van Leeuwen,1999) have focused on the ways in which language and grammar have been used to recontextualize social practices by substituting elements, the actual participants, micro-processes, locations, times, etc., from the actual social practice with others, by deletion, substitutions and additions; a process which reshapes representations to serve the interests of a particular group. In the critical studies of the language used in the call to arms we find the horror of war, what will be the effect on civilian populations, on bodies and on society and what exactly are the benefits and to whom, abstracted and substituted by evil orientalized enemies, sanitized bombardments, the defence of 'freedom' and the psychological ordeal of 'our boys' who serve us.

In this book we have looked at this process of recontextualization through material semiotic choices, carrying out an MCDA of war monuments erected since WWI. The war monuments we have analysed clearly communicate about war differently than speeches and news items. While of course speeches can use metaphors and symbolism to communicate discourses and to carry out the process of recontextualization, monuments use a range of material semiotic resources. The WWI monuments glorify the death of soldiers, linguistically as giving and sacrifice so others might live. The attitudes and values substitute the fear and subjugation that soldiers felt as they died, often in squalor of disease. The reasons for the colonial war are substituted by attitude of selflessness and community belonging. Visually soldiers appear idealized as Classical gods striking impassive poses. The actions that they carried out in war: killing, maiming, destroying and suffering are abstracted to mental states of commitment to the cause. The identities of the participants, scared young men forced from their homes to live like animals in trenches under the threat of execution for 'cowardice' are substituted by beautiful figures who bring with them associations of high ideals that form part of a greater historical destiny. At other times the nature of the nation itself is replaced from a society divided along the lines of wealth and power to be represented as a Classical god of justice. Later monuments draw on some of the same representations although they shift towards greater abstraction and symbolism as they combine warfare with discourses of heritage, sport and more mystical links related to ancient burials and star constellations. Such monuments are often placed at tourism sites where other kinds of history are found that tend towards the ancient or celebratory as opposed to more recent and politically sensitive. But what all of the monuments have in common is that they are placed in public spaces and are produced through official processes which regulate the nature of designs. Since they stand in public spaces they claim to represent our collective ideals and values. They appear to house our shared sense of what is of note in our history and to what we might aspire.

Through this analysis we have shown that multimodal analysis can make a valuable contribution to CDA if the aim is to show what is done with semiotic resources, which semiotic resources are used and what discourses these are used to realize and in whose interests do these serve. It is through prioritizing this aim of revealing ideology and power relations that we best begin to understand the nature of the broader strategic use of semiotic resources in communication. In this book we have taken the principles of social semiotics that communication is accomplished through these broadly shared resources, or meaning potentials, that are continually being remade through use. We have sought to identify some of the meaning potentials available for the monument designer. Some of these appear as options on a continuum, as in angularity versus curvature, and are based more clearly around experiential and associational meanings. Others are based around associations of social relations such as angles of interaction, proximity and gaze. And others are based around provenencial meanings such as the symbolism of Classical architecture and Christian symbolism. Through this we have sought to follow the principles of social semiotics as indicated by Halliday (1985). But what we have not done is taken a model designed to account for linguistics and attempted to apply this to other kinds of communication.

One of the interests in multimodality has been with what different modes can do – what affordances different modes bring (Kress, 2010). Following Forceville (2013) we would suggest that it is not so important to spend time on finding individual modes. Indeed the idea of thinking in terms of 'mode' itself may say more about the nature of linguistic enquiry and its former isolation from other fields where there had been long and taken-for-granted traditions of analysing images and sound alongside language as in film studies and semiotics. In terms of our aims here in MCDA we did find it important and fruitful to look for the affordances brought by different kinds of semiotic resources but not to look for and isolate modes per se. In the case of monuments we found that materials have specific kinds of affordances. A heavy bronze figure of a soldier can communicate heaviness and permanence, something forged in furnaces by traditional processes. Or marble can communicate heaviness, but also something organic of the mountains and something finely sculptured. The use of plastic, however durable or heavy, would simply not do. In language it would in contrast be odd to try to communicate these same kinds of things about the acts and identities of the soldiers – that they belong to a fraternity of ancient warriors and Greek gods and represent the high values of Classical antiquity.

Rather than mode we find here that Kress's (2010) notion of epistemological commitment, as applied more broadly to using different resources in combinations, more useful. In terms of the recontextualization of social practice this is a useful tool since it allows us to think about the way that different semiotic resources can be used for different kinds of abstraction, addition and substitution. So materials provide an addition regarding an evaluation of the importance and nature of the actions of the dead soldiers. But they avoid the epistemological commitment that would be made through language that makes the comparison overt and specific.

Linguistically the inscriptions tend to commit to the idea of there being a nation and a 'we' and of death as a deliberate act of giving. It appears that it was important to commit to this at a linguistic level. But they tend not to commit to the idea of the Classical ideals, the impassive attitude nor the nature of victory that personifications are used to represent. At the visual and material levels in contrast there is no commitment to existential verbs. It is not stated that these Greek figures *are* like your son who died. It is not stated that the war is about high ideals in the manner of ancient Greece and Rome. Specifying transitivity is avoided. There is no commitment to the idea that soldiers only simply *stood impassively* or that in battle there *was no aggression nor fear*. But again we find that looking for how these semiotic choices are used, how they contribute to recontexualization and what ideologies they help to foster and maintain is what helps us to reveal these affordances and the commitments that they bring or avoid. The ideology these material choices help to maintain are where a collective people, who align with higher civilized values and god, must all participate and be prepared to die for other people. These people are the very same as the nation itself and more complex socio-economic differences and political aims are silenced. Death for the nation/people is good and of primary interest beyond the reasons for their death and the broader aims of the conflict. In the terms described by Billig (1995), the placement of these monuments in our public places provides a banal reminder of this ideology, fusing it into our everyday routines.

In the British context the discourses of war that are disseminated through political speeches and news media and also from war monuments rely extensively on discourses of war from previous conflicts. The British experience of war in recent history is one not of military occupation, nor one of living in combat zones, as was the experience of much of Europe. War is not associated with the terrors, humiliations and brutality of such contexts but rather more with one where 'our boys' travel overseas to chase out an evil enemy in acts of protection of the homeland and the people. Kelsey (2012) describes the way that even the bomb attacks on the London underground in 2005 were represented in the press through a set of myths associated with WWII such as the blitz spirit of the brave and unified British public against a cowardly enemy. Such discourses serve only to hamper public understanding of contemporary conflicts. Smith (2001) expresses his concern that the new forms of conflict are reacted to inappropriately since there is no wider understanding at a public and political level that war and therefore the role of the military has changed. When there are no font lines, nor massive rival army equipped with industrial-level weaponry, when this enemy fights among the people and where motivations may lie along complex and uniformly contestable claims to ethnicity, territory, power and political allegiances, the complexity of which lies in centuries of colonial and corporate involvement and boundary shifting then what role can 'our boys' best carry out? As Smith points out, no clear objective is ever now given for the involvement of the British military apart from in the form of broader processes of peacekeeping and humanitarianism. Clearly new discourses of war are needed that better align with the nature of modern conflicts.

What this MCDA approach has also allowed us to do is provide the kind of approach to the study of monuments that has been called for by scholars in this field. This in itself, we feel, being able to show exactly how scholars from other fields studying the same phenomenon can find the new approach useful and valuable, should be something that multimodality can demonstrate. Kress and Van Leeuwen's (1996) work has been taken up in the areas of visual design. Jewitt's (2005) work on classroom layout and interaction has proved groundbreaking in educational studies. This is important as it is in such academic fields they key questions that need to be answered and major obstacles to this being accomplished are laid out. Machin (2009) notes that much work on multimodality suffers as it has largely ignored the very significant body of work going back over 100 years in semiotics which asked many of the same questions and came up against a number of barriers to progress. In such cases, rather than reinventing the wheel, multimodality can show how it is able to learn from what has already gone and show how its approach can take us a step further. As regards monument studies a range of scholars (Danzer 1987; Ashplant et al., 2000, 2004; Niven 2008) have called for the need for a more systematic model to analyse the ways that monuments communicate physically. These scholars also recommend that, due to the dangers of more creative interpretation in textual analysis, it is important that this analysis considers historical matters such as the social and political climate at the time of design and the commission and design issues that lead to the completed monument. It is only through this process that we will be able to understand how 'official' forms of commemoration achieve their subjective hold on viewers (Reynolds 1996; Rowlands 2001).

But we feel we have begun to show in this book that MCDA must be developed to think more about the way that discourses are realized in different genres of communication, through different kinds of semiotic resources. Discourses are communicated not only through political speeches and news items but through all kinds of media. And as Iedema (2001) has argued it is the way they are realized through things like play, entertainment, fashion and material objects that they become institutionalized and naturalized. It is the objects around us and our leisure and entertainments that are the resources for us knowing ourselves. We do not know who we are independent from the meanings of the environments in which we live. In this sense what if all of our cities and towns contained statues dedicated to those who profit from war, those who commit genocide in war, those whose bodies were brutalized and humiliated through war? In the introduction to this book we considered a cartoon by Arthur Stadler in 1915 depicting a crucified soldier surrounded by gloating elite from different countries. What if this image had become that universally realized in the form of monuments and placed in public places? If war was not recontextualized through Classical ideals and of contemporary monuments instead of abstract symbolism and reified ethnic histories, sitting alongside other celebratory heritage experiences, how would this have changed our response to calls for our heroes to serve us in the next conflict, whose name will be added to the next generation of monuments or to the lengthening lists on the WWI monuments?

REFERENCES

Abousnnouga, G. (2005), *Discourses of Soldiery in Contemporary British Military Recruitment*. Unpublished MA thesis, Cardiff University.

Abramson, D. (1996), 'Maya Lin and the 1960s: Monuments, time lines and minimalism', *Critical Inquiry*, 22/4: 679–709.

Anderson, B. (1983), *Imagined Communities: Reflections on the Origin and Spread of Nationalism*. London: Verso.

Argyle, M. (1975), *Bodily Communication*. London: Methuen and Co Ltd.

Arnheim, R. (1982), *The Power of the Center: A Study of Composition in the Visual Arts*. Berkeley, CA: University of California Press.

— (1997), *Film Essays and Criticism*. Madison, WI: University of Wisconsin Press.

Arnot, R. Page (1967), *The Impact of the Russian Revolution in Britain*. London: Lawrence and Wishart.

Arthur, M. (2002), *Forgotten Voices of the Great War, a New History of WW1 in the Words of the Men and Women who Were there*. London: Ebury Press.

— (2009), *We Will Remember them, Voices from the Aftermath of the Great War*. London: Wiedenfeld and Nicolson.

Ashplant, T. G., Dawson, G. and Roper, M. (2000), *The Politics of War Memory and Commemoration*. London: Routledge.

— (2004), *The Politics of Memory: Commemorating War*. New Brunswick, NJ: Transaction Publishers.

Bagnold, E. (1978), *Diary without Dates*. London:Virago.

Baldry, A. (2004), 'Phase and transition, type and instance: Patterns in media texts as seen through a multimodal concordancer'. In L. O'Halloran (ed.), *Multimodal Discourse Analysis: Systemic Functional Perspectives*. London: Continuum, pp. 83–108.

Baldry, A. and Thibault, P. (2006), *Multimodal Transcription and Text Analysis: A Multimedia Toolkit and Coursebook*. Sheffield: Equinox Publications.

Barthes, R. (1973), *Mythologies*. New York: Hill and Wang.

— (1977), *Image, Music, Text*. London: Fontana.

Bateman, J. (2008), *Multimodality and Genre: A Foundation for the Systematic Analysis of Multimodal Documents*. London: Palgrave.

— (2011), *Multimodal Film Analysis: How Films Mean*. London: Routledge.

Beddoe, D. (2000), *Out of the Shadows, a History of Women in Twentieth-Century Wales*. Cardiff: University of Wales Press.

Billig, M. (1995), *Banal Nationalism*. London: Sage Publications.

Blair, C. (1994), 'Public memorializing in postmodernity'. In Nothstine, W. L. Blair, and G. Copeland (eds), *Critical Questions: Invention, Creativity, and the Criticism of Discourse and Media*. New York: St Martin's Press, pp. 345–82.

Blair, C., Jeppeson, M. and Pucci, E. (1991), 'Public memorializing in postmodernity: The Vietnam Veterans Memorial', *The Quarterly Journal of Speech*, 77/3: 263–88.

Boorman, D. (2005), *A Century of Remembrance, One Hundred Outstanding British War Memorials*. London: Barnsley, Yorks, Pen and Sword Books Ltd.

Borg, A. (1991), *War Memorials*. London: Barnsley, Yorks, Leo Cooper (imprint of Pen & Sword Books Ltd).

Bourke, J. (1996), *Dismembering the Male: Men's Bodies, Britain and the Great War*. London: Reaktion.

Bown, M. C. and Taylor, B. (1993), *Art of the Soviets Painting, Sculpture, and Architecture in a One-Party State, 1917–1992*. Manchester: Manchester University Press.

Braybon, G. and Summerfield, P. (1987), *Out of the Cage, Women's Experiences in Two World Wars*. London: Pandora Press (Routledge & Kegan Paul Inc).

Breverton, T. (2000), *The Book of Welsh Saints*. Bro Morganwg: Glyndwr Publishers.

Burgett, D. (2001), *The Road to Arnhem*. London: Barnes and Noble.

Calder, A. (2004), *Disasters and Heroes: On War, Memory and Representation*. Cardiff: University of Wales Press.

Calkins, S. (2006), 'Women in service during World War I'. In B. A. Cook (ed.), *Women and War: A Historical Encyclopedia from Antiquity to the Present*. Santa Barbara, CA: ABC-CLIO Ltd, pp. 237–41.

Carlson, A. C. and Hocking, J. E. (1988),'Strategies of redemption at the Vietnam veterans' memorial', *Western Journal of Speech Communication*, 52:203–15.

Chouliaraki, L. (2005), 'Spectacular ethics, on the television footage of the Iraq war', *Journal of Language and Politics*, 4/1: 143–59.

Cirlot, J. E. (2002) (republication of 2nd edn), *A Dictionary of Symbols*. Mineola, NY: Dover Publications Inc.

Cobley, P. and Randviir, A. (2009), 'Introduction: What is sociosemiotics?', *Semiotica*, 173/1: 1–39.

Cohen, E. (1988), 'Authenticity and commoditization in tourism', *Annals of Tourism Research*, 15/3: 371–86.

Compton, A. (1985), *Charles Sargeant Jagger: War and Peace Sculpture*. London: The Imperial War Museum.

— (2004), *The Sculpture of Charles Sargeant Jagger*. Aldershot: Lund Humphries.

Cook, B. (ed.) (2006), *Women and War, a Historical Encyclopedia from Antiquity to the Present*, Vol. 1A–K. Santa Barbara, CA: ABC-CLIO Inc.

Crabb, B. J. (2006), *Beyond the Call of Duty, the Loss of British Commonwealth Mercantile and Service Women at Sea during the Second World War*. Donington: Shaun Tyas.

Crofton, E. (1997), *The Women of Royaumont, a Scottish Women's Hospital on the Western Front*. East Lothian: Tuckwell Press.

Curran, J. and Seaton, J. (1977), *Power without Responsibility*. London: Routledge.

Danzer, G. (1987), *Public Places, Exploring their History*. Walnut Creek, CA: AltaMira Press.

Dark, J. (1991), *The Monument Guide to England and Wales*. London: MacDonald Illustrated.

Darrow, M. H. (1996), 'French volunteer nursing and the myth of war experience', *The American Historical Review*, 101/1: 80–106.

Davis, W. (1989), *The Canonical Tradition in Ancient Egyptian Art*. Cambridge: Cambridge University Press.

Dewey, P. E. (1984), 'Military recruiting and the British labour force during the First World War', *The Historical Journal*, 27(1), 199–233.

Dicks, B. (2003), *Culture on Display: The Production of Contemporary Visitablility*. Maidenhead: Open University Press.

Doerr, P. W. (2006), 'Great Britain, women in service during the Second World War'. In B. Cook (ed.), *Women and War, a Historical Encyclopedia from Antiquity to the Present*, Vol. 1A–K. Santa Barbara, CA: ABC-CLIO Inc, pp. 235–46.

Fairclough, N. (1992), *Discourse and Social Change*. Cambridge: Polity Press.

— (1995), *Critical Discourse Analysis, the Critical Study of Language*. London and New York: Longman.

— (2000), *New Labour, New Language?* London: Routledge.

— (2003), *Analysing Discourse, Textual Analysis for Social Research*. London: Routledge.

Fairclough, N. and Wodak, R. (1997), 'Critical discourse analysis'. In T. A. Van Diijk (ed.), *Discourse as Social Interaction: Discourse Studies: A Multidisciplinary Introduction*, Vol. 2. London: Sage, pp. 258–84.

Forceville, C. (2010), 'Review of Carey Jewitt (ed.), *Routledge Handbook of Multimodal Analysis* (2009)', *Journal of Pragmatics*, 42: 2604–8.

Fowler, R., Hodge, R., Kress, G. and Trew, T. (1979), *Language and Control*. London: Routledge & Kegan Paul.

Furlong, J., Knight, L. and Slocombe, S. (2003), '"They shall grow not old': An Analysisanalysis of Ttrends in memorialisation based on information held by the UK National Inventory of War Memorials', *Cultural Trends*, 12/45: 1–42.

Gaffney, A. (1998), *Aftermath, Remembering the Great War in Wales*. Llandybie, Dyfed: Dinefwr Press.

Gage, J. (1993), Colour and culture: Practice and meaning from antiquity to abstraction. London: Thames and Hudson.

Gellner, E. (1983), *Nations and Nationalism*. Oxford: Blackwell.

Gibbs, Phillip, Carlisle, ca/c10/12/1, unititled and undated press cutting, in King, A. (1998), *Memorials of the Great War in Britain. The Symbolism and Politics of Remembrance*. Oxford and New York: Berg.

Graham, P., Keenan, T. and Dowd, A. (2004), 'A call to arms at the end of history: A discourse-historical analysis of George W. Bush's declaration of war on terror', *Discourse & Society*, 15/2–3: 199–221.

Graham, P. and Luke, A. (2003), 'Militarizing the body politic: New mediations as weapons of mass instruction', *Body and Society*, 9/4: 149–68.

Gramsci, A. (1971), *Selections from the Prison Notebooks*, ed. and trans. Q. Hoare and G. Nowell-Smith. London: Lawrence & Wishart.

Grayzel, S. R. (1999), *Women's Identities at War, Gender, Motherhood and Politics in Britain and France during the First World War*. Chapel Hill, NC: The University of North Carolina Press.

Gregory, A. (1994a), *The Silence of Memory, Armistice Day 1919–1946*.
Oxford: Berg Publishers.

Greer, T. H. and Lewis, G. (2004), *A Brief History of the Western World*.
Belmont, CA: Wadsworth.

Griswold, C. L. (1986), 'The Vietnam veterans memorial and the Washington
mall: Philosophical thoughts on political iconography', *Critical Inquiry*, 12:
688–719.

Haines, H. W. (1986), 'What kind of war? An analysis of the Vietnam veterans
memorial', *Critical Studies in Mass Communication*, 3/1: 1–20.

Hall, S. (1974), 'The television discourse – encoding and decoding'. In A. Gray
and J. McGuigan (eds), *Studies in Culture: An Introductory Reader*. London:
Arnold, pp. 28–34.

Halliday, M. A. K. (1978), *Language as Social Semiotic: The Social
Interpretation of Language and Meaning*. London: Edward Arnold.

— (1985), *An Introduction to Functional Grammar*. London: Edward Arnold.

Hard, R. (2003), *The Routledge Handbook of Greek Mythology: Based on
H. J. Rose's Handbook of Greek Mythology*. Abingdon, NY: Routledge,
Taylor & Francis.

Harris, S. and Platzner, G. (2003), *Classical Mythology: Images and Insights*.
New York: McGraw Hill.

Hobsbawm, E. (1990)nd, *Nations and Nationalism since 1780: Programme,
Myth, Reality,* 2nd edn. Cambridge: Cambridge University Press.

— (1992), *Nations and Nationalism since 1780: Programme, Myth, Reality*.
Cambridge: Cambridge University Press.

Hobsbawm, E. and Ranger, T. (eds) (1983), *The Invention of Tradition*.
Cambridge: Cambridge University Press.

Hodge, R. and Kress, G. (1979), *Language as Ideology*. London: Routledge.

Hodges, A. (2007), 'The political economy of truth in the "War on Terror"
discourse: Competing visions of an Iraq/al Qaeda connection', *Social
Semiotics*, 17/1: 5–20.

Holoka, J. P. and Weil, S. (2003), *Simone Weil's the Iliad or the Poem of Force:
A Critical Edition*. New York: Lang.

Housely, W. and Wahl-Jorgensen, K. (2008), 'Theorizing the democratic
gaze: Visitors' experiences of the new Welsh Assembly', *Sociology*, 42/4:
726–44.

Iedema, R. (2001), 'Analysing film and television: A social semiotic account
of hospital: An unhealthy business'. In T. Van Leeuwen and C. Jewitt (eds),
Handbook of Visual Analysis. London: Sage, pp. 183–206.

Jagger, Charles, Royal Artillery, Central Committee Minutes, 12 Nov 1924, in,
King, A. (1998), *Memorials of the Great War in Britain. The Symbolism and
Politics of Remembrance*. Oxford and New York: Berg.

Jaworski, A. and Thurlow, C. (eds) (2010), *Semiotic Landscapes Language,
Image, Space*. London and New York: Continuum International Publishing
Group.

Jencks, C. (1987), *Post-modernism: The New Classicism in Art and Architecture*.
New York: Rizzoli.

Jenkins, R. (2002), *Churchill*. London: Pan Macmillan.

Jewitt, C. (2005), *Techonology, Literacy, Learning – A Multimodal Approach*.
Abingdon, NY: Routledge.

Jewitt, C. and Oyama, R. (2001), 'Visual meaning: A social semiotic approach'. In T. Van Leeuwen and C. Jewitt (eds), *Handbook of Visual Analysis*. London: Sage, pp. 134–56.

Jewkes, Y. (2011), *Media and Crime*, rev. 2nd edn. London: Sage.

Johnson, R. (2002), 'Defending ways of life: The (anti-)terrorist rhetorics of Bush and Blair', *Theory, Culture and Society*, 19/4: 211–31.

Kapferer, B. (1988), *Legends of People, Myths of State: Violence, Intolerance, and Political Culture in Sri Lanka and Australia Edition*, illustrated. Washington, DC: Smithsonian Institution Press.

Karp, I. and Lavine, D. (eds) (1991), *Exhibiting Cultures: The Poetics and Politics of Museum Display*. Washington, DC: Smithsonian Press.

Keegan, J. (2001), *The First World War: An Illustrated History*. New York: Random House.

Keene, J. (2001), *Doughboys, the Great War and the Remaking of America*. Baltimore: Johns Hopkins University Press.

Kelsey, D. (2012), 'Pound for pound champions: The myth of the Blitz spirit in British newspaper discourses of the City and economy after the 7 July bombings', *Critical Discourse Studies*, 9/3: 285–99.

Kidd, W. (1997), 'Memory, memorials and commemoration of war memorials in Lorraine, 1908–1988'. In M. Evansand and K. Lunn (eds), *War and Memory in the Twentieth Century*. Oxford: Berg, pp. 144–51.

King, A. (1998), *Memorials of the Great War in Britain. The Symbolism and Politics of Remembrance*. Oxford and New York: Berg.

— (1999), 'Remembering and forgetting in the public memorials of the Great War'. In A. Forty and S. Kuchler (eds), *The Art of Forgetting*. London: Bloomsbury, pp. 147–70.

King, George, Hackney, SN/W/1/11, list of suggestions received by the Borough Council up to 18 Mar 1919, in, King, A. (1998), *Memorials of the Great War in Britain. The Symbolism and Politics of Remembrance*. Oxford and New York: Berg.

Kirshenblatt-Gimblett, B. (2006), *Destination Culture: Tourism, Museums and Heritage*. Berkeley and Los Angeles, CA: University of California Press.

Kohn, M. (2003), *Radical Space: Building the House of the People*. Ithaca, NY: Cornell University Press.

Konstantinidou, C. (2008), 'The spectacle of suffering and death: The photographic representation of war in Greek newspapers', *Visual Communication*, 7/2: 143–69.

Korpela, K. M. (1989), 'Place-identity as a product of environmental self-regulation', *Journal of Environmental Psychology*, 9: 241–56.

Kress, G. (1989), *Linguistic Processes in Sociocultural Practice*. London: Oxford University Press.

— (2001), 'Sociolinguistics and semiotics'. In P. Cobley (ed.), *The Routledge Companion to Semiotics and Linguistics*. London: Routledge, pp. 66–82.

— (2010), *Multimodality, a Social Semiotic Approach to Contemporary Communication*. Abingdon, NY: Routledge.

Kress, G. and Van Leeuwen, T. (1996, 2006), *Reading Images*, 2nd edn. Abingdon, NY: Routledge.

— (2001), *Multimodal Discourse, the Modes and Media of Contemporary Communication*. London: Arnold.

Kruk, S. (2008), 'Semiotics of visual iconicity in Leninist "monumental" propaganda', *Visual Communication*, 7/1: 27–56.

— (2010), 'Profit rather than politics: The production of Lenin monuments in Soviet Latvia', *Social Semiotics*, 20/3: 247–76.

Laybourn, K. (1997), *The Rise of Socialism in Britain 1881–1951*. Stroud, Gloucester: Sutton.

Lazar, A. and Lazar, M. (2004), 'The discourse of the new world order: "Out-casting" the double face of threat', *Discourse and Society*, 15/2: 223–42.

Leach, E. (1964), *Anthropological Aspects of Language: Animal Categories and Verbal Abuse*. Massachusetts: MIT Press.

Leneman, L. (1994), *In the Service of Life, the Story of Elsie Inglis and the Scottish Women's Hospitals*. Edinburgh: Mercat Press.

Lennon, J. and Foley, M. (2000), *Dark Tourism, the Attraction of Death and Disaster*. London and New York: Continuum.

Loverance, R. (2007), *Christian Art*. London: British Museum Press.

Macdonald, J. M. (2009), *The Uses of Symbolism in Greek Art*. Charlston, SC: Bibliolife, LLc.

Machin, D. (2007a), 'Visual discourses of war: Multimodal analysis of photographs of the Iraq occupation'. In A. Hodges and C. Nilep (eds), *Discourse, War and Terrorism*. Amsterdam, PA: John Benjamins Publishing Co., pp. 123–42.

— (2007b), *Introduction to Multimodal Analysis*. London: Hodder Education.

— (2009), 'Multimodality and theories of the visual'. In C. Jewit (ed.), *The Routledge Handbook of Mmultimodal Analysis*. Abingdon, NY: Routledge, pp. 181–90.

Machin, D. and Mayer, A. (2012), *How to do Critical Discourse Analysis. A Multimodal Introduction*. London: Sage.

Machin, D. and Richardson, J. E. (2012), 'Discourses of unity and purpose in the sounds of fascist music: a multimodal approach', *Critical Discourse Studies*, 9/4: 329–45.

Machin, D. and Sulleiman, U. (2006), 'Arab and American computer war games: The influence of a global technology on war discourse', *Critical Discourse Studies*, 3/1: 1–22.

Machin, D. and Van Leeuwen, T. (2005), 'Computer games as political discourse: The case of black hawk down', *Journal of Language and Politics*, 4/1: 119–41.

— (2007) *Global Media Discourse*. London: Routledge.

— (2009), 'Toys as discourse: Children's war toys and the war on terror', *Critical Discourse Studies*, 6/1: 51–63.

Maddrell, A. (2007), 'The "Map Girls". British women geographers' war work, shifting gender boundaries and reflections on the history of geography', *Transactions of the Institute of British Geographers*, 33/1: 127–48.

Marx, K. (2013), *Capital: Volumes One and Two*. Hertfordshire: Wordsworth Editions Limited.

McIntyre, C. (1990), *Monuments of War: How to Read a War Memorial*. Tunbridge Wells: Hale.

McKibbin, R. (1974), *The Evolution of the Labour Party 1910–1924*. London: Oxford University Press.

Michalski, S. (1998), *Art in Political Bondage 1870–1997*. London: Reaktion Books Ltd.

Michaud, E. (2004), *The Cult of Art in Nazi Germany*. Stanford, CA: Stanford University Press.

Minkes, J. and Minkes, L. (2008), *Corporate and White Collar Crime*. London: Sage.

Moeller, S. D. (2009), 'The politics of coverage'. In S. D. Moeller (ed.), *Packaging Terrorism: Co-opting the News for Politics &Profit*. New York: Wiley, pp. 37–45.

Moriarty, C. (1995), 'The absent dead and figurative First World War memorials', *Transactions of Ancient Monuments Society*, 39: 7–40.

— (1997), 'Private grief and public remembrance: British First World War memorials'. In M. Evansand and K. Lunn (eds), *War and Memory in the Twentieth Century*. Oxford: Berg, ch. 8.

Morris, D. (2002), *People Watching, the Desmond Morris Guide to Body Language*. London: Vintage.

Mosse, G. L. (1990), *Fallen Soldiers, Reshaping the Memory of the World Wars*. New York: Oxford University Press.

Newsinger, J. (1997), *Dangerous Men: The SAS and Popular Culture*. London: Pluto.

Niven, B. (2008), 'War memorials at the intersection of politics, culture and memory', *Journal of War and Culture Studies*, 1/1: 39–45.

Noakes, L. (2006), *Women in the British Army. War and the Gentler Sex, 1907–1948*. London: Routledge.

Norris, S. (2004), *Analysing Multimodal Interaction*. London: Routledge.

O'Halloran, K. L. (ed.) (2004), *Multimodal Discourse Analysis*. London: Continuum.

— (2011), *Multimodal Studies: Exploring Issues and Domains*. London: Routledge.

O'Toole, M. (1994), *The Language of Displayed Art*. London: Leicester University Press.

Panofsky, E. (1970), *Meaning in the Visual Arts*. London: Penguin.

— (1972), *Studies in Iconology: Humanistic Themes in the Art of the Renaissance*. New York: Harper and Row.

Peirce, C. S. (1931–58), *Collected Writings* (8 vols), ed. Charles Hartshorne, Paul Weiss and Arthur W. Burks. Cambridge, MA: Harvard University Press.

Penny, N. (1981), 'English sculpture and the First World War', *Oxford Art Journal*, 4/2: 36–42.

Posen, B. R. (1993), 'Nationalism, the mass army, and military power', *International Security*, 18/2: 80–124.

Quinlan, M. (2005), *British War Memorials*. Hertford: Authors Online Ltd.

Raivo, P. J. (1998), *In this Very Place: War Memorials and Landscapes as an Experienced Heritage*. Lancaster: Lancaster University Press.

Rausch, H. (2007), 'The nation as a community born of war? Symbolic strategies and popular reception of public statues in late nineteenth-century Western European capitals', *European Review of History*, 14/1: 73–101.

Remarque, E. M. (1987), *All Quiet on the Western Front*. London: Ballantine Books.

Reynolds, D. M. (1996), *"Remove not the ancient landmark" Public Monuments and Moral Values*. Amsterdam: Gordon and Breach Science Publishers SA.

Reynolds Stephens, undated reprint included in Wirral, zwor16 with a letter dated 13 Oct 1918, in, King, A. (1998), *Memorials of the Great War in Britain. The Symbolism and Politics of Remembrance*. Oxford and New York: Berg.

Richardson, J. (2007), *Analysing Newspapers: An Approach from Critical Discourse Analysis*. London: Palgrave.

Roderick, I., (in press) 'Military hardware as affective objects: Towards a Social Semiotics of militainment television'. In D. Machin (ed.), *Visual Communication*. Berlin: De Gruyter.

Rodríguez, L.M.L., (2006), 'Female iconography and subjectivity in Eavan Boland's "In her own image"', *ATLANTIS*, 28/1 (June): 89–100.

Rojek, C. and Urry, J. (1997), 'Transformations of travel and theory'. In C. Rojek and J. Urry (eds), *Touring Cultures*. London and New York: Routledge, pp. 1–22.

Rowlands, M. (2001), 'Remembering to forget: Sublimation as sacrifice in war memorials'. In A. Forty and S. Kuchler (eds), *The Art of Forgetting*. Oxford and New York: Berg, pp. 129–47.

Rudy, C. (1918), 'Concerning Tommy', *Contemporary Review*, 545–52 (n.b.: full publication details [volume and issue] lost during wartime bombing of publisher's offices).

Sack, R. D. (1992), *Place, Modernity and the Consumer's World: A Relational Framework for Geographical Analysis*. Baltimore, MD: John Hopkins University Press.

Sajer, G. (2001), *The Forgotten Soldier*. Hernden, VA: Potomac Books.

Sapir, E. (1929), 'The status of linguistics as a science'. In E. Sapir (1958), *Culture, Language and Personality*, ed. D. G. Mandelbaum. Berkeley, CA: University of California Press, pp. 65–77.

Saussure, F. (1959), *Course in General Linguistics*. New York: Philosophical Library.

Scarry, E. (1985), 'Injury and the structure of war', *Representations*, 10: 1–51.

Shaw, M. (2003), *War and Genocide*. Cambridge and Malden, MA: Polity Press.

Sir George Frampton, Wirral, zwo/16, letter from Frampton to Sir A. V. Paton 2 Mar 1921, in, King, A. (1998), *Memorials of the Great War in Britain. The Symbolism and Politics of Remembrance*. Oxford and New York: Berg.

Smith, A. (2001), *Nationalism*. Cambridge and Malden, MA: Polity Press.

Souhami, D. (2010), *Edith Cavell: Nurse, Martyr, Heroine*. London: Quercus.

Stafford, B. M. (1998), *Good Looking: Essays on the Virtue of Images*. Massachusetts: MIT Press.

Stenglin, M. (2009), 'Space Odyssey: Toward a social semiotic model of 3D space', *Visual Communication*, 8/1: 35–64.

Stewart, T. A. (1997), 'A satisfied customer is never enough', *Fortune* (21 July): 112–13.

Summerfield, P. (1997), 'Gender and war in the twentieth century', *The International History Review*, XIX(1): 1–15.

Takacs, S. (2009), 'The body of war and the management of imperial anxiety in US television', *International Journal of Contemporary Iraqi Studies*, 3/1: 85–105.

Teo, P. (2000), 'Racism in the news: A critical discourse analysis of news reporting in two Australian newspapers', *Discourse & Society*, 11/1: 7–49.

Turner, J. (ed.) (1996), *The Grove Dictionary of Art*. London: Grove.

— (2003), 'War rhetoric of a little ally. Political implicatures of Aznar's legitimization of the war in Iraq', *Journal of Language and Politics*, 4(1): 65–92.

— (2006), 'Discourse and manipulation', *Discourse and Society*, 17/3: 359–83.

Van Leeuwen, T. (1996), 'The representation of social actors'. In C. R. Caldas-Coulthard and M. Coulthard (eds), *Text and Practices: Readings in Critical Discourse Analysis*. London: Routledge, pp. 32–70.

— (2001), 'Semiotics and iconography'. In T. Van Leeuwen and C. Jewitt (eds), *Handbook of Visual Analysis*. London: Sage, pp. 92–119.

— (2005), *Introducing Social Semiotics*. Abingdon, NY: Routledge.

Van Leeuwen, T. and Wodak, R. (1999), 'Legitimizing immigration control: A discourse-historical analysis', *Discourse Studies*, 1/1: 83–118.

Van Straten, R. (1994), *An Introduction to Iconography*. Amsterdam: Gordon and Breach Science Publishers SA.

Watson, J. (2004), *Fighting Different Wars: Experience, Memory and the First World War in Britain*. Cambridge: Cambridge University Press.

Wingate, J. (2005), 'Over the top the Doughboy in World War I memorials and visual culture', *American Art Journal*, 19/2: 27–47.

Winter, J. (1998), *Sites of Memory, Sites of Mourning, the Great War in European Cultural History*. Cambridge: Cambridge University Press.

— (1999), 'Forms of kinship and remembrance in the aftermath of the Great War'. In J. Winter and E. Sivan (eds), *War and Remembrance in the Twentieth Century*. Cambridge: Cambridge University Press, pp. 40–60.

Wodak, R. and Meyer, M. (2001), *Methods of Critical Discourse Analysis*. London: Sage.

Wodak, R. and Van Leeuwen, T. (1999), 'Legitimizing immigration control: A discourse-historical analysis', *Discourse Studies*,1/1: 83–118.

Wulf, H. (2005), *Internationalizing and Privatizing War and Peace*. London: Palgrave Macmillan.

INDEX